Plate I.

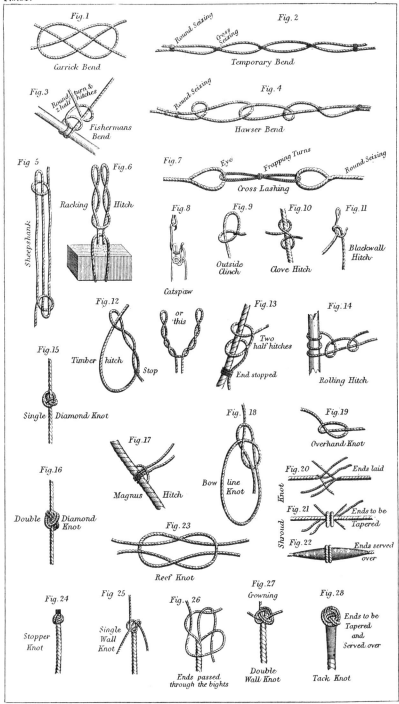

Fig.1 Carrick Bend

Fig. 2 Temporary Bend
Round Seizing Cross Seizing

Fig.3 Fishermans Bend
Round turn & 2 half hitches

Fig. 4 Hawser Bend
Round Seizing

Fig 5 Sheepshank

Fig.6 Racking Hitch

Fig.7 Cross Lashing
Eye Frapping Turns Round Seizing

Fig.8 Catspaw

Fig. 9 Outside Clinch

Fig.10 Clove Hitch

Fig.11 Blackwall Hitch

Fig.12 Timber hitch Stop
or this

Fig.13 Two half hitches End stopped

Fig.14 Rolling Hitch

Fig.15 Single Diamond Knot

Fig.16 Double Diamond Knot

Fig.17 Magnus Hitch

Fig. 18 Bow line Knot

Fig.19 Overhand Knot

Fig. 20 Ends laid
Fig. 21 Ends to be Tapered
Fig. 22 Ends served over
Shroud Knot

Fig. 23 Reef Knot

Fig. 24 Stopper Knot

Fig 25 Single Wall Knot

Fig. 26 Ends passed through the bights

Fig. 27 Crowning Double Wall Knot

Fig. 28 Tack Knot Ends to be Tapered and Served over

THE
ART OF RIGGING

containing an

EXPLANATION OF TERMS AND PHRASES

and the

PROGRESSIVE METHOD OF RIGGING
EXPRESSLY ADAPTED FOR
SAILING SHIPS

BY

CAPT. GEORGE BIDDLECOMBE, R.N.

WITH AN INTRODUCTION BY

CAPT. ERNEST H. PENTECOST, R.N.R.

DOVER PUBLICATIONS, INC.
New York

Published in Canada by General Publishing Company, Ltd., 30 Lesmill Road, Don Mills, Toronto, Ontario.

This Dover edition, first published in 1990, is an unabridged republication of the work first published by The Marine Research Society, Salem, Massachusetts, in 1925. The arrangement of a few plates has been changed for reasons of space, but nothing has been omitted.

Manufactured in the United States of America
Dover Publications, Inc.
31 East 2nd Street
Mineola, N.Y. 11501

Library of Congress Cataloging-in-Publication Data

Biddlecombe, George, 1807–1878.
 The art of rigging : containing an explanation of terms and phrases and the progressive method of rigging expressly adapted for sailing ships / by George Biddlecombe ; with an introduction by Ernest H. Pentecost.
  p.   cm.
 Developed from The elements and practice of rigging and seamanship by David Steel first published in London in 1794.
 Reprint. Originally published: Salem, Mass. : Marine Research Society, 1925. (Publication number 8 of the Marine Research Society)
 ISBN 0-486-26343-6
 1. Masts and rigging.   I. Steel, David. Elements and practice of rigging and seamanship.   II. Title.
VM531.B53   1990
623.8′62—dc20   90-39121
                                                     CIP

PREFACE

THIS work was originally compiled for the use of the students in a Naval Academy and it is believed by modern experts to be the best manual ever produced on rigging the sailing ship. At the present time there is a constant demand from builders of ship models for a good handbook on rigging — comprehensive as to details and yet simple to understand. In the following pages it is believed that the model builder will find the solution of his problem.

The PROGRESSIVE METHOD OF RIGGING worked out in this book teaches the beginner first to rig the bowsprit; then the lower rigging; then the topmasts up; and so on in the correct order. Reeving the gear and bending the sails are described in detail and for the benefit of the more advanced student there are tables giving the quantities and dimensions of the standing and running rigging of various types of vessels.

The nucleus from which this book developed may be found in *The Elements and Practice of Rigging and Seamanship* by David Steel, published in London, in 1794, in two quarto volumes containing three plates devoted to rigging. At that time the author wrote — "There is no one undeviating mode which is pursued in the progressive rigging of ships." Six years later this work was republished in four volumes, in an octavo edition, of which the third volume was devoted to the art of rigging, and the number of plates was increased to eleven. It was published at the Navigation Warehouse, No. 1, Union Row, Minories, Little Tower-Hill, London, 1800.

As the years passed, various improvements were made in the rigging of vessels and in 1848, Charles Wilson, of the well-known firm of Norie & Wilson, chart-sellers and publishers of books on navigation, decided to issue a new edition of *The Art of Rigging* and the revision of the work was entrusted to Capt. George Biddlecombe, who had been in the merchant service for many years and afterwards became a Master in the Royal Navy. He found it necessary to make extensive alterations and additions so that the new and enlarged edition may be regarded as a new work, although the same form of arrangement was followed. The number of plates was increased and they were engraved from new drawings.

In publishing the present edition of THE ART OF RIGGING, the Society has had access to Captain Biddlecombe's own copy and corrections in the text, made in his handwriting, have been incorporated. The INTRODUCTION is by Capt. Ernest H. Pentecost, R. N. R., formerly commander of the well-known Cunarder "Saxonia" — a man who began his career in the sailing ship and who speaks from well-trained personal experience. The Society desires to express its thanks not only to Captain Pentecost, but also to Mr. Malcolm B. Stone of Boston, Mr. William E. Northey of Salem, and to all others who have aided or encouraged the republication of this book.

INTRODUCTION

THE very numerous articles and operations which belong to the Rigging of a Ship, render it somewhat difficult to arrange this subject.

The progressive connection of the whole should be shown; and yet it should be so disposed as to be easy of reference to any particular.

To unite these two objects has been our care; and, with that view, we have divided the Art of Rigging Ships and Vessels into Five Parts.

The First Part contains an Alphabetical Explanation of Terms and Phrases used in Rigging.

The Second Part consists of Directions for the Performance of Operations incidental to Rigging, and preparing it on shore; with a Table of the comparative strength of Chain and Rope.

The Third Part contains the Progressive Method of Rigging Ships.

The Fourth Part contains a Description of Reeving the Running Rigging and Bending the Sails; also, the Rigging of Brigs, Yachts, and small Vessels.

The Fifth Part comprises Tables of the Quantities and Dimensions of the Standing and Running Rigging of Ships, Brigs, Fore-and-Aft Schooners, and Cutters; with the species, size, and number of Blocks, Hearts, Dead-Eyes, &c.

INTRODUCTION TO THIS EDITION

"Is tight, and yare, and bravely rigg'd, as when
We first put out to sea." — *The Tempest, Act. V.*

THE art of rigging ships with rope, other than wire, is now lost, never to return, since the necessity for it has departed; although there are still a few old "shell backs" drifting around who could "clap two ends of a rope together," put a gang of rigging over a mast-head and set it up "as well as e'er a' he that ever crossed salt water."

Few, today, can realize how important was the art of rigging a ship and reeving her gear in the days just old when all aloft was wood and hemp; or how great the part it has played in the building of Empire.

It was a great work to mast and rig a full-rigged ship when all was done by hand; but it was a small matter when compared with the work of care and maintenance required to make each rope, spar and canvas do its work and live its life. No baby was swaddled with greater care than that bestowed on shrouds and backstays by the mariners when paying, parcelling, worming and serving. The ship's boys were taught to

"Worm and parcel with the lay,
Serve and turn the other way."

The boatswain of a large sailing ship was a busy man for the rigging, standing and running, was his charge. Chief to be guarded against was chafe and a cross-strain on ropes which was said to take the heart out of them. According to sailors, everything on board a ship has a heart. The old-time mariners spoke of the heart of a spar and when a ship was hard-pressed with canvas and shipping water, the Captain was said to be "breaking her heart" or "taking the heart out of her." Then there was the heart-yarn of a mainstay — the sailor's emblem of constancy in days gone by.

"Do you think your girl's playing true to you, Bill?"

"True! Ay! As true as the heart-yarn of a mainstay."

The writer remembers an old sailor telling a shipmate that a certain landlady of Wapping had a heart as hard as the heart of a marling spike, which instrument, as the reader probably knows, is made of iron.

Before the days of iron hulls and steel masts, ships returned from long voyages were stripped to a girt-line; that is, all the yards and upper masts with their gear, were sent down, overhauled and stowed away until fitting-out time, when the ships were again made ready for sea. The work of stripping and rigging in home ports was done by men called "riggers." They were sailors who had "swallowed the anchor" and were usually "spliced." A sailor is said to have "swallowed the anchor" when he "knocks off going to sea" and to be "spliced" when he is moored fore and aft to a female craft. The work done by the riggers was rough but strong and was known as rigger's work. One could always tell a rigger's splice or seizing by its lack of fine finish for they never took the trouble to hide the ends. When a ship got into "flying fish weather," many of the rigger's splices were drawn and tucked again in neater style.

The fancy work done on board ships known as "Flash Packets," was a delight to a sailor's eye. There every rope's end was pointed instead of the usual twine whipping. No shore craftsman ever put more into his job than did the old-time mariner when splicing a rope, sticking a cringle or doing any of the hundred and many other jobs of sailoring, and when it came to decorating rope or canvas he was an artist of the deep waters.

The old art of rigging is lost to those who now "do business on the great waters," but fortunately for us and for posterity there are men who devote their spare time to the rigging of ship models. To the riggers of ship models and others who would learn the seaman's secrets, this book, complete and wonderfully clear, is recommended by an old seafaring man who first went to sea in a ship rigged in the old style with not a fathom of wire rope aboard her.

ERNEST H. PENTECOST.

CONTENTS

PART I

ALPHABETICAL EXPLANATION OF THE TERMS AND PHRASES USED IN RIGGING

PART II

DIRECTIONS FOR THE PERFORMANCE OF OPERATIONS INCIDENTAL TO RIGGING; AND FOR PREPARING IT ON SHORE

PART III

PROGRESSIVE METHOD OF RIGGING SHIPS

PART IV

DESCRIPTION OF REEVING THE RUNNING RIGGING AND BENDING THE SAILS

DESCRIPTION OF THE RIGGING OF BRIGS, YACHTS, AND SMALL VESSELS

RIGGING CUTTERS OR VESSELS WITH ONE MAST

PART V

ERRATA

Plate VI, Fig. 1. The engraver has made an error in indicating the course of the cable. It should pass *under* the cross-piece of the bitts and up abaft it. — G. B.

THE ART OF RIGGING

PART I

EXPLANATION OF THE TERMS AND PHRASES USED IN RIGGING

ABAFT or AFT. — The hinder part of a ship, or all those parts which lie towards the stern. Frequently used to signify further aft, or nearer the stern.

ABAFT the BEAM implies that the relative situation of the object spoken of is contained between a line drawn at right angles to the keel and the point to which the ship's stern is directed.

ABOARD or INBOARD. — The inside of a ship; hence, *The riggers are aboard* — signifying they are in the ship; but when an enemy enters in the time of battle, he is said to board — a phrase which always implies hostility.

ABREAST. — Side by side, or opposite to. The situation of two or more ships with their sides parallel to each other, their heads equally advanced: they are then said to be abreast; also of any other object in a line with the beam of a ship.

A-HEAD signifies further onward, or more toward the head of the ship; as, *Go further a-head,* means to go further forward. *A-head* is also used in opposition to *A-stern:* the former implies at any distance before the ship; the latter expresses the situation of any object behind the ship.

ALOFT. — Up in the tops; at the mast-head, or anywhere in the rigging.

ALOOF. — At a distance.

AMIDSHIPS is used when speaking of the middle of the ship, either with regard to her length or breadth; as, *The enemy boarded us amidships* — that is, midway between the stem and stern; *Put the helm amidships* — that is, in the middle, or in a line with the keel.

ANCHOR-STOCK TACKLE. — A tackle used to cant the anchor-stock into its place.

AN-END. — The situation of any mast or boom when perpendicular to the plane of the deck, tops, &c. The top-masts are said to be *an-end* when swayed up to their usual station at the head of the lower-masts.

ATHWART. — Across; as, *We discovered a fleet steering athwart us* — that is, steering across our way.

AVAST. — The order to stop, or pause, in any exercise or operation; as, *Avast heaving* — that is to say, desist, or stop, from drawing in the cable or hawser, by means of the capstan, &c.

AWNING. — A covering of canvas spread over the decks of the ship, or over a boat, in hot weather, to protect the officers and crew from the heat of the sun. That part of the poop-deck which is continued forward beyond the bulk-head of the cabin, is also called the *awning*.

BACKSTAYS *(Breast* and *Standing)* are stays which support the top-masts, top-gallant, and royal-masts from aft; they reach from the heads of their respective masts to the channel on each side of the ship, and assist the shrouds when strained by a press of sail, as shown in Pl. 9, figs. 20, 21, 22, 31, 32, 33, 37, 38, 39.

Stay-sail Stays are those stays on which the stay-sails are extended. (Pl. 11, figs. 3, 4, 5, 6, 7, 8, 9).

The *Jib Stay* is similar to the stay-sail stays, and extends from the jib-boom end to the fore-top-mast-head. (Pl. 11, fig. 2).

Preventer, or *Spring Stays,* are subordinate stays, to support their respective stays, and supply their places in case of accident.

BECKETS. — Short ropes used in several parts of a ship, to confine large ropes, &c., or to hang up the weather sheets and lee tacks of the main and fore-sail to the foremost main and fore shrouds. The noose made at the breast of a block, to make fast the standing part of a fall to, is also called a *Becket.* (Pl. 2, fig. 15).

BELAYING. — Fastening a rope, by giving it several cross-turns alternately round two timber-heads, each end of a cleat-pin, &c.; as, *Belay the main brace* — that is, make it fast. (Pl. 4, fig. 8).

BENDING. — Fastening one rope to another, or to different objects, and fastening a sail to its yard. The different sorts of bends are explained under the *Bends,* Part II.

BENDS. — The small ropes used to lash the clinch of a cable. (Pl. 6, fig. 3). *See* Part II.

BIGHT. — The double part of a rope when it is folded in contra-distinction to the end; as, *Her anchor hooked the bight of our cable* — that is, caught any part of it between the ends. Again: *The bight of his cable has swept our anchor* — that is, the double part of the cable of another ship, as she ranged about, has entangled itself about our anchor.

BINDING. — The iron wrought round the dead-eyes, or blocks.

BITTS. — A frame composed of two upright pieces of timber, called the pins, and a cross-piece, fastened horizontally near the head of them; they are used to belay cables or ropes to. *Bowline* and *Brace Bitts* are situated near the masts. The *Fore-jeer* and *Top-sail Sheet Bitts* are situated on the forecastle and round the fore-mast. The *Main-jeer* and *Top-sail Sheet Bitts* tenon into the foremost beam of the quarter-deck. The *Cable* or *Riding Bitts* are the largest bitts in a ship, and those to which the cable is bitted when the vessel rides at anchor. (Pl. 6, fig. 1).

Bitt the Cable is to put it round the bitts (Pl. 6, fig. 1), in order to fasten it, or slacken it gradually; which last is termed *veering away.*

BLOCKS. — Machines used in ships, and each block having one or more sheaves or wheels in it, through which a rope is put, to increase the purchase. (Pl. 2, figs. 1, 2, 3, 4, 5, 6, 7, 8, 10, 11, 12, 13, 15, 16, 17, 20, 21, 22).

BLOCK-and-BLOCK. — The situation of a tackle when the effect is destroyed, by the blocks meeting together.

BOARDING NETTING is thrown over the sides, to prevent the enemy from boarding. (Pl. 4, fig. 3).

BOAT-SKIDS or BOOM-SKIDS. — Pieces of wood extending athwart the midship part of the ship, and on which the boats, spare masts, &c., are stowed. (Pl. 5, fig. 16).

BOBSTAY. — Stays used to confine the bowsprit down upon the stem, and counteract the force of the stays, which draw it upwards. (Pl. 4, fig. 9, and Pl. 9, fig. 2).

BOLSTERS. — Pieces of wood placed under the shrouds, to prevent their chafing against the trestle-trees; they are covered with well-tarred canvas, to make an easy bed for the shrouds, which is called *clothing.*

BOLT-ROPE. — A rope to which the edges of a sail are sewed, in order to strengthen and prevent them from splitting. That part of a bolt-rope which is on the sides of a square-sail, is called the leech-ropes; that at the top, the head-rope; and that at the bottom, the foot-rope. Stay-sails have no head-rope.

BOOMS. — Long poles rigged out from the extremities of the yards, bowsprit, &c., to extend the feet of particular sails. The *Spanker-boom,* on which the foot of the spanker is extended, is attached to the mizen-mast, and the outer end projects over the stern. The *Jib-boom* is rigged out from the outer end of the bowsprit, and extends to the foot of the jib. The *Main-boom,* used in vessels of one or two masts, is similar to the spanker-boom of a ship; and on this is spread the foot of the fore-and-aft main-sail. The *Ringtail-boom* projects from the spanker or main-boom, to spread the foot of the ringtail-sails. *Studding-sail-booms,* to spread the studding-sails, slide through boom-irons at the extremities of the yards; and the lower booms swing from the vessel's sides, on goose-necks.

BOOM-IRONS. — Two flat iron rings, formed into one piece, and employed to connect the studding-sail-booms to the yards. *Quarter Boom-irons* fasten on the yard with a clamp. (Pl. 7, figs. 4 and 5).

BOOM TACKLE or BOOM JIGGER. — The tackle used to get the studding-sail-booms in or out.

BOWGRACE. — A frame of old rope or junk laid round the bows, stern, and side of a vessel, to prevent her being injured by flakes of ice.

BOWSING. — Hauling or pulling upon a rope or fall of a tackle, to remove a body, or increase the tension.

BOWLINES. — The ropes fastened to the bowline-bridles on the leech or sides of the square-sails. They are used, when the wind is unfavourable, to extend the windward edges of the sails tight forward and steady; without which, they would be all shivering, and rendered useless.

BOWLINE-TACKLE. — The tackle used to bowse out the main bowline, when the ship is upon a wind.

BOWSPRIT. — A large boom, or mast, projecting from the stem, to carry sail forward, in order to govern the fore part of the ship, and counteract the force of the after-sails. It is otherwise of great use, in being the principal support of the foremast, which is secured to it. (Pl. 9, fig. 61).

BOWSPRIT-NETTING is fastened, at the outer end of the bowsprit, to the horses, or man-ropes, to stow away the fore-top-mast stay-sail.

BRACE. — A rope, to turn the yards and sails horizontally about the masts, when necessary. *Preventer Brace.* — A rope used in ships-of-war, to supply the place of a brace, should that be shot away, or damaged; they are led the contrary way, to be less liable to detriment at the same time. In the merchant-service they are used in blowing weather, and led as most convenient. (Pl. 10, figs. 8, 10, 12, 17, 20, 23, 25, 28, 31, 34, 37, 41).

BRAILS. — Ropes passed through the blocks on the gaff, and fastened to the after-leech of the fore-and-aft sails, to truss or brail them up. (Pl. 7, fig. 8, and Pl. 11, figs. 50, 51, 52).

BREAST-ROPE. — To secure the leadsman when in the chains, heaving the lead.

BREASTWORK. — The rails and stanchions on the formost end of the quarter-deck and poop.

BREECHING. — A rope used to secure the cannon, and to prevent them from recoiling too much in the time of battle.

BRIDLES. — Short ropes, or legs, which fasten to the cringles on the leeches of the sails, and to which the bowlines are fixed.

BULL'S-EYE. — Similar to a thimble, only made of wood instead of iron. (Pl. 2, fig. 18).

BUMPKINS or BOOMKINS. — A short boom, or beam of timber, projecting from each bow of a ship, to extend the clue, or lower edge of the foresail, to windward; for which purpose there is a large block fixed on its outer end, through which the tack is passed, which, being tight down, brings the corner of the sail close to the block; the tack is then said to be *aboard*. The *Bumpkin* is fitted above the main rail in the head, and secured by an iron-brace, which confines it downward to the ship's bow, in order to counteract the strain it bears from the fore-sail above, dragging it upward. (Pl. 9, fig. 72).

BUMPKIN SHROUDS, to support the bumpkins, have their after ends hooked to eye-bolts, one into the bows, the other in the cutwater; at the fore part is seized in a thimble, which sets up with a laniard to a triangle in an iron strop fixed round the outer end of the bumpkin.

BUNTLINES are ropes rove through certain blocks above the yards, whence, passing downwards on the forepart of the sail, they are fastened to the lower edge in several places of the boltrope, where cringles are worked. (Pl. 12, figs. 22, 28, 31, 34, 37, 40, 43).

BUOY. — A kind of cask, or block of wood, fastened by a rope to the anchor, to point out its situation, that the ship may not come too near it, as to entangle her cable about the stock or flukes of the anchor. Buoys are of various kinds, and have the following names — *Cable Buoy, Can Buoy, Floating Buoy, Life Buoy, Nun Buoy, and Wooden Buoy.* (Pl. 6, figs. 10 and 11).

BUOY-ROPE. — The rope which fastens the buoy to the anchor. It should be a little more than equal in length to the depth of the water where the anchor lies, as it is intended to float near, or immediately above the bed of it, that the pilot or officer may at all times know the situation thereof. It should be always of sufficient strength to weigh the anchor, if necessary. (Pl. 6, fig. 10).

BURTON TACKLES. — Tackles used to set up the top-mast shrouds, support the top-sail-yards, &c. (Pl. 9, figs. 15, 16, 59).

BUTTON and LOOP. — A short piece of rope, having on one end a wall-knot, crowned; and at the other end an eye. It is used as a becket, to confine ropes in.

BUTTONS. — Small pieces of thick leather under the heads of nails that are driven through ropes.

CABLE. — A large rope, usually 120 fathoms in length, to which the anchor is fastened, and used to retain a ship at anchor. Cables are of various sorts and sizes, and were generally manufactured of hemp; but of late years chain cables have become in common use. Every hemp cable, of whatever thickness it may be, is generally formed of three ropes, twisted together, which are then called strands; each of these is composed of three smaller strands, all containing a certain number of ropeyarns, the number being, more or less, in proportion to the size of the cable required. (Pl. 6, figs. 1 and 3).

CABLET. — Any cable-laid rope under 9 inches in circumference.

CANT. — A term used to express the position of a piece of timber, or other article, that does not stand square; and *canting* is the act of turning anything over, to see the other side.

CAPS. — Short thick blocks of wood, with two holes in them — one square, the other round — used to confine the masts together.
   To Cap a Rope — To cover the end with canvas. (Pl. 4, figs. 1 and 5).

CAPSIZE. — To upset, or turn over; as, *Capsize that coil of rope,* signifies to turn it over; or, *Capsize the boat,* is to place it bottom uppermost.

CAPSTAN or CAPSTERN. — A machine for heaving up anchors, or to effect other great strains.

To CARRY AWAY. — To break; as, *That ship has carried away her bowsprit* — that is, has broken it off.

CAST-OFF. — To loose a rope, by unseizing it, or by cutting the lashing.

CATHARPINS. — Short ropes, to keep the lower shrouds in tight, after they are braced in by swifters; and to afford room to brace the yards sharp up.

CATFALL. — The rope that forms the tackle for heaving up the anchor from the water's edge to the bow. (Pl. 6, fig. 4).

CATHEADS. — Two strong beams of timber, projecting almost horizontally over the ship's bows, being like two *radii,* which extend from a centre taken in the direction of the bowsprit. The catheads rest upon the forecastle, and are securely bolted to the beams; the outer end has two, three, or four sheaves of brass, or strong wood, through which the catfall passes, and communicates with the cat-block. The catheads also serve to suspend the anchor clear of the bows, when it is necessary to let it go. (Pl. 6, fig. 4).

CHAIN CABLES are of different sizes, corresponding to the size of the vessel. Every link of the chain has a bar placed across, to prevent them from being drawn together; and at every length of 12 or 13 fathoms, a shackle: thus it may be used for a mooring-chain, or for any other purpose. A swivel is also placed midway between each length. (Pl. 6, figs. 1 and 6).

CHAIN PLATES. — Thick iron plates bolted to the ship's sides, and to which the chains and dead-eyes, that support the masts by the shrouds, are connected. (Pl. 4, fig. 1).

CHAIN SHEETS. — Now in common use, instead of ropes, and fastened to the clues of sails, to extend the foot of the sails along the yards.

CHAIN SLINGS. — Short chains, used to hang the lower yards to the masts, in lieu of ropes. (Pl. 10, figs. 13, 14, 15).

CHEERLY implies heartily, cheerfully, or quickly; as, *Row cheerly in the boats,* and *Lower away cheerly* — that is, pull heartily; lower speedily or briskly, &c.

CHESTREES. — Pieces of oak, fitted and bolted to the topsides of vessels abaft the fore channels, with a sheave in the upper end.

They confine the clues of the main-sail, by hauling home the main tack through the sheaves.

CHOAKING THE LUFF. — Placing the bight of the leading part or fall of a tackle close up between the next part and jaw of the block.

CHOCK-A-BLOCK is the same as block-and-block (which article see).

CHOCKS of the RUDDER are large pieces of timber, kept in readiness to stop the motion of the rudder, in case of an accident, and while shipping a new tiller, &c.

CLAMP. — A crooked iron plate, fastened to the after end of the main cap of brigs, to secure the try-sail-mast-head.

CLAP ON is to fasten, or lay hold of; as, *Clap on the stoppers before the bitts* — that is, fasten the stoppers: *Clap on the catfall* — that is, lay hold of the catfall.

CLEATS. — Pieces of wood, various shapes, used for stops, and to make ropes fast, to, viz.: — *Arm or Sling Cleats* are nailed on each side of the slings of the lower yard, and have an arm at one end, which lies over the straps of the jeer-blocks, to prevent their being chafed. *Belaying Cleats* have two arms, or horns, and are nailed through the middle to the ship's sides, or elsewhere, to belay ropes to. *Comb Cleats* are semi-circular, and hollowed out in the middle, to confine a rope to one place. *Range Cleats* are shaped like belaying cleats, but are much larger, and bolted through the middle. *Shroud Cleats* have two arms, similar to belaying cleats; the inside is hollowed, to fit the shroud, and grooves are cut round the middle and ends, to receive the seizings which confine them to the shrouds. (Pl. 5, fig. 18). *Stop Cleats* are nailed to yard-arms, to prevent the rigging from slipping, and the gammoning, and to stop collars on masts, &c. *Thumb Cleats* are shaped like sling cleats, but are much smaller.

CLINCH. — A particular method of fastening large ropes, by a kind of knot, and seizings, instead of splicing. It is chiefly used to fasten the cable to the ring of the anchor, and the breechings of guns to the ring-bolts in the ship's side. (Pl. 6, fig. 3).

CLUE of a SAIL. — The lower corner of the square-sails, but the aftermost only of stay-sails, the other lower corner being called the tack, and the outer lower corner of studding-sails. (Pl. 4, fig. 7).

CLUE-LINES are for the same purpose as clue-garnets, only that the latter term is solely appropriated to the courses; while the word clue-lines is applied to those ropes on all the other square-sails.

COAT. — A piece of canvas nailed round that part of the masts and bowsprit which joins the deck, or lies over the stem. Its use is to prevent the water running down between the decks. There is also a coat for the rudder, nailed round the hole where the rudder traverses in the ship's counter.

COIL. — The manner in which all ropes are disposed on board ships, for the convenience of stowage. Coiling is a sort of surpentine winding the ropes, by which they occupy a small space, and are not liable to be entangled one amongst the other in working the sails. Each winding of this sort in a cable is called a *fake*.

COIN or QUOIN is the wedge laid under the breech of a gun, for the purpose of elevating or depressing it at pleasure. Quoins (besides those used to elevate or depress the gun) are tapered pieces of wood, like wedges, that are thrust under the trucks of carriages, and there kept, by being nailed to the deck; they are used in keeping the gun securely housed in very bad weather.

Guns are housed or secured by taking out the quoins, and lowering the breech, so that the muzzle may take the upper part of the port; when thus placed, the two sides of the breeching are frapped under the gun at the muzzle, near the breast part of the carriage. The muzzle of the gun is confined by several turns of a rope or gasket made fast to it, and the eye-bolts that are fixed in the ship's side, over the midships of the port. The lower-deck guns are usually kept housed and secured when at sea.

COLLAR. — The upper part of a stay; also a rope, formed into a wreath, by splicing the ends together with a heart or dead-eye, seized in the bight to which the stay is confined at the lower part. (Pl. 4, fig. 5).

COME HOME. — The anchor is said to come home when it loosens from the ground by the effort of the cable, and approaches the place where the ship floated at the length of her moorings.

COME-UP the CAPSTERN is to turn it the contrary way to that which it was heaving, so as to slacken or let out some of the rope which is about it.

Come-up the tackle-fall handsomely. — The order to slacken it gently.

CONTLINE. — The spiral intervals that are formed between the strands of a rope, by their being twisted together.

CORDAGE is a general term for the running rigging of a ship, or all that part of her rigging which is employed to extend, contract, or traverse the sails; as also for the rope which is kept in reserve to supply the place of such as may be rendered unserviceable.

CREEPER is an instrument of iron, resembling a grapnel, having a shank, with four hooks, or claws. It is used to drag a river or harbour, with a rope to it to hook and draw up anything from the bottom.

CRINGLES. — Small loops made on the bolt-rope of a sail, used to fasten different ropes to, hook the reef-tackles to, for drawing the sail up to its yard, to fasten the bridles of the bowlines to, and to extend the leech of the sail, &c.

CROTCHES. — Pieces of wood, or iron, the upper part of which is composed of two arms, resembling a half-moon; they are chiefly used in boats, of the larger size, to support spare masts, &c.

CROSSTREES. — Short, flat pieces of timber, let in and bolted athwart-ships to the trestle-trees, at the mast-head, to support the tops, &c.

CROW-FOOT. — An assemblage of small cords, which reeve through holes made, at regular distances, through the uphroe. Its use is to suspend the awnings, and keep the foot of the topsail from striking under the tops (now seldom used).

CROWN OF THE CABLE. — The bights which are formed by the several turns.

CROWNING is the finishing part of a knot made on the ends of a rope; it is performed by interweaving the ends of the different strands artfully among each other, so that they may not become loosened or untwisted. The design of these knots is to keep the end of the rope fast in some place assigned for it; they are more particularly useful in all kinds of stoppers. (Pl. 1, figs. 27 and 28).

CRUTCH. — A support for the main-boom of a sloop, brig, or cutter, &c., and for the spanker-boom of a ship, when their respective sails are furled.

CUT-AND-RUN is to cut the cable, and make sail instantly, without waiting to weigh anchor.

DAVIT is a piece of timber, used as a crane, to hoist the flukes of the anchor into its proper berth, without injuring the ship's side as it ascends — an operation which is called *fishing the anchor*.

The anchors being situated on each bow, the davit may be shifted to either side of the ship, according to the position of that anchor on which it is to be employed. The anchor being first *catted*, the fish-hook is fastened on its fluke, and is, by means of the fish-pendant and tackle, drawn up sufficiently high upon the bow to be made fast by the *shank-painter*. (Pl. 6, fig. 4).

DEAD-EYES. — Wooden blocks, with flat sides, having three or four holes, instead of sheaves, through which the laniards reeve when setting up the shrouds or stays. The power gained by the dead-eyes is as the number of parts of the laniards rove through them; but if the laniards be not well greased, the power will be greatly lost by friction; so that they are never applied as purchases, but merely for the better keeping the quantity gained of any shroud or stay when set up, and are much stronger than blocks with sheaves, the strain not lying on a single pin. (Pl. 4, figs. 1 and 10).

DEAD-LIGHTS are wooden ports, made to fit the cabin windows, in which they are fixed on the approach of bad weather and high sea, to prevent the water coming into the ship.

DERRICK. — A diagonal shore, as a support to shears; also a single spare top-mast, or boom, raised upright, and supported by the guys at the head, whence hangs a tackle over the hatchway the heel working in a socket of wood, fastened on the deck.

DISMANTLE is to *unrig* a ship, and take out all her guns, stores, &c., in readiness for being laid up in ordinary, or for any other purpose.

DRIVER, or SPANKER BOOM. — (See Boom).

DOLPHIN. — A rope lashed round the mast, as a support to the pudding.

DOLPHIN-STRIKER. — A strong bar of wood (in smaller vessels, iron), hung down from the lower side of the bowsprit, at its extremity, inside the cap, and by which the martingale supports the jib-boom. (Pl. 9, fig. 47).

DOWN-HAULLER. — A rope which hauls down the stay-sails, studding-sails, and jibs, to shorten sail, &c.

DOWN-HAUL TACKLE. — A tackle employed to haul down the top-sail-yards in severe blowing weather, in order to reef the sails, when the violence of the wind prevents the weight of the yard from having its natural effect in descending, when the ropes by which it is suspended are slackened.

EARINGS. — Small ropes employed to fasten the upper corners of sails.

EASE-OFF, or VEER-AWAY. — To slacken a rope gradually.

ELBOW in the HAWSE. — This expression is used when a ship, mooring in a tide-way, turns twice round the wrong way, thereby causing the cables to take half a round-turn on each other.

END-FOR-END is applied to a rope; as, *Unreeve it, and shift it end for end* — which signifies, to change or reverse the ends of a rope.

ENSIGN. — The flag carried at the stern, or gaff of a ship, to denote what nation she belongs to.

EQUIP. — A term usually applied to the business of fitting a ship for sea, or arming her for war.

EYE of a SHROUD. — The upper part which is formed into a sort of collar, to go over the mast-heads. (Pl. 4, figs. 1 and 2).

EYELET-HOLES. — The holes made in the heads and reefs of sails.

FAG-END of a ROPE. — The end of any rope which has become untwisted by frequent use; to prevent which, the ends are wound with pieces of twine: this operation is called *whipping*.

FAKE. — One of the turns of a rope when stowed away, or coiled.

FALL. — The rope that connects the blocks of a tackle: but the fall sometimes implies only the loose part which is pulled upon, to produce the desired effect. (Pl. 7, figs. 1, 2, 3).

FANCY LINES are used to overhaul the brails of some fore-and-aft sails.

FANGS or LEE-FANGS. — A rope, fastened to a cringle, near the foot of a ketch's wing-sail, to haul in the foot of a sail, for lacing on the bonnet, or taking in the sail.

FENDERS. — Pieces of wood or old cable, bags of old rope-yarn, shakings, cork, or other materials, hung by a laniard over the vessel's side, to prevent her being damaged. (Pl. 2, fig. 28).

FATHOM. — A measure, of six feet, used to regulate the length of the cables and rigging. Lead-lines are marked off in fathoms, &c.

FID. — A square bar of iron or wood, driven through a hole in the heel of a top-mast, when raised at the head of a lower-mast; it rests on the trestle-trees, and supports the top-masts, &c. Top-gallant and royal-masts are secured in the same manner at the head of the top-mast. *Fids* likewise are round tapering pins, made of iron or hard wood, and used for splicing cordage.

Plate II.

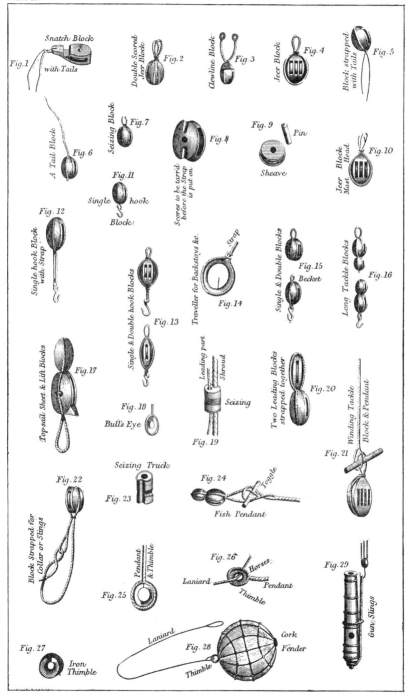

Fig. 1 — Snatch Block with Tails

Fig. 2 — Double Scored Jeer Block

Fig. 3 — Clewline Block

Fig. 4 — Jeer Block

Fig. 5 — Block strapped with Tails

Fig. 6 — A Tail Block

Fig. 7 — Seizing Block

Fig. 8 — Scores to be tarr'd before the Strap is put on

Fig. 9 — Sheave — Pin

Fig. 10 — Jeer Block Mast Head

Fig. 11 — Single hook Block

Fig. 12 — Single hook Block with Strap

Fig. 13 — Single & Double hook Blocks

Fig. 14 — Traveller for Backstays &c. — Strap

Fig. 15 — Single & Double Blocks — Becket

Fig. 16 — Long Tackle Blocks

Fig. 17 — Top-sail Sheet & Lift Blocks

Fig. 18 — Bull's Eye

Fig. 19 — Leading part — Shroud — Seizing

Fig. 20 — Two Leading Blocks strapped together

Fig. 21 — Winding Tackle Block & Pendant

Fig. 22 — Block Strapped for Collar or Slings

Fig. 23 — Seizing Truck

Fig. 24 — Fish Pendant — Toggle

Fig. 25 — Pendant & Thimble

Fig. 26 — Laniard — Horses — Pendant — Thimble

Fig. 27 — Iron Thimble

Fig. 28 — Laniard — Cork Fender — Thimble

Fig. 29 — Gun Slings

Plate III

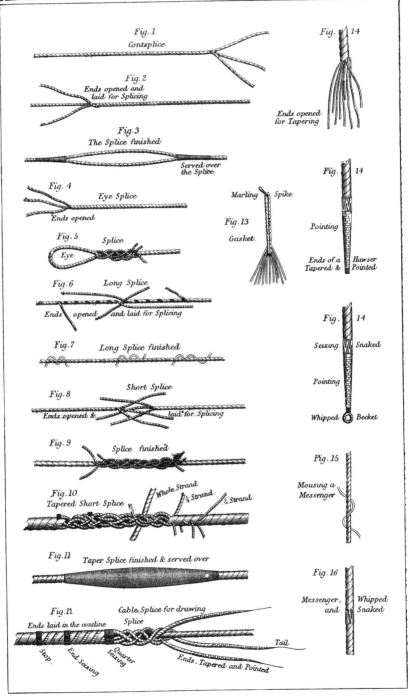

Fig. 1
Contsplice

Fig. 14
Ends opened
for Tapering

Fig. 2
Ends opened and
laid for Splicing

Fig. 3
The Splice finished
Served over
the Splice

Fig. 4
Eye Splice
Ends opened

Marling   Spike

Fig. 13
Gasket

Fig. 14
Pointing
Ends of a   Hawser
Tapered &   Pointed

Fig. 5
Splice
Eye

Fig. 6
Long Splice
Ends   opened   and laid for Splicing

Fig. 14
Seizing   Snaked
Pointing
Whipped   Becket

Fig. 7
Long Splice finished

Fig. 8
Short Splice
Ends opened &   laid for Splicing

Fig. 9
Splice finished

Fig. 15
Mousing a
Messenger

Fig. 10
Tapered Short Splice   Whole Strand   ⅓ Strand   ⅔ Strand

Fig. 11
Taper Splice finished & served over

Fig. 16
Messenger,   Whipped
and   Snaked

Fig. 12
Cable Splice for drawing
Ends laid in the contline   Splice
Stop   End Seizing   Quarter Seizing
Ends, Tapered and Pointed
Tail

FISH. — A strong purchase, employed to hoist up the flukes of an anchor towards the bow, in order to stow it, after it has been *catted*. It is composed of four parts, viz.: — the pendant, block, hook, and tackle, which, with their several uses, are described under the article DAVIT. (Pl. 6, fig. 4).

FLAG-STAFF. — (See STAFF).

FLEETING. — Changing the situation of a tackle, by placing the blocks farther asunder, the force being destroyed by the blocks meeting, called *block-and-block*.

FLY OF A FLAG. — The opposite part to the hoist.

FLYING OF SAILS. — Setting them in a loose manner; as royal-sails without lifts or sheets, the clues being lashed to the top-gallant yards; jibs without stays, and studding-sails without booms.

FORE BRACES are ropes rove through blocks at the fore-yard arms, to change the position of the fore-sail, as necessary. (Pl 10, fig. 8).

FOUL ANCHOR implies that the cable is twisted round the stock, or one of the flukes, and thereby endangers the ship's drifting.

FOUL HAWSE. — (See the article ELBOW in the HAWSE).

FRAPPING. — Take several turns round the middle of a lashing, or any number of ropes, and drawing the several parts tight together. (Pl. 1, fig. 7).

Frapping a Ship is performed by passing a number of turns of a cable over the gunwale and round the hull, and heaving it tight, by thrusting a capstan-bar through the middle of the turns, and twisting them together. The turns are then secured, by stopping the end of the bar. This is mostly used when the upper works of a ship are not strong enough to resist the violent shocks of a heavy sea.

FRESHEN HAWSE is to relieve the chafe off that part of the cable which has for some time been exposed to the friction in one of the hawse-holes, when a ship rolls and pitches at anchor in a heavy sea.

FURLING. — Wrapping or rolling a sail close up to its yard, mast, or stay, and fastening it up with gaskets, lines, &c.

FURLING-LINE. — A cord employed in the operation of furling. Those which are used for the larger sails are generally flat, and better known by the name of *gaskets*.

FUTTOCK PLATE. — A narrow plate of iron, having a dead-eye

bound in the upper end. An eye is made in the lower end, which is put through a mortice in the sides of the top, to hook the futtock shroud to.

FUTTOCK SHROUD. — A great improvement in the manner of fitting futtock shrouds has been adopted in the Royal Navy and merchant-service. (Pl. 9, figs. 51, 52, 53). [For particulars, see Part II, under this head].

FUTTOCK STAVE. — A short piece of wood or iron, served over with spunyarn, to which the shrouds are confined at the catharpins. (Pl. 9, fig. 54).

GAFF. — A pole used to extend the head of the spanker, or mizen, of a ship; and the fore-and-aft main-sails of smaller vessels. (Pl. 10, fig. 67).

GAMMONING. — The rope which binds the inner quarter of the bowsprit close down to the stem, that it may rest well in its bed. (Pl. 6, fig. 4).

GANGWAY is that part of a ship's side, both within and without, by which persons enter and depart; it is provided with a sufficient number of steps, or cleats, nailed on the ship's side, nearly as low as the surface of the water. Gangway also implies a thoroughfare, or narrow passage, of any kind.

GASKETS. — Braided cordage, used to confine the sail to the yard, when furled, &c. *Arm Gaskets* are those used at the extremities of the yards. *Bunt Gaskets* are used in the middle of the yards. *Quarter Gaskets* are those used between the middle and extremities of the yards. (Pl. 3, fig. 13).

GIRTLINES is a rope rove through a single block, occasionally lashed to the mast and sheer-heads, to hoist up rigging, &c.

GOOSE-NECK. — A kind of iron hook, fitted on the inner end of a boom, and introduced into a clamp of iron or eye-bolt, so that it may be unhooked at pleasure.

GRAPNEL. — A small anchor, with four or five flukes, and no stock, commonly used in boats.

GRIPES are ropes used to secure the boats and booms upon the deck, to prevent them breaking adrift, by the labouring of a vessel, in heavy weather. The hooks which are spliced in their ends, are hooked to ring-bolts in the deck on each side of the boat; whence, passing over the middle and extremities, they are set-up by means of laniards rove through the dead-eyes, so as to render the boats and booms firm and secure. (Pl. 5, fig. 16).

GROMMET. — A kind of ring, or small wreath, formed of a strand of rope, laid thrice round, and used to fasten the upper edge of a sail to its respective stay in different places; by means of which the sail is accordingly hoisted or lowered.

GROUND-TACKLE. — A general name given to all sorts of ropes and furniture belonging to the anchors, or which are employed in securing a ship in a road or harbour, as cables, hawsers, tow-lines, warps, and buoy-ropes.

GUDGEONS or BRACES. — Certain clamps of iron, or other metal, bolted on the stern-post of a ship, whereon to hang the rudder; for which purpose there is a hole in each of them, to receive a corresponding pintle, bolted on the back of the rudder, according to her size; which turns thereby, as upon hinges.

GUN-SLINGS. — Similar to bale-slings, and used for hoisting in the guns. (Pl. 2, fig. 29).

GUYS.—Ropes, to steady shears, davits, or derricks, when charged with any weighty body. (Pl. 8, fig. 3).

HAG'S TEETH. — Those parts of pointing, matting, or the like, which are intertwisted with the rest, in an irregular manner, so as to spoil the uniformity of the work.

HALLIARDS. — Ropes or tackles employed to hoist or lower yards, sails, and flags upon the masts, yards, stays, &c.

HANDSOMELY signifies moderately; as, *Lower away handsomely; Heave in handsomely,* &c.

HANDSPIKE. — A wooden bar, used as a lever, to heave about the windlass, in order to draw up the anchor from the bottom, particularly in merchant-ships. It is also employed as a lever on many other occasions, as stowing the anchors, provisions, or cargo in the ship's hold.

HANKS are wooden or iron rings, fixed upon the stays, to confine the stay-sails thereto, at different distances. They are used in lieu of grommets. [See Grommet].

To HAUL. — An expression peculiar to seamen, implying to pull a single rope; as *Haul in; Haul down; Haul aft; Haul altogether,* &c.

HAWSEBAGS are canvas bags filled with oakum; they are used in a heavy sea to stop the hawse-holes, and thereby prevent the admission of the water.

HAWSER. — A kind of small cable, used on various occasions, as swaying up the top-masts, &c.

HEAD-ROPES are the ropes sewed along the upper edge of sails, &c., to strengthen them; when applied to flags, are termed *Head-lines*.

HEART. — A peculiar sort of dead-eye, resembling a heart; it has one large hole in the middle to contain the laniard, by which the stays or shrouds are extended. (Pl. 4, fig. 5).

HEAVER, or WOOLDER. — A short wooden staff, or treenail, used as a lever in setting up the top-mast shroud, by a Spanish windlass, or strapping of blocks and seizing the rigging, &c. (Pl. 5, fig. 9).

HEAVING. — The act of turning about a capstan, or windlass, by means of bars, or handspikes.

HELM. — The helm is usually composed of three parts, viz.: — the rudder, the tiller, and the wheel, except in small vessels, where the wheel is unnecessary.

HINGES are iron joints, used for sundry purposes in and about a ship, of which there are several sorts; as the butt and dovetail hinges, scuttle hinges, locker joint hinges, port side hinges, &c.

HITCH. — A noose, by which one rope is fastened to another, or to some object; as a ring, post, timber-head, &c., and has several names; as, half-hitch, clove-hitch, rolling-hitch, and timber-hitch, &c. (See Pl. 1).

HOIST of a FLAG, or SAIL. — That part which is toward the staff, or bent to a mast or stay.

HOISTING. — Drawing up a weight by tackles. (Pl. 6, fig. 12).

HOLDING-ON. — The act of pulling back and retaining any quantity of rope, acquired by the effort of a capstan, or tackle; also the end of a stopper, nipper, &c., held by the hand.

HOOK. — A crooked piece of iron, of which there are several kinds, of different shapes, used at sea; as, *boat-hooks, can-hooks, cat-hooks, chain-hooks,* &c.

HOOPS. — Thin bars of iron, of circular and other shapes. *Clasp-hoops* are similar to other hoops, but open with a hinge. *Buoy-hoops* are the iron hoops that confine the buoy; and the wreaths of rope that go round the buoy, to which the straps are fastened, are also called hoops. *Wooden hoops* are those which encircle masts, and to which the fore leech of some sails are bent.

HORNS. — The jaws, or semicircular inner ends of booms and gaffs.

HORSE. — A machine with which the operation of woolding is performed. (Pl. 5, fig. 9).

HORSES. — *Bowsprit horses,* or *Man-ropes,* are made fast at the
ends, at a parallel height from the bowsprit, and serve as rails for
the men to hold by when going out upon the bowsprit. *Flemish
horses* are small horses under the yards, without the cleats. *Jib
horses* hang under the jib-boom, and are knotted at certain distances, to prevent the men's feet from slipping. *Traverse horses,*
or *Jack-stays,* are of rope or iron, for sails to traverse on, &c.:
the one of rope is extended up and down the mast on the fore
side; it is for hoisting or lowering the square-sail, of which yard
is attached to the horse by a traveller, and slides up and down
occasionally. Horses of iron are thick iron rods, fastened at the
ends athwart the deck of single-mast vessels before the masts, for
the fore-sail sheet to travel on; and that abaft the mast, across
the inside of the stern, on which the main-sheet block travels.
Yard-horses are ropes depending from the yards, for the men to
stand upon in loosing, reefing, or furling the sails.

HOUNDS. — A name given to those parts of a mast-head which
gradually project on the right and left side beyond the cylindrical,
or conical surface, which it preserves from the partners upwards.
The hounds, whose upper parts are also called *cheeks,* are used
as shoulders to support the frame of the top and trestle-trees,
together with the top-mast, and the rigging of the lower masts.

INHAULER. — A rope employed to haul in the jib traveller, &c.

To JAMB. — This expression is usually applied to the situation of
a running rope, when it is so compressed by other bodies as to be
incapable of traversing in the blocks, till it is released from this
confinement. In this sense, *jambing* is opposed to *render.*

JAWS. — Two cheeks, forming a semicircle, which enclose the
after part of the mast, so as to confine, by the help of the parral,
the inner end of the boom, or gaff. (See Horns).

JEERS. — Tackles by which the lower yards of a ship are hoisted
up along the mast to their usual station, or lowered from thence
as occasion requires; the former of which operation is called
swaying, and the latter, *striking.* (See Sway).

JEWEL BLOCKS. — Small blocks seized to eye-bolts in the extremities of the upper yards, for hoisting the studding-sails by
the halliards which reeve through them. (Pl. 7, fig. 6).

JIB-GUYS. — (See Guys, Part II).

JIGGER. — A short rope, fitted with a block and a sheave, for holding on a cable as it is hove in by the windlass.

JIGGER TACKLE or WATCH TACKLE. — A small light tail tackle, consisting of a double and single block, and used by seamen on sundry occasions.

JUNK. — Unserviceable cables and other ropes, used for making mats, rope-bands, points, gaskets, oakum, &c.

KECKLING. — Any old rope wound about a cable, to preserve the surface of it from chafing against the ship's bow or bottom.

KEVELS. — Two crooked pieces of timber, whose lower ends rest in a step, or foot, nailed to the ship's sides; the head branches out like horns, to belay the ropes to.

KINKING. — The curling up of a rope when twisted too hard, or drawn hastily out of the coil.

KNITTLES, or NETTLES, are small lines, composed of two or three ropeyarns, either plaited or twisted, and used for various purposes at sea, particularly to fasten the service on the cable; to reef the sails by the bottom, and to sling the sailors' hammocks between decks. Knittle is also a name given to the loops, or buttons of a bonnet; likewise to bend the square-sails to the jack-stays, in lieu of rope-bands.

KNOT. — A large knot formed on the extremity of a rope, generally by unlaying the ends thereof, and interweaving them regularly amongst each other. There are several sorts of knots, which differ materially in form, size, and name, according to the uses for which they are designed; as, *bowline-knot, buoy-rope-knot, diamond-knot, reef-knot, stopper-knot,* &c. (See Pl. 1, figs. 15, 16, 24, 25, 26, 27, 28).

To KNOT. — Signifies to tie two ropes together, or the end of a rope to a bight in the same. (See BEND and HITCH).

LACING. — Fastening the head of a sail to a mast, yard, gaff, &c., by a line turned spirally round them, and rove through the eyelet-holes in the sail.

LANIARDS. — Pieces of rope applied for various purposes; as the *laniards to the port,* the *laniard of the buoy,* the *laniard of the stoppers,* &c. The principal laniards used in a ship are those employed to extend the shrouds and stays of the masts, by their communication with the dead-eyes and hearts, so as to form a sort of mechanical power, resembling a tackle. (Pl. 4, figs. 1 and 5). [See DEAD-EYES and HEARTS].

LASHERS. — The ropes employed to lash or secure particular objects; as jeers, &c.

LASHING denotes a piece of rope used to fasten or secure any moveable body in a ship, or about her masts, sails, and rigging.

LASHING OF BOOMS. — That is, the spare top-mast, yards, &c., stowed on the boat-skids on each side. They are first secured in different places with several turns of lashing on one side, independent of the other; then cross-lashed together, and well frapped in the middle. In gales of wind, to prevent the boom shifting, several turns with a hawser are taken round the booms and through large triangular ring-bolts in the sides, and sometimes the turns are passed through an opposite port, and round the side; the turns are then hove tight, frapped, and belayed.

LAUNCH HO! — The order to let go the top rope after any mast is fidded.

LEADING-PART. — That part of a tackle which is hauled upon. (Pl. 7, fig. 3).

LEECH LINES are ropes used to truss up the leeches of the courses. (Pl. 12, figs. 21 and 27).

LEECH ROPE. — (See BOLT ROPE).

LEGS. — Short ropes which branch out into two or more parts; as the *bowline legs* or *bridles, buntline legs, crow-foot legs*, &c.

LIFE LINES are for the preservation of seamen upon the yards.

LIFTS. — Certain ropes descending from the cap and mast-head to the extremities of the yard immediately under; they are used to keep the yard horizontal, or to pull one of its extremities higher than the other, if occasion requires, but particularly to support the weight of it when a number of seamen are employed thereon, to furl or reef the sail. (Pl. 10, figs. 7, 9, 11, 16, 19, 22, 24, 27, 30).

LINES. — Cordage, smaller than ropes, and formed by two or more fine strands of hemp; as *houseline,* made of three strands, used to seize blocks into their straps and the clues of sails, and to marl the skirts of sails to their bolt-ropes, &c.; *log-line,* made of three or more strands, and used for the log, &c.; *marline,* made of two strands, and used for the same purposes as houseline.

LIZARD. — An iron thimble, spliced into the main bowlines, and pointed over to hook a tackle to; or any thimble with a sail spliced into it.

LOOP. — A noose made in a rope.

LOOSING THE SAILS. — Unfurling them for setting, or for drying, when wet.

LUFF TACKLE. — A name given to any large tackle that is not destined for a particular place, but may be variously employed as occasion requires; it generally consists of a double and single block, but sometimes of two double blocks. [See TACKLE]. (Pl. 7, fig. 2).

MAIN TACKLE. — A large strong tackle, hooked occasionally upon the main pendant, and used for various purposes, particularly in securing the mast, setting up the rigging, stays, &c. (Pl. 9, fig. 58).

MAN-ROPES. — A general name given to the small sets of ropes, used for ascending or descending a ship's side, hatchway, &c. Bowsprit horses are also called man-ropes.

MARLINE SPIKE. — A tapered iron pin, used to make openings between the strands of ropes, for introducing the ends of others through them; it is sometimes used as a lever, to strain tight seizings, &c. (Pl. 3, fig. 13).

MARTINGALE. — The name of the rope extending downwards from the jib-boom end to the dolphin striker; its use is to confine the jib-boom down in the same manner as the bobstays retain the bowsprit. [See BOWSPRIT]. (Pl. 9, fig. 46).

MASTS. — Long cylindrical pieces of timber, to which are fastened the yards, sails, and rigging.

MAST COATS. — (See COAT).

MAT. — A thick texture, made of spunyarn, strands of rope, or foxes, woven or plaited together, and fastened upon masts, yards, &c., to prevent their chafing. (Pl. 5, fig. 17).

MAUL. — A large iron hammer, used for various purposes of driving bolts, &c. *Top Maul* is distinguished from above by having an iron handle with an eye at the end, by which it is made fast to the mast-head, to prevent accidents by its falling out of the top; it is particularly used to drive the fid in or out of the top-mast, or for keeping the top down when setting up the top-mast-rigging.

MESHES. — The space between the lines of a netting.

MESSENGER. — A large rope or chain, used to unmoor, or heave up the anchors, by transmitting the efforts of the capstan to the cable. This operation is performed by fastening one part of the messenger to the cable in several places, by a particular kind of rope, called nippers, and by winding another part thereof three or four times about the capstan, which answers the same purpose as if the cable itself were in that manner wound round the capstan; and the messenger being much lighter and more pliant, it is infinitely more convenient. The rope messenger has an eye spliced at each end, through which several turns of a strong lashing are passed; and the chain has a shackle to connect its ends, thereby forming a continuation whereby a quantity passes forward on one side equal to what is hove in on the other. (Pl. 3, figs. 15 and 16).

MOUSING A HOOK. — Taking several turns of spunyarn round the back and point of a hook, and fastening it, to prevent its unhooking.

NAVE LINE is a rope on a bight thrown over a yard, &c., to help it up and down.

NETTING. — A fence made by seizing together the bights of small ropes, leaving uniform spaces or meshes between; it is used in different parts of a ship. *Forecastle, gangway, quarter,* and *waist-nettings,* are used to keep the hammocks in the stanchions.

To NIPPER, OR NIP ROPES, is to stop them with several turns of ropeyarn alternately round each, and the ends made fast.

NIPPERS. — Selvagees, 12 or 14 feet long, used in heaving in the cable by the messenger.

NORMAN. — A short wooden bar, with a head, used in one of the holes of the windlass, when there is little strain on the cable, to stopper it. It is sometimes used in the capstan holes when at sea, to belay the fore-braces to.

OAKUM. — The substance into which old ropes are reduced, when they are untwisted, loosened, and drawn asunder. It is principally used in caulking the seams of vessels.

OVERHAUL. — Is to extend the several parts of a tackle, or other assemblage of ropes, communicating with blocks, or dead-eyes, so that they may be again placed in a state of action.

OUTHAULER. — A rope made fast to the traveller of the jib, to haul it out by.

OUTRIGGER. — (See Part II, under GUYS and OUTRIGGERS).

PAINTER. — A rope secured to the stem of a boat, to make her fast with.

PANCH. — A covering of wood, or thick texture made of plaited ropeyarn, larger than a mat, to preserve the masts, &c., from chafing.

PARBUCKLE. — A contrivance to hoist or lower bodies, by fastening the bight of a rope over fixed objects, and passing the ends of it under the body or article to be hoisted, &c.: they are then turned upward toward the bight, and hauled upon or slackened, as occasion requires. (Pl. 5, fig. 1).

PARCELLING. — A name given to long narrow slips of tarred canvas, and bound about a rope, in the manner of bandages, previous to its being sewed. It is laid in spiral turns, as smoothly upon the surface as possible, that the rope may not become uneven and full of ridges. (Pl. 5, fig. 2).

PARRAL. — A sort of collar, by which the yards are fastened at the slings to the masts, so that they may be hoisted or lowered with facility. (Pl. 5, figs. 14 and 15). [See Part II].

PARRAL TRUCKS. — [See Trucks]. (Pl. 5, fig. 15).

PASSAREE. — Any rope fastened round the cat-head and fore-tack, to keep tight the leech of the sail in light winds.

To PAY OUT. — To let a cable or other rope run out of the vessel.

PEAK HALLIARDS. — The ropes by which the outer end of a gaff or yard that hangs obliquely to a mast that is hoisted. (Pl. 10, fig. 46).

PENDANTS. — Large but short ropes which go over the mastheads, and to which are hooked the main and fore-tackles. There are besides many other pendants, with a block or tackle attached to one end, all of which serve to transmit the effort of their tackles to some other object; such as the *bill pendant; burton pendants; fish pendants; main* and *fore pendants; main stay tackle pendants; quarter tackle pendants; top-rope pendants; truss pendants; winding tackle pendants;* and *yard tackle pendants.* (For the preparation of these pendants, see Part II).

PINS, for belaying ropes to, are wooden or metal, with a shoulder near the middle; the small end is driven through racks of plank made on purpose. Pins for blocks are of wood or iron, driven through the shell, and form the axis on which the sheaves turn.

POINTING. — Tapering the end of a rope or splice, and work over the reduced part, a small close netting, with an even number of knittles twisted from the same, to prevent the end untwisting, and to go more easily through a block or hole. (Pl. 3, fig. 14).

POINTS are pieces of braided cordage plaited together, with an eye in one end, and tapering toward the other, used to reef the sails.

PORT PENDANTS. — Ropes spliced into the rings on the outside of the port-lids; they lead through the lead pipes in the ship's side, and are used to haul up the port-lids, by the assistance of port-tackles.

PREVENTER. — An additional rope, employed sometimes to support, or answer the purpose of, another that has a great strain upon it, or is injured: such as the *preventer braces, shrouds, stays,* &c.

PREVENTER STAYS. — (See SPRING STAYS).

PURCHASE. — Tackles frequently employed in fixing or extending the rigging of a ship. They are also used to remove or raise heavy bodies, with the assistance of other mechanical powers; such as the *capstan, windlass, screw, handspike,* &c.

QUARTER TACKLES are used to hoist water, provisions, &c., in or out of the ship.

RACK. — A short thin plank, with holes made through it, containing a number of belaying pins, used instead of cleats. It sometimes contains a number of sheaves for leading ropes through, instead of blocks, which are belayed to pins in the same rack.

RACKING A TACKLE. — Fastening together the fall of a tackle, or any two ropes, by passing two or more cross-turns with rope-yarn round each part, and as many round-turns above them, making fast the ends with a reef-knot.

RATLINES OR RATLINGS.—Small ropes which cross the shrouds horizontally, at equal distances, from the deck upwards, forming ladders to go up or down from the mast-heads.

To RATTLE DOWN THE SHROUDS, is to fix the ratlines to them. They are firmly attached by a hitch, called a *clove-hitch,* to all the shrouds, except the foremost and aftermost, where both ends, being fitted with an eye-splice, are fastened with seizings.

REEF. — That portion of a sail contained between the head or foot, and a row of eyelet-holes parallel thereto; which portion is taken up to reduce the surface of the sail, when the wind increases. Sails according to their sizes, have from one to four reefs. *Bag Reef* is the fourth or lower reef of a top-sail. *Balance*

Reef crosses the boom-main-sails diagonally from the nock to the end of the upper reef band, on the after leech.

REEF TACKLE. — A rope which passes from the deck through a block in the top-mast rigging, and thence through a sheave-hole in the top-sail-yard-arm, and is afterwards attached to a cringle a little below the lowest reef, and used to draw the leeches of the sail up to the extremities of the yard, in order to lighten the sail at the time of reefing.

To REEVE, is to pass the end of a rope through any hole or channel of a block, the cavity of a thimble, ring-bolt, cringle, &c. Hence, to pull a rope out of a block, hole, &c., is termed *un-reeving*.

RELIEVING TACKLES. — Tackles used to the fore end of the tiller, in action, or bad weather.

RIBS OF A PARRAL. — Short, flat pieces of wood, having a hole near each end, through which the parral rope is rove. (Pl. 5, fig. 14).

RIDGE TACKLE. — The tackle used to suspend the awning in the middle or sides.

To RIG. — To fit the shrouds, stays, braces, &c., to their respective masts and yards.

RIGGING. — A general name given to all the ropes employed to support the masts, and to extend or reduce the sails.

RIGGING-HOUSE OR LOFT. — A place on shore, in which much of the rigging is prepared for fitting on board. At the upper end of it is a windlass; and at certain distances down the middle are two rows of large strong posts, for stretching ropes and laying on service. On each side of the house are berths, for the men to prepare small rigging in; such of the rigging as is here prepared is fully explained in Part II; but as that is dispersed in alphabetical order, it may be convenient perhaps to present, at one view, a list of those articles which are thus previously prepared on shore. They consist of the following, viz.: — *Back-stays* — standing back-stays for top-masts and top-gallant-masts; *Bob-stays; Breast back-stay runners; Buoy-hoops; Buoy-ropes; Buoy slings; Catharpin legs; Collars* for bob-stays, bowsprit shrouds, fore-stay, fore spring-stay, main-stay, main spring-stay, top-mast stays, and top-mast spring-stays; *Davit guys; Fore tack; Futtock staves; Horses* for the jib-boom and lower yards; jeers for the lower yards; *Main tack; Parral ropes; Pend-*

ants — fish-tackle pendant, fore-tackle pendants, main-stay-tackle pendants, main-tackle pendants, mizen burton pendants, quarter-tackle pendants, rudder pendants, top-rope pendants, truss pendants, vang pendants, and yard-tackle pendants; *Puddening of Anchors; Runners of Tackles; Shrouds* — bowsprit shrouds, futtock shrouds, the lower, top-mast and top-gallant shrouds; *Slings* — butt and hogshead slings, can-hook slings, and gun slings; *Spans* about the masts, and long and short spans; *Stays* for the lower-masts and top-gallant-masts; *Stoppers* — deck and bitt stoppers; *Strapping* of blocks; *Ties* for top-sail-yards, &c., &c. (See Part II).

ROLLING TACKLE. — A purchase, occasionally fastened to that part of a yard which is to windward of the mast, in order to confine the yard close over to leeward, to steady it.

ROPE-BANDS. — Braided cordage, having an eye at one end: they are used to fasten the heads of the sails to their respective yards. (See KNITTLES).

ROPES. — All cordage in general, above one inch in circumference, which bear different names, according to their various uses. *Bolt Rope* is the rope sewed to the skirts or edges of sails. *Buoy Rope.* — A rope fastened to the buoy of the anchor. *Breast Rope* is fastened along the laniards of the shrouds, for safety, when heaving the lead in the chains. *Davit Rope* is the lashing which secures the davit to the shrouds, when out of use. *Entering Ropes* hang from the upper part of the stanchions alongside the ladder at the gangways. *Guest Rope* is fastened to an eye-bolt in the ship's side, and to the outer end of a boom, projecting from the ship's side, by guys, to keep the boats clear off the sides. *Heel Rope* is to haul out jib-booms, and the bowsprits of cutters, &c. *Passing Ropes* lead round the ship, through eyes in the quarter, waist, gangway, and forecastle stanchions, forward to the knight-heads. *Ring Ropes* are occasionally made fast to the ring-bolts in the deck, and by cross-turns round the cable, to confine it securely in stormy weather. *Slip Rope* is to trice the bight of the cable into the head, and is also employed in casting off a vessel in a tide-way, &c. *Tiller Rope* is the rope by which the tiller is worked. (Explained in Part III). *Top Rope* is a rope rove through the heel of a top-mast, to raise it by its tackle to the mast-head.

ROPEYARN is one of the threads of which a rope is composed.

ROUGH-TREE RAIL. — A rail, breast high, along the sides of the poop and quarter-deck.

ROUND-UP implies, to gather in the slack of any rope which passes through one or more blocks in a perpendicular direction; and is particularly applied to a tackle; as, *Round up the main tackle.*

ROUNDING. — A name given to old ropes wound closely about that part of the cable which lies in the hawse, or athwart the stem, &c. It is used to prevent the cable from being chafed in those places. (See Keckling and Service).

ROUND-TURN. — The situation of the cables of a ship, which, when moored, has swung the wrong way, and twisted round each other, by the force of the wind, tide, or current. (See Hawse). *Round-Turn* is also the passing of a rope once round a timber-head, &c., in order to hold on.

To ROWSE. — To pull together upon a cable, hawser, tackle, &c., without the assistance of a capstan, windlass, or other mechanical power; as, *Rowse hearty.*

RUDDER-COATS. — (See Coat).

RUDDER TACKLES. — Tackles used to save or direct the rudder, when any accident happens to the tiller.

RUNNER. — A single rope, connected with a tackle, which transmits its effort the same as if the tackle was the whole length; such as the *Breast backstay runner, runners of tackles,* &c.

RUNNER TACKLES. — Tackles used to set up the shrouds, and to get the mast-heads forward, for staying the masts.

RUNNING-RIGGING is that which is fitted for the purpose of arranging the sails, by passing through various blocks, in different places about the masts, yards, shrouds, &c.; as the *braces, sheets, halliards,* &c.

SADDLES for BOOMS. — A small block of wood, hollowed on the lower and upper sides, and nailed on the bowsprit, for retaining the jib-boom in a steady position.

SCIATIC STAY or SPAN. — A strong rope, fixed from the main to the fore-mast-head in merchant ships, when loading or unloading; it serves to sustain a tackle, which, travelling upon it, may be shifted over the main or fore hatchways as occasion requires.

SEIZING. — Joining two ropes, or the two ends of one rope, together, &c., by taking several close turns of small rope, line, or spunyarn round them. *End Seizing* is a round seizing on the end of a rope. *Throat Seizing* is the first seizing clapped on where a rope or ropes cross each other. *Middle Seizing* is a seizing between a throat and end seizing. *Eye Seizing* is a round seizing, next the eye of a shroud, &c. (Pl. 4, fig. 1).

SELVAGEE. — Several ropeyarns turned into a circular form, and marled together with spunyarn. It is used to attach the hook of a tackle to any rope, shroud, or stay, to extend or set them up, not being so likely to slip as rope; two or more turns of the selvagee are taken round the same, in which the hook is fixed. (Pl. 5, fig. 11).

To SERVE is to wind round spunyarn, &c., by means of a mallet, to prevent it from being rubbed. The materials used for the purpose are called *service*. (Pl. 5, fig. 3).

SERVICE. — A term given to all sorts of stuff, whether of old canvas, mat, plat, hide, parcelling, spunyarn, &c., when put round the cables, or other ropes, in order to preserve them from being chafed.

SERVING MALLET. — A cylindrical piece of wood, with a handle in the middle; it is used for serving, and has a groove along the surface, opposite the handle, which fits the convexity of the rope to be served. (Pl. 5, fig. 3).

SETTING THE SAILS. — Loosing and expanding them.

SETTING UP. — Increasing the tension of the shrouds, stays, and back-stays, to secure the masts by tackles, laniards, &c.

SHACKLES are made of iron, with a bolt and pin, and are used to connect the different lengths of a chain cable; there are several sorts of shackles. (Pl. 6, figs. 6 and 7).

SHANK-PAINTER. — A short rope and chain, bolted to the ship's sides above the fore-channels, to hang or secure the shank of an anchor to, the flukes resting in a chock on the gunwale.

SHEAVE. — A solid cylindrical wheel, fitted in blocks, &c., and moveable about an axis, called the pin. (Pl. 2, fig. 9).

SHEEP-SHANK. — A sort of knot made on backstays, to shorten them, when the masts are struck, by bending part of the back-stay, &c., in three parts, and taking a half-hitch over the end. (Pl. 1, fig. 5).

SHEERS are used for masting vessels when there is no sheer-hulk. They are generally composed of two hand-masts, or top-masts, or other large spars, erected on the vessel whose masts are to be fixed or displaced; the lower ends or heels rest on opposite sides of the deck, upon which thick plank is laid, sufficiently long to extend over two or three beams, shored underneath. The two hand-masts cross each other at the upper end, and are securely lashed, as represented in Pl. 8, fig. 4. The sheers are secured by guys, of proportionable rope, extending fore and aft to the opposite extremities of the vessel; and the heels are lashed also.

Method of taking out a first-rate's main-mast, by means of two top-masts. — The top-masts of a first-rate are about seventy feet long, and strong enough to take the main-mast out; therefore, after securely lashing the top-masts together, near the head, or upper end, so as to form sheers, as above described, and lashing the blocks at the sheer-head, measure the distance from the heel of the mast to the upper side of the quarter-deck, which will be found to be about forty-five feet; then set off that distance down the mast from the lower part of the sheer-head blocks, and let that be the upper part of the lower blocks on the mast, allowing for the lashing stretching, and a few feet spare if possible: that will be sufficient to clear the heel of the quarter-deck and the gunwale on either side, as represented in Pl. 8, fig. 2. As the blocks on the mast are lashed nearer to the heel than the head, the head of course must be the heaviest: to steady which, let a tackle be lashed at each sheer-head, and likewise on the mast (to avoid unhooking), to act as steadying-tackles in lowering the masts, as in fig. 3, Pl. 8. But before the heel of the mast is clear of the upper deck, there must be, as represented in fig. 2, two luff-tackles lashed, one block to the heel of the mast, the other to the heel of the sheers, if there is no secure place in the ship's side, also two fore-and-aft tackles; so that when the heel of the mast is clear of the deck, the head of the mast may not incline too suddenly, as in fig. 3. In this manner the masts of any ship may be taken in or out with the greatest safety.

SHEET. — A rope or tackle fastened to one or both the lower corners of a sail, to extend and retain it in a perpendicular direction. The square-sails have two sheets. The stay-sails and studding-sails have only one tack and one sheet each. The stay-sail tacks are always fastened forward, and the sheet drawn aft; but the studding-sail tacks draw the outer clue of the sail to the extremity of the boom, while the sheet is employed to extend the inmost.

SHIFTING BACKSTAY TACKLES. — Tackles used to set up the shifting backstays when wanted.

SHIP-SHAPE. — According to the fashion of a ship; as, *That mast is not rigged ship-shape.*

SHROUDS. — A range of large ropes, extended from the mast-head to the port and starboard sides of the vessel, to support the masts, &c. (Pl. 9, figs. 7, 8, 9). The shrouds are denominated from the places to which they belong; thus, the *fore, main,* and *mizen shrouds; fore, main,* and *mizen top-mast shrouds,* &c. (Pl. 9, figs. 17, 18, 19). *Bowsprit Shrouds* are those which support the bowsprit. (Pl. 9, fig. 3). *Bumpkin Shrouds* are those which support the bumpkins. *Futtock Shrouds* are shrouds which connect the efforts of the top-mast shrouds to the lower shrouds or masts. (Pl. 9, figs. 51, 52, 53).

SLABLINE is a rope used to trice up the foot of courses occasionally.

SLACK implies a decrease in tension of a rope; as, *Slacken the laniards of the lower rigging.*

SLACK OF A ROPE is that part which hangs loose, as having no strain or stress upon it.

SLACK RIGGING implies that the shrouds, stays, &c., are not so firmly extended as they ought to be.

SLINGS. — Short ropes, used to hang the yards to the masts, &c., or to encircle a bale or cask, and suspend it whilst hoisting or lowering; and also to secure buoys, &c. (Pl. 5, figs. 6, 7, 8, &c.).

SLIP-KNOT is one which will not bear any strain, but will either become untied, or will traverse along the other part of the rope.

SLIP-ROPE is a rope used to trice up the bight of other ropes; as, *Get a slip rope round the bight of a cable, and trice it up into the head.*

To SLUE. — To turn a mast or boom about in its cap, or boom-iron, &c.

SNAKING. — A sort of fastening, to confine the outer turns of seizings, &c. (Pl. 6, fig. 2).

SNAKING THE STAYS, or ropes on the quarters, instead of netting, is seizing proportioned sized rope at angles from one stay or rope to the other alternately, in a parallel direction along the whole length. Its use to stays is, that one part may remain perfect and independent of the other, should it be shot away. (Pl. 5, fig. 10).

SNOTTER. — A short rope, spliced together at the ends, and served with spunyarn, or covered with hide; it is seized to the size of the mast, leaving a bight to fit the lower end of a sprit, which it confines to the mast.

SPANS. — Short ropes, having a block, thimble, or eye spliced into each end; the middle is hitched round a mast, yard, gaff, cap, or stay, whence the ends branch out. Spans are sometimes fastened at both ends, and have a block in the bight. They are used to lead ropes through, which pass through the blocks or thimbles to increase power, or to prevent their swinging about.

SPANNING of BOOMS. — Confining them by ropes.

SPANNING of RUNNERS. — Taking several turns with small ropes round both runners abaft the mast, and frapping the turns.

SPANISH WINDLASS. [See Windlass]. (Pl. 5, fig. 9).

SPARS. — Small trees.

SPILLING LINES are certain ropes, fixed occasionally to the top-sails and courses of a ship, in tempestuous weather, for reefing or furling them more conveniently.

SPLICING. — Joining one rope to another, by interweaving the ends, or uniting the end of a rope into another part of it. There are different sorts of splices, viz.: — The *Cont Splice,* which forms an eye in the middle of a rope. (Pl. 3, figs. 1, 2, 3). The *Eye Splice* forms an eye or circle, at the end of a rope on itself, around a block, &c. (Pl. 3, figs. 4 and 5). The *Long Splice* is made to rejoin a rope or ropes intended to reeve through a block, without increasing its size. (Pl. 3, figs. 6 and 7). The *Short Splice* is made by unlaying the ends of a rope, or of two ropes, and placing the strands of one between those of the other. (Pl. 3, figs. 8 and 9). The *Tapered Splice* is chiefly used on cables, and is made as the short splice, but is gradually tapered towards each end, by cutting away some of the ropeyarns, and is served over. (Pl. 3, figs. 10 and 11). The *Drawing Splice* is a splice used for joining cables together, and is esteemed the best for this purpose, as it may be readily undone. (Pl. 3, fig. 12).

SPRING STAYS. — Assistant stays, extending in a direction nearly parallel to the principal stays; they are sometimes less in circumference than the others, and used to the lower-masts and top-masts, for hoisting the stay-sail upon.

SPRIT. — A small yard or pole, by which the sprit-sails are extended. The foot of it is fixed in a snotter, which encircles the

Plate IV

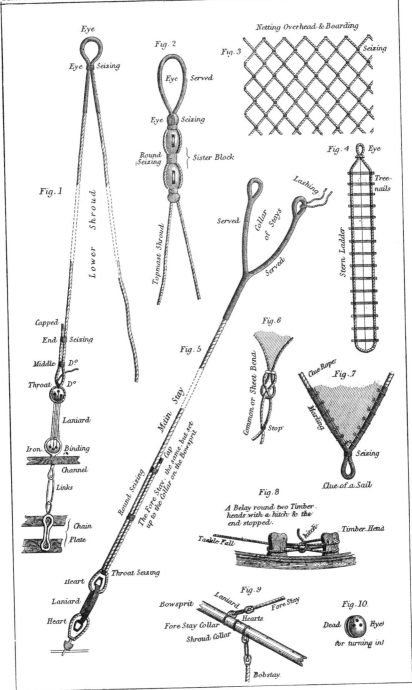

Netting Overhead & Boarding

Fig. 3

Seizing

4

Fig. 2

Eye

Eye   Served

Eye   Seizing

Round
Seizing   } Sister Block

Topmast Shroud

Eye

Eye

Eye   Seizing

Fig. 1

Lower Shroud

Capped
End   Seizing

Middle   Dᵒ

Throat   Dᵒ

Laniard

Iron   Binding

Channel

Links

Chain
Plate

Fig. 4   Eye

Tree-
nails

Stern Ladder

Fig. 5

Main Stay

Round Seizing

The Fore Stay, the same, but set
up to the Collar on the Bowsprit

Heart   Throat Seizing

Laniard

Heart

Collar
of Stays

Lashing

Served

Served

Fig. 6

Common or Sheet Bend

Stop

Clue Rope   Fig. 7

Marling

Seizing

Clue of a Sail

Fig. 8

A Belay round two Timber
heads with a hitch & the
end stopped.

Tackle Fall   hitch   Timber Head

Fig. 9

Bowsprit   Laniard   Fore Stay

Hearts

Fore Stay Collar

Shroud Collar

Bobstay.

Fig. 10.

Dead   Eye

for turning in!

Plate V.

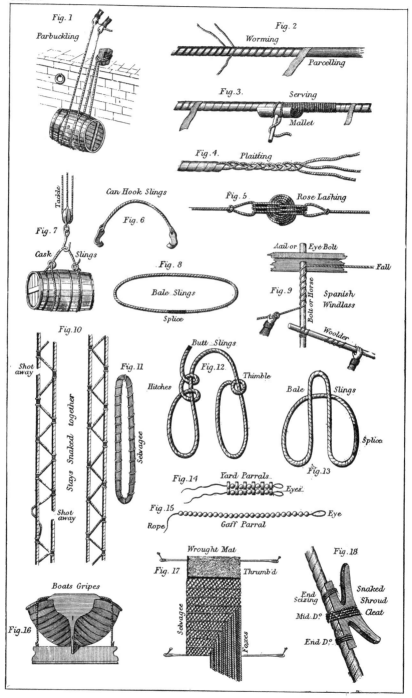

Fig. 1
Parbuckling

Fig. 2
Worming
Parcelling

Fig. 3.
Serving
Mallet

Fig. 4.
Plaiting

Tackle
Can Hook Slings
Fig. 6

Fig. 7
Cask Slings

Fig. 5
Rose Lashing

Fig. 8
Bale Slings
Splice

Rail or Eye Bolt
Fall
Fig. 9
Bolt or Horse
Spanish Windlass
Woolder

Fig. 10
Shot away
Stays Snaked together
Shot away

Fig. 11
Selvagee

Butt Slings
Fig. 12
Hitches
Thimble

Bale Slings
Fig. 13
Splice

Fig. 14
Yard Parrals
Eyes

Fig. 15
Rope
Gaff Parral
Eye

Wrought Mat
Fig. 17
Thrumb'd
Selvagee
Foxes

Fig. 18
End Seizing
Snaked Shroud Cleat
Mid. D.º
End D.º

Boats Gripes
Fig. 16

mast, and it crosses the sail diagonally; the upper end being attached to the peak.

SPUNYARN. — A small line or cord, formed of two or three rope-yarns, twisted together by a winch. The yarns are usually drawn out of the strands of old cables, knotted together, and tarred. It is employed for several purposes, particularly for seizing; to fasten one rope to another; to seize blocks to the shrouds; and to serve ropes which are liable to be chafed, &c.

SQUARE-RIGGED. — A term applied to those ships which have yards at right angles with the length of the keel and lower-mast; it is thence used in contra-distinction to those vessels whose sails are extended by stays between yards, &c.

SQUARE-SAIL BOOM. — A boom extended to windward in vessels carrying a square-sail, supported by guys, to spread the foot of the sail to windward; it is also used in small square-rigged vessels, lashed to the foot of the fore-sail, to avoid tacks and sheets.

STAFF. — A light pole, on which the flags are hoisted. The *Ensign Staff* is the principal staff, and is erected on the stern, within side of the tafferal, to display the ensign. (Pl. 9, fig. 60). The *Jack Staff* is a short staff, erected on the aft-side of the bowsprit cap, to expand the jack.

STAGE. — A small platform, made of grating or of short bands, for men to stand upon to fix the rigging towards the outer end of the bowsprit, &c.

STANDING-PART. — That part of a tackle which is made fast. (Pl. 7, figs. 1, 2, 3).

STANDING-RIGGING is that which is employed to sustain the masts, and which remains in a fixed position; as the *shrouds, stays,* and *backstays.*.

STANDING PART of a ROPE (in the making of knots, &c.), means the principal part of a rope; or it may be said to be that part of a rope which is at rest, and is acted upon by the end.

STANCHIONS of the NETTINGS. — Square wooden pillars, let into the upper part of the ship's side, or small pillars of iron, used to support the nettings, awnings, &c .

STAYS. — Strong ropes, to support the masts forward, which extend from their upper part, at the mast-head, toward the fore part of the ship. Stays are denominated from the masts; as, *lower stays, top-mast stays, top-gallant stays,* or *royal stays,* &c.

(See Pl. 9, figs. 10, 11, 12, 13, 14, 23, 24, 25, 26, 27, 34, 35, 36, 40, 41, 42).

STAY-SAIL STAY TACKLES. — Tackles used to set up the jib and other stay-sail stays.

STAY TACKLES (MAIN and FORE HATCH). — Tackles used for hoisting anything out of the main and fore hold and for hoisting the boats in or out.

STERN-FAST. — A rope to confine or secure the sterns of vessels, or boats, &c.

STIRRUPS. — Short ropes, which have an eye in their upper ends; which eye is put over an eye-bolt in the yards. Eyes are made in their lower ends, through which the horses are rove, to keep them parallel to the yards.

STOCK TACKLE is used to keep the stock clear of the ship's side, when fishing the anchor.

STOOLS. — Small channels fixed to the ship's sides, to contain the dead-eyes for the backstays.

STOP. — Several turns of spunyarn taken round the end of a rope, similar to a seizing, to fasten it to another rope. Also a projection left on the upper part of top-gallant masts, &c., to prevent the rigging from sliding down.

STOPPERS. — Short ropes, used to check the cable, suspend weighty bodies, and retain the shrouds, &c., in a fixed position, after being damaged or otherwise. *Anchor Stoppers* are used to suspend the anchor, when catted. *Bitt Stoppers* are those stoppers used to check the cable. *Deck Stoppers* are used to retain the cable when the ship is riding at anchor. *Shroud Stoppers* are used to confine a shroud together, when damaged or shot. *Fore Tack* and *Sheet Stoppers* are for securing the tacks and sheets, until belayed.

STRAND. — (See CABLE).

STRANDED. — Speaking of a cable or rope, signifies that one of its strands is broken.

STRAPS. — Wreaths of rope, spliced round blocks, or encircling a yard, or any large rope, by which tackles, &c., may be connected to them, as in setting up the rigging where one hook of the tackle is fixed in a strap, applied to the particular shroud, and the other to the laniard. (See Pl. 2, figs. 1, 2, 3, &c.).

To SURGE. — To slack gently a cable or rope, so that it may slide up the capstan, round which it is turned; as, *Surge the Messenger*.

SWAB. — A large bunch of old junk, or ropeyarns, seized round at the bight or upper end, and used to clean the decks, &c., as a sort of mop.

SWAGGING-OFF. — Pulling upon the middle of a tight rope that is made fast at both ends.

To SWAY implies to hoist, and is particularly applied to the lower yards, top-masts, top-sail-yards, and top-gallant-masts and yards; as, *Sway up the lower yards, top-masts,* &c.

SWIFTER. — A strong rope, sometimes used to encircle a boat lengthwise, as well to strengthen and defend her sides, as to enable her the better to resist the impression of other boats which may run against her. It is usually fixed about 10 inches below the boat's upper edge, or gunwale. This rope is oftentimes termed a *fender*. (See FENDER).

SWIFTER. — A rope used to confine the bars of the capstan in their sockets, whilst the men are heaving it round; for which purpose, it is passed through holes in the extremities of the bars, so as to strain them firmly together, like the spokes of a wheel, which operation is called *swifting*.

SWIFTERS are the aftermost shrouds on each side the lower masts; they are above all the other shrouds, and are never confined to the catharpins.

SWIFTERING OF SHROUDS. — Stretching them by tackles, to prevent any future extension; — only done in bad weather.

SWIVEL is a strong link of iron, used in mooring-chains, &c., which permits the bridles to be turned repeatedly round, as occasion requires.

SWIVEL-HOOK. — A hook that turns in the end of an iron block strap, and readily takes the turns out of a tackle.

TACK. — A rope used to confine the foremost lower corners of the courses and stay-sails in a fixed position, when the wind crosses the ship's course obliquely. The same name is also given to the rope employed to pull out the lower corner of a studding-sail to the extremity of the boom. The courses are furnished with a tack on each side, formed of a thick rope tapering to the end, and rove through a block in the clue of the sail; the tack therefore extends the sail to windward, whilst the sheet extends it to leeward. *Tack* is also applied by analogy to that part of any sail to which the tack is fastened.

TACK OF A FLAG. — A line spliced into the eye at the bottom of the tabling, for securing the flag to the halliard.

TACK TACKLE is composed of a double and single block, strapped with hooks and thimbles; it is used for bowsing down the tacks of the principal sails to their respective stations, and particularly attached to the tacks of the main-sails of brigs, sloops, cutters and schooners, for the same purpose.

TACKLE. — A machine formed by the connection of a rope or fall, with an assemblage of blocks. (See Pl. 7, figs. 1, 2, 3. — *See more particularly* Part II, *under the word* TACKLE).

TAIL. — The long end of a block strap, by which the block is attached to any place required. (Pl. 2, figs. 1, 5, 6).

TARPAWLING. — Canvas, payed over with tar, and used to cover hatches, to prevent water from going in; and to cover the blocks at the sheer-heads of hulks, &c.

THIMBLES. — A kind of iron rings, the outsides of which are grooved, to receive ropes of different sizes. They are fixed to the rigging for blocks to be hooked to, and for ropes to reeve through, &c. (Pl. 2, figs. 25 and 26).

THROAT. — A name given to the end of a gaff, which is next the mast.

THROAT-BRAILS are those ropes which are attached to the gaff, close to the mast. (Pl. 11, fig. 50).

THROAT-HALLIARDS are ropes or tackles applied to hoist the inner end of the gaff. (Pl. 10, fig. 47).

THRUMMING. — Interplacing, in a regular manner, through intervals of matting, made by a fid, short pieces of thrums or ropeyarn.

TILLER-ROPE. — (See ROPE).

TIMENOGUY. — A rope fastened at one end to the fore-shrouds, and seized at the other to the anchor stock, on the bow, to prevent the fore-sheet from entangling.

TOGGLE. — A small wooden pin, and usually tapering from the middle, toward the extremities. It is fixed transversely. They are used for the bowlines, sheets, reef-tackles, clue-lines, bunt-lines, &c., by which means, square-sails are bent with astonishing expedition, when compared with the ordinary mode.

TOP. — A platform surrounding the lower mast-heads, from which it projects on all sides like a scaffold. The principal intention of the top is to extend the top-mast shrouds, so as to form a greater angle with the top-mast, in order to give additional support to it.

TOP-ROPE. — A rope employed to sway up a top-mast or top-gallant mast, in order to fix it in its place, or to lower it in tempestuous weather, or when it is no longer necessary. The rope used on this occasion for the top-masts is, on account of their great weight, furnished with a top-tackle at its lower end, to hoist or lower the mast with greater facility.

TOP-ROPE PENDANTS. — (See PENDANTS).

TOP-TACKLE, OR TOP-ROPE TACKLE. — A large tackle hooked to the lower end of the top-mast top-rope, and to the deck, in order to increase the mechanical power in hoisting the top-mast. It is composed of two strong iron-bound double or triple blocks, the hooks of which work on a swivel.

TOPPING. — The act of drawing one of the yard-arms higher than the other, by slackening one lift, and pulling upon the other.

TOPPING-LIFT. — A rope to suspend, or top, the outer end of a gaff, boom, &c. (Pl. 10, fig. 50).

TOWLINE. — A small cable-laid rope, generally used to remove a ship from one part of a harbour or road to another, by means of anchors, capstans, boats, &c.

TRAIN TACKLE is composed of double and single hooked blocks, the latter being hooked to a ring-bolt in the deck, the former to an eye-bolt in the train of the carriage, to prevent the gun from running out of the port whilst loading.

TRAVELLER. — A large iron thimble, the diameter of which is larger than the common thimbles, though the surface is smaller. The *Jib Traveller* is a circular iron hoop, with a hook, to which the jib-stay is made fast, and a shackle to haul out the jib with.

TRAVERSE HORSES, or JACKSTAYS. (See HORSES).

TREENAILS. — The wooden pins, by which the ship's planks are fastened to the timbers.

TRESTLE-TREES. — Two strong pieces of oak, bolted to the sides of the lower-mast-heads, to support the crosstrees top and weight of the top-mast; and to the top-mast-heads, to support the top-gallant-masts, &c.

TRICING-LINE. — A small rope, generally passed through a block or thimble, and used to hoist up any object to a higher station, in order to render it less inconvenient; such as the tricing lines to the yard-tackles, booms, &c.

TRUCKS. — Small pieces of wood, of various shapes, used for different purposes. *Flag-staff Trucks* are round flat pieces of elm, with a small sheave on each side; they are fixed, by a square mortise hole made in the middle, on the upper end of flag-staffs, and are used to reeve the halliards. *Parral Trucks* are round balls of elm or other wood, and have a hole through the middle, through which a rope is rove to form the parrals. (Pl. 5, figs. 14 and 15). *Seizing Trucks* are similar to parral trucks, but have a score round the middle, to admit a seizing; they are used to lead ropes through. (Pl. 2, fig. 23). *Shroud Trucks* are short cylindrical pieces of elm, &c.; they have a hole through the middle, lengthwise; a groove down the side, the size of the shrouds; and a score round the middle, to admit a seizing. They are seized to the shrouds to lead ropes through, that they may be more readily found. (Pl. 2, fig. 19).

TRUSS. — A rope employed to confine or slacken the lower yards to or from their respective masts.

TRUSS TACKLES. — Tackles used to secure the lower yards to their masts. (See TACKLE).

TIE. — A sort of runner, or large rope, used to convey the effort of the tackle to hoist the upper yards and gaff. (Pl. 10, figs. 43, 44, 45).

VANGS. — The braces that keep steady the peak of gaff-sails and fore-and-aft sails. (Pl. 10, fig. 48).

To VEER AWAY. — To let go a rope gently.

VIOL, or VOYL. — A large rope, used to unmoor or heave up the anchors of a ship, by transmitting the effort of the capstan to the cables.

To UNDERRUN a TACKLE is to separate the several parts of which it is composed, and range them in order, from one block to the other, so that the general effort may not be interrupted when it is put in motion.

UPHROE. — An oblong block, made of ash, without sheaves, from nine to thirty inches long, and two to five inches in diameter; it has several holes bored through the middle, at equal distances, and grooved round the outside, to receive the rope by which it is suspended. It is used to suspend the awnings, by extending the small ropes through the holes, lengthwise, along the middle of the awning.

WALL KNOT. — A particular sort of large knot raised upon the end of a rope, by unlaying the strands, and interweaving them among each other. (Pl. 1, figs. 25 and 27).

WARP. — A hawser, used to remove a ship from one place to another.

WARP, or more properly WOOF, is the twine or thread woven across the nettles in pointing.

WARP of SHROUDS. — The length of the shrouds from the bolster at the mast-head to the dead-eyes.

WHIP. — A small single tackle, formed by connecting the fall to a single block; it is used to hoist light bodies out of the hold, &c. (Pl. 6, fig. 12).

WHIPT. — The end of a rope is said to be whipt when several turns of twine, or ropeyarns, &c., have been taken upon it, to prevent its unravelling.

WHIP upon WHIP is formed by fixing the end of one whip upon another whip-fall. Thus two single blocks will afford the same purchase as a tackle having a double and a single block, and with much less friction. This purchase should therefore be used whenever the length of the hoist will admit of it. To top-sail and top-gallant yards that hoist with a single tie, there is sufficient room to apply this purchase as halliards, which will overhaul with great facility. (Pl. 6, fig. 12).

WINDING-TACKLE. — A name usually given to a tackle formed of one triple block and one double or triple. It is principally employed to hoist up heavy articles, such as anchors, guns, &c.

WINDING-TACKLE PENDANT. — This pendant is made fast round the mast-head, with a round-turn and two half-hitches. The strap of the tackle block is thrust through the eye in the pendant, and a toggle driven through the strap. It is guyed out to the lower-yard, that the tackle may hang clear of the side. The fall is led inboard, or wherever necessary. (Pl. 2, fig. 21).

WINDLASS. — A machine used in most merchant-ships to answer the purpose of a capstan. A Spanish windlass is formed of a handspike, which is hove round by a woolder, that acts as a lever for turning it round. It is used to set up rigging, &c. (Pl. 5, fig. 9).

WOOLDING. — When used, winding several close turns of rope, in a tight manner, round masts and yards that are made of several united pieces, to strengthen and confine the same together.

WORMING.—Winding spunyarn close along the contlines of rope to strengthen it, and make a fair surface for service. (Pl. 5, fig. 2).

YARDS. — Long cylindrical pieces of fir timber, hung to the masts of ships, to expand the sails to the wind. The *Lower Yards,* to which the courses are bent, are the largest; such are the main, fore, cross-jack, and spritsail yard, which hang to the masts at right angles with the ship's length. The *Top-sail Yards,* which expand the top-sails, hang to the top-masts next above the lower yards. The *Top-gallant Yards* which expand the top-gallant sails, hang above the top-sail yards; and the *Royal Yards,* which expand the royal sails, are hung above the top-gallant yards. The *Cross Jack-Yard* is used to expand the foot of the mizen top-sail; and also the foot of the top-sail, and head of the square-sail of vessels with one mast. *Studding-sail Yards* hang to the extremities of the yards, and by these are expanded the heads of the studding-sails.

YARD TACKLES. — Tackles used to hoist the boats, &c., in or out; and which are generally, in bad weather, carried aft, and hooked to eye-bolts in the side, to prevent too great a strain on the braces. (Pl. 10, figs. 5 and 6).

YARN. — In rope-making, signifies one of the threads of which a rope is composed. (See CABLE — ROPE YARN).

End of the First Part

THE ART OF RIGGING

PART II

DIRECTIONS FOR THE PERFORMANCE OF OPERATIONS INCIDENTAL TO RIGGING; AND FOR PREPARING IT ON SHORE

Much of the Rigging of all Ships is previously prepared on shore, in a house or loft; and before a person can possibly arrive at the knowledge of fitting rigging on board, he must not only be acquainted with all that is thus prepared on shore, but must also know how to perform the various other operations incidental to Rigging. Such preparatory knowledge, therefore, may be gained by a perusal of this Second Part, alphabetically arranged.

BALE SLINGS are spliced together with a short splice, then served with spunyarn over the splice. (Pl. 5, fig. 8).

BENDS. — *Common Bend* (Pl. 4, fig. 6). — Pass the end of a rope through the bight of another rope, then round and underneath the standing part; but to prevent it jambing, pass it round again under the standing part. The sheet of a sail has the end passed up through the clue, then round the clue, and underneath the standing part. The rope of a buoy is passed as a sheet, and has the end stopped. *Bends of a Cable Clinch* are passed as a seizing. (Pl. 6, fig. 3). *Carrick Bend* (Pl. 1, fig. 1). — Lay the end of a rope or hawser across its standing part; then take the end of another rope or hawser, and lay it under the first standing part, at the cross, and over the end; then through the bight under the standing part; then over its own standing part, and underneath the bight again. It is often used in haste, to form a greater length to warp or tow with. *Fishermen's Bend* (Pl. 1, fig. 3). — Take a round-turn with the end of a rope or hawser through the ring of an anchor, or round a spar, &c., and a half-hitch through both parts, and another half-hitch round the standing part; then stop the end. *Hawser Bend* (Pl. 1, fig. 4) is a hitch, with a throat and end-seizing made on one end, and the end of another hawser rove through the bight, and hitched with another throat and end-seizing. *Temporary Bend* (Pl. 1, fig. 2). — Commonly made to reeve through large blocks, thus: — Lay three fathoms of the end of two hawsers together, and put on a round-seizing in the middle; then reverse the ends to each standing part, and put on a throat-seizing between each end and the middle, and a round-seizing on each end.

BOBSTAYS are wormed, parcelled, and served with spunyarn three-fourths of the length, then led through a hole in the cut-water, and have the two ends spliced together. A dead-eye or heart is seized in with a round-seizing, the splice laying on the upper side of it. A laniard is spliced into the dead-eye, which is rove through a dead-eye or heart, the collar of which is lashed to the bowsprit. (Pl. 4, fig. 9).

BOBSTAY COLLARS are wormed, parcelled, and served, having an eye spliced at each end. A dead-eye or heart is placed in the bight; and a round-seizing is clapped on, which fitted, thus lies underneath the bowsprit; and the lashing is passed through the eyes over the upper part of it. Vessels are fitted with a number of bobstays and collars, according to their size. (Pl. 4, fig. 9).

BREAST BACKSTAYS are served with spunyarn over the eye, and continued about three feet below the cross-trees; also in the wake of the tops and lower yards, to prevent chafing, according to the size of the ship. They have a single or double block spliced into their lower ends.

BREAST BACKSTAY RUNNERS. — A rope rove through the single block, which is spliced into the end of the breast backstay, the end of which is knotted into the channels; the other end has a single or double block spliced into it, for use as a tackle in setting it up.

BUOY-HOOPS AND SLINGS (Pl. 6, figs. 10 and 11). — Each hoop is fixed its breadth within the second iron hoop, at each end; the whole length of the rope required for the slings and hoops, is eleven times the length of the buoy; they are wormed and served, and cross each other. The hoops are drawn asunder sufficiently to force the buoy between them; are then put over the ends of the buoy, and the slings and hoops got into their places, as nearly as possible. The slings are placed on the quarters, equally between each other; and the bights fixed in scores in the ends of the buoy. It is next got upon the stretch; one end of the sling is made fast to a post, and the other end to a tackle, the fall of which is swayed tight, or hove so by a heaver. When the buoy is thus set tight, the hoops are driven by a mallet into their places; and the bight of the slings is seized well together, with an eye in each end. Large buoys have seven under and six riding turns; smaller buoys, six under and five riding; the end of the seizing crossed each way, and the end knotted and crowned. A fid is driven in the eye, to make it round; then driven out, and the two bights marled together, to bend the buoy rope to. *Iron Buoys* are now in general use.

BUTT AND HOGSHEAD SLINGS. — Each pair has a thimble spliced in one end, which is served with spunyarn over the splice; the other end is whipt. (Pl. 5, fig. 12).

CAN-HOOK SLINGS. — A flat broad iron hook, with an eye in one end, is spliced through the eye in each end of the slings, and sometimes with a thimble seized in the bight. (Pl. 5, fig. 6).

CATHARPIN-LEGS are seldom used at present; a necklace of chain being placed round the lower mast, to secure the futtock rigging to, instead (when they are used): the foremost is the shortest; and they increase as they go aft. They have an eye spliced in each end for seizing; are wormed, parcelled, and served from end to end: they are occasionally used by being doubled with a thimble seized in the bight, and sets up with a laniard. Each vessel has a number of catharpin-legs, corresponding to the number of top-mast shrouds that she carries. The foremost shroud is never catharpinned in. (See FUTTOCK SHROUDS).

CATS-PAW, *for setting-up shrouds,* &c. (Pl. 1, fig. 8). — Lay the end of a rope or fall over the standing part and middle of the bight, then turn it three times over both parts, and hook the tackle through both bights.

CLINCHES. — *Inside Clinch* (Pl. 6, fig. 3). — The end of a cable is passed through the hawse-hole, and rove through the ring of the anchor; then passed round the standing part, through the bight, and a circle, which is called the *clinch,* formed, of the same size as the ring of the anchor. A throat and end bend is then clapped on opposite each other, and a seizing of spunyarn close to the end. All other inside clinches are stopped, similar to the bends of this clinch, with small rope or spunyarn. *Outside Clinch* (Pl. 1, fig. 9) only differs from an inside clinch by passing the end on the outside, and not through the bight, for the more readily casting it off.

CLOTHING the BOLSTERS. — (See BOLSTERS, Part I).

COLLARS. — *Fore-stay Collars* are fitted in various ways, and spliced together at the ends; wormed, parcelled, and served the whole length. In some cases they are doubled, and a heart seized in the bight. The splice is to lie on the back of the heart, with quarter-seizings, a score being cut, on each side of the heart, large enough to admit from nine to twelve turns of seizing. The seizing is to be snaked on the back, to lie closely. *Main-stay Collars* are fitted in different ways, but generally, the main-stay is secured to the bitts, before the fore-mast, with seizings to its own parts. (Pl. 4, fig. 5). *Bowsprit-shroud Collars* are fitted to the circumference of the bowsprit. They have an eye spliced in each end; are then wormed, parcelled, and served from eye to eye, and a heart seized in the bight, with a long and short leg, with seven under and six riding turns, well strained, and crossed with two turns; the ends whipt, and secured with a wall knot, crowned. (Pl. 4, fig. 9). *Main-top-mast* and *Spring-stay Collars* have an eye spliced in each end; are wormed, and served with spunyarn, and have a single block seized in the bight.

CROWNING, or FINISHING, a WALL KNOT (Pl. 1, fig. 27). — Lay the first strand over the walling, and the second strand across over the first, and the third strand across over the second, and through the bight of the first, then haul the ends tight.

DAVIT GUYS have an eye spliced in one end to the circumference of the davit-head; are served with spunyarn over the splice, and a thimble and laniard in the other end.

FLEMISH-EYE, or MADE EYE. — Open the end of a rope, then open the yarns, dividing them into two parts, and laying one part over the other; or place them together, one part in the other; then well marl, parcel, and serve them together.

FUTTOCK SHROUDS (Pl. 9, figs. 51, 52, 53). — The length allowed is divided into the number of top-mast shrouds the vessel carries, and cut in the bights. Each length has a hook and thimble spliced into each end, and the ends of the splices stopped with spunyarn; then doubled, and a spunyarn tied in the middle for the cutting mark. The hooks are then hooked in each other, and got upon the stretch. They should be well hove out, to try the hooks and splices, as the top-mast depends very much thereon. If a hook should break, or the splices draw, the former must be shifted, and the latter hauled tighter through. After they are sufficiently stretched, the ends of the splices are tapered, marled down, and served with spunyarn, within two feet of the cutting mark; they are cut asunder, and have an eye spliced in the ends when on board.

The above is correct, according to the old general practice on board ships, but of late years several other plans have been adopted, either by having a chain necklace, or iron hoop, around the lower mast, to set the futtock shrouds up to; thereby avoiding the catharpin-legs. Some have the futtock shrouds seized to the lower rigging at the futtock stave, and then short legs hooked to the necklace, with an eye in its upper part, to set up to the futtock stave. This latter plan is preferable, as in the event of carrying away the necklace, the lower shrouds may be swifted in at the futtock staves, by tackles, in a few moments.

FUTTOCK STAVES. — (See Part I).

GASKETS are made with three-yarn foxes. (Pl. 3, fig. 13). Those for large ships consist of nine foxes, those for smaller, of seven. Place four foxes together, but lay them of unequal lengths; mark the middle of the whole length, and plait four foxes together for eight or nine inches; then double it, and plait the eight parts together for five inches, and work in the odd fox. The whole is then plaited together for eighteen inches in length; then leave out one fox, and so keep lessening one fox at a time, till you come to five. If the foxes work out too fast, others must supply their places till the whole length is worked, which is from five to seven fathoms long. To secure the ends, make a bight by turning upwards one of the foxes, and plait the others through the bight, then haul tight upon that laid up.

GUN-SLINGS are spliced together with a short splice. (Pl. 2, fig. 29).

GUYS. — Jib-guys, with sprit-sail-yards, are fitted with an eye to go over the jib-boom end, and wormed, parcelled, and served for about a fathom in the wake of where the thimbles act on the sprit-sail-yard, to prevent friction. They are generally set up with a tackle, and secured to their own parts, through an eye-bolt in the bows.

When no spritsail-yard is carried, the jib-boom is secured by guys to the outriggers, commonly called *whiskers,* which are placed just inside the bowsprit-cap. This method has been generally adopted, on account of the great weight of a yard being so far out, when a ship is pitching in a head sea, the outriggers being easily got in. The outriggers have back-ropes, which lead inboard. Whiskers are sometimes made of iron, when they generally extend out from the fore part of the cat-heads, and have sheaves at its extremity, through which the jib-guys lead, and are set-up inboard.

HITCHES. — *Clove-hitch* (Pl. 1, fig. 10) is two half-hitches one at the back of the other, made by the ratlings round the shrouds, and by buoy-ropes round anchors. *Blackwall-hitch* (Pl. 1, fig. 11).—Take the end of a rope, or fall of a tackle, round the back of a tackle-hook, and jamb it underneath the standing part. *Half-hitch* (Pl. 1, fig. 3). — Pass the end of a rope over the standing part, and through the bight, and lay it up to the standing part, and repeat it for two half-hitches. *Magnus-hitch* (Pl. 1, fig. 17). — Take two round-turns through the ring of an anchor, &c., and bring the end over the standing part, then round the ring and through the bight. *Racking-hitch,* for shortening slings (Pl. 1, fig. 6). — Lay the bight over both parts, and turn it over several times; then hook the tackle through the bights. *Rolling-hitch* (Pl. 1, fig. 14). — Take two round-turns round a mast, &c., and make two half-hitches on the standing part. *Timber-hitch* (Pl. 1, fig. 12). — Lay the end over the hauling part, and pass it through the bight; then take several turns round the standing part, and stop the end. The bight serves as a sling for bales, drawing of timber, &c.

HORSES for the YARDS have an eye spliced in one end, the circumference of the yard-arm, and served with spunyarn over the splice; the inner end is fitted with a thimble and laniard, to set it up by. *Flemish Horses* are spliced in the eye-bolt at the yard-arm; and an eye at its end, which is seized to the yard.

JACKSTAYS. — *Jackstays for Yards* have an eye in one end, to fit the yard-arm, and a thimble spliced in the other. It is used for the purpose of bending the sail to with rope bands. The eye is put over the yard-arm before the horse; the other end is rove through pieces of hide, nailed to, or through bolts driven in the yard, before the thimble is spliced in the end, by which it is set up to the eye of the opposite one, over the strap of the tie block or slings of the yard.   There are various other jackstays, such as *Square-sail Jackstays* and *Try-sail Jackstays*.

JUMPER has an eye spliced in one end, and a thimble in the other.   The eye is seized to the main-stay nearly abreast the fore-mast, and the thimble at the lower end has a laniard spliced into it, which is rove alternately through an eye-bolt in the deck, and a thimble, which keeps the stay from working too much while the ship labours in a heavy sea.

KNOT. — *Bowline Knot* (Pl. 1, fig. 18). — Hold the end of the rope in the right hand, and the standing part in the left; then pass the end under the standing part in the left hand, and over through the bight; then bring it over the standing part, and pass it again through the bight, and haul the parts taut. *Running-bowline Knot* has the knot made in the bight instead of the standing part, round which it makes a bight. *Bowline Knot* upon the bight of a rope. — Take the bight in one hand, and the standing part in the other; throw a kink or bight over the bight with the standing parts, the same as for the single knot. Take the bight round the parts, and over the large bights, bringing it up again, which makes the knot complete. *Buoy-rope Knot* (Pl. 6, fig. 10). — One end is unstranded for one yard in length, stopped with ropeyarn, and one of the nine smaller strands taken out of each of the larger strands, which are then laid together again.   The three smaller strands are doubled-walled, right-handed, close to the stop, and then laid upon their contlines. *Diamond Knot, Single* (Pl. 1, fig. 15). — The strands of the rope are unlayed to where the knot is designed to be made; then form bights, by laying the strands down the sides of the rope, and keep them fast, then pass the end of the first strand through the second bight, missing the first; and the end of the second strand through the third bight, round the second; and the end of the third strand round the second and third bight: then pass the ends through the first bight, and haul tight.   The strands are then twisted together to the next knot. *Diamond Knot, Double* (Pl. 1, fig. 16), is made by the several strands following their respective places through the bights of the single knot, and led up through the middle, and the strands twisted together to the place of the next knot. These knots are used as ornaments upon bell and side ropes. *Matthew Walker's Knot* is made by separating the strands of a rope, taking the end round the rope, and through its own bight; the end underneath through the bight of the first, and through its own bight; and the end underneath through the bights of the strands, and through its own bight. Haul them taut, and they form the knot. The ends are cut off. It is a handsome knot for the end of a laniard. *Overhand Knot* (Pl. 1, fig. 19) is made by passing the end over the left hand, and through the bight. *Reef Knot* (Pl. 1, fig. 23) is to attach the two ends of a rope together; and, in making, observe to pass both parts of the rope on one side in the bight of the other, thus: — Turn up one end and form a bight, and put the other up through the bight, take it round underneath, and pass it through the bight again. *Shroud Knot* (Pl. 1, figs. 20, 21, 22). — The two ends are opened about four feet, and interplaced one in the other, as for splicing; then a single wall knot is made with the ends on each part, and the end laid in the contline, tapered, and served over with spunyarn. *Sprit-sailsheet Knot.* — The ends of the rope are first thrust through holes, one on each side of the sprit-sail-sheet block; then unlayed about two feet, and the six strands walled together and crowned at top, thus: — Lay four strands over the walling, two to the right and two to the left; the remaining two strands are woven contrariwise over and under the other strands, and hauled tight; the block is then seized in the bight. *Stopper Knot* (Pl. 1, fig. 24) is made the same way as a double wall knot, and the ends put up through the heart, and whipt at top. *Tack Knot* (Pl. 1, fig. 28) is made by unlaying the strands sufficiently, and there making a stop with ropeyarn; then single wall and crown, then double wall and double crown, and haul the end tight, and jamb the knot: then the strands are led down through the walling, and laid down in the contline; tapered, marled, and served over with spunyarn. *Wall Knot, Single* (Pl. 1, fig. 25), is made by unlaying the ends of a rope, and making a bight with the first strand; then passing the second over the end of the first, and the third strand over the end of the second, and through the bight of the first, and haul the ends tight. *Wall Knot, Double* (Pl. 1, fig. 27), is made by passing the ends, singly, close underneath the first wall, and thrusting them upwards through the middle, only the last end comes up under two bights. *Double Crown.* — This knot the same as a tack knot, above described.

LASHING. — *Lashing of Blocks.* — Take a number of turns, parallel to each other, through the eye oi the block-strap and round any object, as a mast, yard, &c.; and to strengthen the lashing, take several cross-turns with the end, and make fast.

LINES, *used in the Rigging-Loft.* — Cordage, smaller than ropes, and formed of two or more fine strands of hemp; as *House-line* made of three strands, used to seize blocks into their straps and the clues of sails, and to marl the skirts of sails to their bolt-ropes, &c. *Log-line,* made of three or more strands, and used for the log, &c. *Marline,* made of two strands, and used for the same purposes as house-line.

MARLING (Pl. 4, fig. 7) is winding any line round a rope, and securing every turn by a hitch, so that they may be independent of each other, and remain fixed, should either be cut through by friction. It is principally used to fix on the clues of sails and the foot-rope of top-sails. Splices are marled down for serving with ropeyarn or twine.

MATS are made thus (Pl. 5, fig. 17): — A small rope or line is first tightly extended, horizontally, at nearly a man's height, and made fast at each end, across which foxes are placed in a regular manner and hang down from their middles; then, beginning with the first next the left hand, it is crossed or plaited with that which is next the right hand, then taking that which was to the right hand, and crossing it with its next, and so on in succession. This will make the mat downwards; and, when finished to the length intended, it is begun again at top till its breadth is completed. Each twist is to be pressed tight, and each couple of foxes is to be twisted together at the bottom, to keep in their twists till the next in succession are interwoven with them. When the mat is completed to its depth, the bottom is selvaged, by placing another small rope or line across in a tight manner, similar to the head-line, round which one fox is half-hitched while the next fox is laid up at the back of it, and so on alternately. When mats are thrummed, it is thus performed:—Short pieces of the foxes are thrust under every other overlay of the foxes in every other row. To receive the thrums, a hole is opened with a small marline-spike; the thrums are afterwards cut off to an equal length, and their ends opened.

MOUSING a MESSENGER. — Open every other strand for three strands, and thrust in the ends of a small rope or strand, in order to form a projection on the surface, to prevent the nippers from slipping. The ends are not cut off close. (Pl. 3, fig. 15).

OUTRIGGER. — A strong beam of timber, of which there are several fixed on the side of a ship, and projecting from it, in order to secure the masts in the act of careening, by counteracting the strain they suffer from the effect ot the careening-tackles, which, being applied to the mast-head, draw it downwards, so as to act upon the vessel with the power of a lever, whose fulcrum is in her centre of gravity.

Outrigger is also a small boom, occasionally used in the tops, to thrust out the breast-backstays to windward, in order to increase the angle of tension, and thereby give additional security to the top-masts. This machine is thrust out a proper distance beyond the top-brim, where it is securely fastened; after which, the backstays are placed in the notches, or scores, and set up below, by means of their tackles in the chains.

Outriggers, or *Whiskers*, are generally used to support the jib-boom. (See Guys).

PARRALS. — There are four sorts of parrals, viz.:—*Parral-ropes*, formed of a single rope, well served and finished, with an eye at each end; this being passed round the yard, is seized on: the two ends are placed round the after-part of the mast, one of them being taken under and the other over the yard; the two eyes are lashed together on the upper side. *Parrals* with *Ribs* and *Trucks* (Pl. 5, fig. 16) is formed by passing the two parts of the parral rope through the two holes in the ribs, observing that between every two ribs is strung a truck on each part of the rope. The ends of the parral-rope are made fast with seizings. These are chiefly used on the top-sail yards. *Parrals* with *Trucks* (Pl. 5, figs. 16 and 17) is composed of a single rope, passing through a number of trucks, sufficient to embrace the mast. These are calculated for the cheeks of a gaff. *Truss Parral* is formed by fixing a rope upon the middle of the yard, which, passing at the back of the mast, is rove through an iron thimble, spliced into another rope (also fastened upon the yard), and communicates with a tackle reaching to the deck, whereby it may be occasionally hauled taut, or slackened; large ships generally have two of

Plate VI.

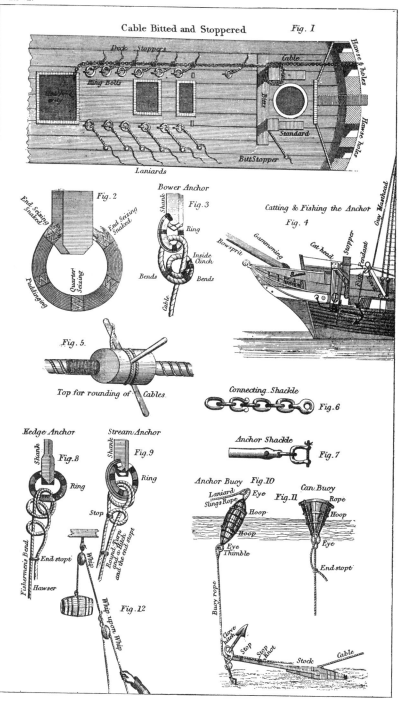

Cable Bitted and Stoppered — Fig. 1

Deck Stoppers
Hawse holes
Cable
Ring Bolts
Bitts
Standard
Hawse holes
Laniards
Bitt Stopper

Fig. 2
End Seizing
Snaked
End Seizing
Snaked
Quarter Seizing
Puddening

Bower Anchor
Fig. 3
Shank
Ring
Inside Clinch
Bends
Bends
Cable

Catting & Fishing the Anchor
Fig. 4
Gog Masthead
Gammoning
Bowsprit
Cat head
Stopper
Fish Pendant

Fig. 5
Top for rounding of Cables

Connecting Shackle
Fig. 6

Kedge Anchor
Shank
Fig. 8
Ring
Fisherman's Bend
End stopt
Hawser

Stream Anchor
Shank
Fig. 9
Ring
Stop
Round a Hitch
and the end stopt
Whip
Whip upon Whip
Fig. 12

Anchor Shackle
Fig. 7

Anchor Buoy Fig. 10
Laniard
Slings Rope
Eye
Hoop
Hoop
Eye
Thimble
Buoy rope
Clove hitch
Stop
Stop Knot

Can Buoy
Fig. 11
Rope
Hoop
Eye
End stopt

Stock
Cable

these, one leading on each side. These are peculiar to the lower yards.

PENDANTS. — *Bill Pendant* has a hook and thimble spliced in one end, and served with spunyarn over the splice. *Fish-Tackle Pendant* has a large iron hook, with a thimble spliced in one end, and the ends of the splice tapered, marled down, and served over with spunyarn. *Fore* and *Main Tackle Pendants* (Pl. 9, figs. 4 and 5) are wormed, parcelled, and served with spunyarn in the way of the contsplice. They are then spliced in the middle to the circumference of the mast-head; have large thimbles spliced into their lower ends (in large ships they have an eye and splice); they are wormed, parcelled, and served with spunyarn the whole length. Large ships having two pairs of pendants to the main and foremasts, the after pendants are longer than the foremost ones. *Guy Pendants* are doubled, and served with spunyarn in the bight, one fathom in length. *Main-stay Tackle Pendants* (Pl. 9, figs. 48 and 49) have a hook spliced in one end, and a double block in the other, and served with spunyarn over the splices. *Mizen Burton Pendants* (Pl. 9, fig. 6) have a contsplice in the middle to the circumference of the mast-head; thimbles spliced in the lower ends, and served with spunyarn over the splices. *Top-mast Burton Pendants* (Pl. 9, figs. 15 and 16) are the same as mizen burton pendants. *Top-rope Pendants* have a large iron thimble spliced in the lower ends; are marled over the splice, and pointed. *Truss Pendants* are doubled and cut in the bight; they have an iron thimble spliced into one end, and are served with spunyarn two-thirds of the length. *Winding Tackle Pendant* (Pl. 2, fig. 21) has an eye spliced in one of the ends; the ends put in three times, and cut off short; the other end is whipt. *Yard Tackle Pendants* (Pl. 10, figs. 5 and 6) have an eye spliced in one end to the size of the yard-arm, and a double block in the other end. The splices are served over with spunyarn.

PLAITING. — Braided cordage, made by ropeyarns, and twisted together, and then laid one over the other alternately; or the end of a rope opened, and the strands placed together in the same manner.

PUDDENING of ANCHORS. — Worn hawser-laid rope is cut into lengths three times the diameter of the ring; and as many of these lengths as will cover the ring, which is about thirteen. (Pl. 6, fig. 2). The ring is first chocked upright, by wedging it in the hole of the shank; then well tarred, and parcelled with worn canvas twice round, and marled close down with spunyarn. The turns of the puddening are then passed, one turn and a-half each way from the middle of the ring; then hove tight by a heaver, and well seized with two quarter and two end-seizings, that are snaked all round. The ends remaining are opened out, and payed all over with a good coat of tar.

RUNNERS OF TACKLES have a double block spliced in one end, and served with spunyarn over the splice, and the other end whipt or pointed. (Pl. 9, fig. 58).

SEIZING is joining two parts of a rope together with spunyarn, house-line, marline, or small cordage. To make a round-seizing, splice an eye in the end of a seizing, and taking the other end round both parts of the rope, reeve it through the eye: render it round as many turns as you are to have; then make a kind of cats-paw on the seizing, by the marline-spike, laying the end part over the standing part, pushing the marline-spike down through the bight again. Heave these turns well taut by the heaver or marline-spike, making six, eight, or ten turns, according to the size of the rope; then push the end through the last turn; over these pass five, seven, or nine more (which are termed Riders), always laying one less above than below. These are not to be hove too taut, that those underneath may not be separated. The end is now pushed up through the seizing, and two cross-turns between the two parts of the rope and round the seizing (leading the end through the last turn), and hove well taut. If the seizing be small cordage, a wall knot is cast in the end; but if spunyarn, an overhand knot. When the seizing is clapped on the two ends of a rope, it is called an *End-Seizing*. (Pl. 4, fig. 1). A *Throat-Seizing* is with riding-turns, but not crossed. A bight is formed, by laying the end over the standing-part; the seizing is then clapped on, the end put through the last turn of the riders, and knotted. The end part of the rope is turned up, and fastened to the standing-part; this is used for turning in dead-eyes, hearts, blocks, or thimbles. (Pl. 4, figs. 1 and 5).

SENNIT is braided cordage, made by plaiting from five to thirteen ropeyarns together, one over the other, according to the size and length, always keeping an odd yarn.

SERVING is encircling a rope with line or spunyarn, &c., to keep it from rubbing and chafing. The end of the spunyarn, for service, is placed under the two or three first turns, to keep it fast; then two turns are taken round the rope and mallet, on each side of and round the handle. The mallet is then gradually turned round the rope by its handle, while another person passes the ball of spunyarn; and this is continued until the rope is covered the length required. When the mallet is within a few turns of the end, take the turns off the mallet, and pass them by hand, and heave the ends well through, where it is made fast, as at first. (Pl. 5, fig. 3).

SHROUDS. — The *Lower Shrouds* (Pl. 9, figs. 7, 8, and 9, and Pl. 4, fig. 1). — The rope is warped round two iron fids, fixed in the floor, as distant from each other as the first warp is long. The length is the distance from the top of the bolsters at the mast-head, to the foremost dead-eye. One end of the cablet is made fast to the lower fid, and passed round the upper fid, and so on alternately, one turn close to the back of the other, and each hauled tight by hand. The additional length gained by the turns lying round each other, is sufficient for the lengthening of each pair of shrouds, as they rake aft. When the whole gang of shrouds are warped out, the bights of the lower end are cut through in a straight direction with the fids.

The upper bights are designed for the eyes, and are marked round the middle, beginning at the inner one, with one piece of spunyarn knotted, two for the second, and so on for the number required. The outer turn is called *Swifters;* and they are left four or five feet at each end longer than the shrouds, and have an eye spliced in them the circumference of the mast-head. The shrouds, when cut up to the length, are got up, and stretched thus for worming: at the end of each is made a bend; one end is passed through a pair of slings, fixed round a post at the lower end of the house, and the other end through the strap of a treble block, and a fid thrust through each bend. The treble block is connected by its fall to a double block, lashed round a post, at the upper end, thus: — The standing part of the fall is fastened to the becket, at the arse of the double block; then rove through the first sheave of the treble block, then through the first sheave of the double block on the same side, and so on alternately, and the fall carried and attached to the windlass by three or four round-turns. The windlass is put in motion by men, with levers or handspikes, and each length thus stretched hand-tight. The

rope used for the fall is commonly white rope. All shrouds are
wormed with double, treble, or four-yarn spunyarn, one-fourth
the length from the centre to the eye, on each side; but the foremost shrouds are wormed all the way to the end. Each length,
after being wormed, is hove out by the same purchase, till each
pair has acquired, by stretching, once and a half the length of the
eye; and should remain on that stretch twenty-four hours before
the service is laid on. Shrouds are wormed before they are hove
out to lengthen, because the worming increases in tension with
the rope, and thereby draws smooth and even into the contline.
The eyes of all the shrouds are parcelled with worn canvas, well
tarred, about one fathom and a half on each side of the middle,
for large ships, and proportionably for smaller; and then served
with spunyarn one-fourth of the length; each turn of their serv-
ing· is laid close, and strained tight round, to prevent the water
from penetrating. The foremost shroud is served the whole
length. Swifters, when stretched have the length of the splice
set off on each side of the middle; and likewise the length of the
eye or circumference of the mast-head. The latter is parcelled
and served as above. They are then cut asunder in the middle,
and spliced to the circumference of the mast-heads; then got on
the stretch, and served over the splice one-fourth of the length.
   The bights of shrouds are seized together to the circumference
of the mast-heads; the seizing of the first shroud is put on below
the bolster, or trestle-trees, with seven under and six riding
turns, and a double cross-turn over all. The seizing of each
shroud is to be laid its breadth below the next, and clear of each
other, to prevent chafing. Vessels having four pairs of shrouds,
the foremost shroud and pendant are in one. *Top-mast Shrouds*
(Pl. 9, figs. 17, 18, 19, and Pl. 4, fig. 2) are warped out on the
floor, as the lower shrouds are, and fitted to the circumference of
the top-mast-head. In the foremost part of shrouds, on each
side is seized a sister-block, below the futtock staff. *Top-gallant
Shrouds* are fitted as the top-mast shrouds are, except that, instead of a sister-block, a thimble is seized in the two foremost
pair on each side, close up to the hounds. They lead through
holes in the cross-trees and over the futtock-stave, down to the
top, where they are set up with laniards. *Bowsprit Shrouds* (Pl.
9, fig. 3) have an iron hook and thimble spliced in the inner ends,
and are served over the splice. The outer end has a dead-eye

spliced into it, with a laniard to set it up to the collars.

SLINGS *for Lower Yards* are generally of chain (round the middle of the yard), with a shackle or slip, to connect it with the mast-head slings, which are also of chain. The mast-head slings are either passed over the lower cap, or abaft the lower mast-head, and down before the foremost cross-tree, where they are connected with the slings of the lower yard. Ships that carry sprit-sail-yards, usually have an iron strap, which goes round the bowsprit-end. The strap has an eye-bolt to which the sprit-sail-yard is shackled. The sprit-sail-yard slings (or iron hoop in its centre) has a shackle for that purpose.

SPANS ABOUT THE MAST have a single block spliced in each end, and generally covered with canvas, or served with spunyarn the whole length.

SPLICING. — The *Cont Splice* (Pl. 3, fig. 3) forms an eye in the middle of a rope, &c., as the eye-splice doth at the end, by interlaying the ends between the strands of the rope, &c., at certain distances from each other, so that the rope becomes double in the extent of the splice. This splice is occasionally used for pendants; also for lead-lines, log-lines, and fishing-lines, where the short-splice would be liable to separate. *Eye Splice* forms an eye, or circle, at the end of a rope, on itself or round a block, &c. (Pl. 3, figs. 4 and 5). The strands are unlayed, and their ends pushed through intervals made in the strands by a fid or marline-spike, at that distance on the rope which the eye may require; observing to put the middle strand through first, then pass it over the surface of the second strand, and push it through the third; repeat the same with the two other ends, laying them fair asunder. The ends of this splice are tapered, by gradually reducing the yarns, then placed smooth along the rope; then marled, and served with spunyarn. *Long Splice* is made to rejoin a rope or ropes, intended to reeve through a block, without increasing its size. (Pl. 3, figs. 6 and 7). The ends are opened from one-half to a whole fathom in length, and placed close together regularly one in the other; one strand is then unlaid, and the opposite strand laid up its intervals each way, and the two strands knotted together at the ends and middle of the splice; the ends are then halved, and pushed under the next strand. *Short Splice* (Pl. 3, figs. 8 and 9) is made by unlaying the ends of two ropes, or the two ends of one rope, and placing the strands of one opposite to and between the strands of the other; draw them close together, and push the strands of one under the strands of the other, the same as the eye-splice. This splice is used for block-straps, slings, &c., and the ends are tapered and served. *Tapered Splice* (Pl. 3, figs. 10 and 11), mostly used on cables, is made by unlaying a certain length of each cable, then placing them together, and interplacing the strands, as in the short-splice, twice each way, and hauled tight each time; then inlay the strands, or ends, successively, and reduce them, by cutting away one strand; then interplace the two remaining strands, and reduce them to a single strand, which is again thrust through, and cut off. The splice is then served over with spunyarn, something more than the whole length. *Drawing Splice* (Pl. 3, fig. 12), used on cables, is made by unlaying about three fathoms of the ends; then place them together, and make a short splice: then leave about one fathom, and thence reduce each strand to a long taper, by gradually cutting away as many yarns as necessary, and neatly point over the taper; then lay the ends up the contlines, and clap on a quarter-seizing at each end of the splice, an end-seizing at the beginning of the pointing, and a stop at the ends of the tails. This is the best splice for cables, as it may be readily taken asunder. Another good method of making a *Cable Splice* is to put the ends in twice each way; then to pick out the strands, worm part of them round the cable, and taper away the rest, which should be marled close down; then clap on a good throat and two end-seizings of ratline. Cables are often connected by splicing *Elliot's* thimble into them, and then shackling them together.

STANDING BACKSTAYS, for *Top-masts* (Pl. 9, figs. 20, 21, 22), are wormed, and served with spunyarn over the eye, and in the way of the top-brim and lower yard. They are fitted as the shrouds are, except that if there is a third pair, they are tongued together the circumference of the top-mast-head. The tongue is a short piece of rope of the same size as the stay, and is spliced into the strands of the stay. *Standing Backstays*, for *Top-gallant-masts* (Pl. 9, figs. 31, 32, 33), are fitted as the shrouds are; wormed, and served in the way of the top-brim.

STAYS (Pl. 9, figs. 10, 11, 12, 13, 14) for the *Lower Masts* are fitted with two legs and lashing eyes, which form the collar, the lashing being cast abaft the mast-head; the stay is got upon the stretch, and hove well out with a windlass, as the shrouds are. The collar, and one fathom below it, is then wormed with spun-yarn, parcelled with canvas well tarred, and served over with spunyarn. (See Pl. 4, fig. 5). *Stays* for the *Top-masts* (Pl. 9, figs. 24, 25, 26, 27) are fitted as the lower stays are. The collar is in proportion to the top-mast head. *Preventer* or *Spring Stays* (Pl. 9, fig. 23), the same as the stays. *Stays* for *Top-gallant-masts* (Pl. 9, figs. 34, 35, 36) have an eye spliced in the upper end to the circumference of its mast-head, and served with spun-yarn over the splice.

STERN LADDERS (Pl. 4, fig. 4) are made of cable-laid rope, thus: — Double the rope, that it may be long enough to reach the water, nearly, from the upper part of the stern; then splice an eye in each end, or make an eye in the middle, by splicing the ends together, and a seizing. The steps are commonly tree-nails, thrust horizontally through the strands of the rope on each side, sixteen inches asunder, and a score is cut round the middle for the concluding line, or middle rope, which is fastened round every step with a clove-hitch in the score. The ladders are lashed to an eye-bolt in upper part of the quarter-piece, or stern, one at each side.

STOPPERS, Deck and Bitt. (Pl. 6, fig. 1). — The long stoppers, from a first-rate ship to a sloop, are, when knotted, about twelve feet; the short stoppers, when knotted, about five feet long. One end of each stopper has a double wall knot, and the ends led up through the middle, and whipt with spunyarn, and the other end is only whipt with spunyarn, being generally seized into the ring-bolts of the deck.

STRAPPING of BLOCKS. — The whole length of all the dif-ferent sizes of block-strapping is got upon the stretch, and hove out tight for worming and serving; it is then wormed and served, and cut into shorter lengths, to suit the different blocks.

The strapping of all large blocks is wormed, parcelled, and served. Strapping of four inches in diameter, and above, is wormed and served: and all under four inches is only served with spunyarn, except the sprit-sail brace, bunt-line, and leech-line blocks, that are lashed under the tops, which are only served with spunyarn over the splice. Purchase or jear-blocks are double scored; and the double and treble blocks are strapped with a double strap, thus: — It is spliced together at the ends, and when doubled, to be the size of the block and circumference of the yard; it is then doubled, and the block seized in the bight, with a long and short leg, the splice laying in the arse of the block. (Pl. 2, fig. 2). The scores of all blocks are to be well tarred, and the pin and sheave to be examined, before the strap is put on. (Pl. 2, fig. 9). The block is set well into the strap with wedges, thus: — The four parts are frapped together with ropeyarn under the block, with a chock between, and the wedges are set between the breast of the block and chock. Then the strap is nippered with a heaver round the block, the wedges, chock, and frapping taken away, and the block hung upon the stake-head, or post, and the strap well seized together, close under the block, with nine under and eight riding turns; every turn strained tight round by a heaver, and cross each way with two turns. Jear-blocks for the mast-heads are strapped with long eyes, to receive many turns of the lashing, and the block is seized into the strap, as before; as are all seizing-blocks in proportion to their size. The straps are cut agreeably to the following

TABLE of the Dimensions of Straps and Seizings for Single and Double Blocks

Size of Blocks.	Size of Strap.	Length to marry for Single Blocks.		Seizing for Single Blocks.		Length to marry for Double Blocks.		Seizing for Double Blocks.	
Inches.	Inches.	Ft.	In.	*Marline.*		Ft.	In.	*Marline.*	
5	1½	1	5	6 feet.		1	7	6 feet.	
6	2	1	6	6 „		1	9	6 „	
7	2	1	9	7 „		2	0	7 „	
8	2½	2	0	9 „		2	3	10 „	
9	3	2	3	11 „		3	0	13 „	
10	3	3	0	13 „		3	3	15 „	
				Rope.				*Rope.*	
				In.	Fms.			In.	Fms.
11	3½	3	3	½	2½	3	6	½	3
12	4	3	6	¾	3	3	9	¾	3½
13	4	3	9	¾	3½	4	3	¾	3½
14	4½	4	2	1	3½	4	6	1	3½
15	5	4	5	1¼	3½	4	9	1¼	3½
16	5½	4	8	1¼	4	5	1	1¼	4
17	6	5	1	1½	4	5	7	1½	4
18	6½	5	7	1½	4	6	2	1½	4
19	7	6	1	1½	4	6	9	1½	4
20	7½	6	9	2	3½	7	4	2	3½

NOTE.—From the 3-inch rope upwards, 18 inches more length will be required for splicing, &c.; under 3-inch, 12 to 15 inches.

Plate VII.

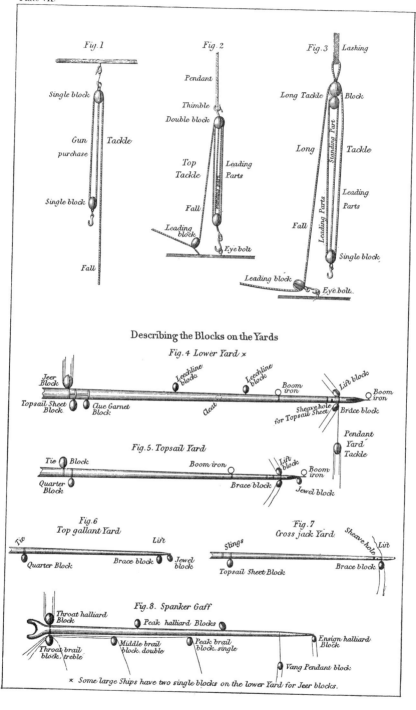

Fig.1

Single block

Gun
purchase

Tackle

Single block

Fall

Fig.2

Pendant

Thimble

Double block

Top
Tackle

Leading
Parts

Fall

Leading
block

Eye bolt

Fig.3 Lashing

Long Tackle   Block

Long   Standing Part   Tackle

Leading
Parts

Leading Parts

Fall

Single block

Leading block   Eye bolt

Describing the Blocks on the Yards

Fig. 4 Lower Yard ✕

Jeer
Block

Leechline
block   Leechline
block   Boom
iron   Lift block

Boom
iron

Topsail Sheet
Block   Clue Garnet
Block   Cleat   Sheave hole
for Topsail Sheet   Brace block

Pendant
Yard
Tackle

Fig. 5. Topsail Yard

Tie   Block   Boom iron   Lift
block   Boom
iron

Quarter
Block   Brace block   Jewel block

Fig. 6
Top gallant Yard

Tie   Lift

Quarter Block   Brace block   Jewel
block

Fig. 7
Gross jack Yard

Slings   Sheave hole   Lift

Topsail Sheet Block   Brace block

Fig. 8. Spanker Gaff

Throat halliard
Block   Peak halliard Blocks

Throat brail
block. treble   Middle brail
block. double   Peak brail
block. single   Ensign halliard
Block

Vang Pendant block

✕ Some large Ships have two single blocks on the lower Yard for Jeer blocks.

Blocks, strapped with eyes or thimbles spliced in the ends, are seized tight into the bight, and the legs left long enough to lash through the eyes, round a mast, yard, &c., as the top-sail clue-lines, clue-garnets, &c. Blocks, strapped with a thimble or hook and thimble, have the strap spliced together at the ends. The block is fixed in one bight, for the splice to lay on the arse of the block, and the thimble in the other bight; the seizing is put on between the block and the thimble, with eight under and six riding turns, according to the size of the block, each turn strained tight by a heaver; the turns double crossed, and the ends stopped with a wall knot crowned. Some hook blocks (unless for luff-tackles) have the strap between the seizing, and the thimble left the length of the block. Blocks, strapped with double tails, are fixed in the strap, similar to blocks with eye-straps; and those with a single tail are spliced in, and served with spunyarn over the splice. (Pl. 2, figs. 5 and 6). *Girtline Blocks* are strapped with a lashing eye or tail, and the girtlines rove.

TACKLE. — The number of parts of the fall of a tackle is more or less, in proportion to the effects intended to be produced. That part of the fall which is fastened to one of the blocks is called the standing part, and the other parts of it are called the running part. (Pl. 7, figs. 2 and 3). Tackles are used to stretch the rigging in the house, &c., to raise or remove weighty bodies, to support the masts, extend the rigging, or expand the sails. They are either moveable, as connecting with a runner, or have one part fixed to an immoveable station by a hook, lashing, &c. A tackle is a convenient kind of purchase, but subject to much friction. Its power will be (the friction not considered) as the number of the parts of the fall that are applied to sustain the weight. If a tackle consists of a double and a single block, as pl. 7, fig. 3, and the weight to be hoisted is hung to the single block, there will be four parts of the fall; and the weight resting upon four ropes equally stretched, each must bear the same part of the weight. Thus, suppose the weight hung to the single block be 4 cwt., then 1 cwt. applied to the hauling part of the fall will suspend it; and, if as much more power be applied as will overcome the friction, it will purchase the weight; but had the weight been hooked to the double block, it would have rested on three ropes only, each of which would bear one-third of the weight; therefore one-third of the weight being applied to the

hoisting part of the fall, would suspend the weight when hooked
to the double blocks; and as much more power being applied as
will overcome the friction, would purchase the weight. Ropes,
if tight laid, will not easily bend round small sheaves, but will
take up a considerable part of the power to force them into their
proper direction; hence it follows, that blocks with small pins,
large sheaves, and slack-laid ropes, are the best materials to
obviate friction and make tackles with. The blocks that are
fixed, commonly called leading-blocks, are only for the convenience of turning the direction of the fall; they add nothing to
the power of the purchase, but, on the contrary, destroy so much
as is necessary to overcome their friction, and are therefore to
be avoided as much as possible. It may be here remarked, that
the blocks of all the standing and running rigging are generally
strapped and prepared in the house.

The *Anchor-stock Tackle* is composed of a double block and a
single block, strapped with a hook and thimble. *Boom Tackles*
are composed of double and single blocks, strapped with tails.
Bowline Tackle is composed of a long tackle and a single block,
strapped with a hook and thimble. *Burton Tackles* are composed of double and single blocks, and are used with pendants.
A *Fish Tackle* is composed of a long tackle and a single block,
strapped with eyes, and is used with a pendant. (Pl. 6, fig. 4).
Jigger Tackles are composed of double and single blocks, strapped
with tails. *A Long Tackle* is composed of two blocks, — a long
tackle-block, and a common single-hook block. The long-tackle
block is double, but it resembles two single blocks, joined together
at their ends. (Pl. 7, fig. 3). *Luff Tackles* are composed of
double and single blocks, strapped with a hook and thimble.
Outhauler Tackle is composed of two single blocks, strapped
with tails. *Quarter Tackles* are composed of a double block,
strapped with eyes, and a single block with a hook and thimble,
having a long strap. *Reef Tackles* (Pl. 13, figs. 22 and 33) are
composed of two single blocks; one block has a thimble seized
to it, which the reef tackle is rove through, and the other is
strapped with an eye round the top-sail yard-arm, if the sister
block is not used. *Relieving Tackles* are the same as luff tackles.
Ridge Tackle is composed of a double block and single block,
strapped with an eye. *Rolling Tackles* are the same as luff
tackles. *Rudder Tackles* are composed of long tackle blocks

and single blocks, strapped with hooks and thimbles. *Runner Tackles* are composed of double and single blocks and a pendant; the lower blocks are strapped with a hook and thimble. *Stay Tackles,* main and fore, are composed of double and single blocks: the double blocks are spliced into a pendant; the single blocks have a long strap, like pl. 9, figs. 48, 49, 50. The pendants have a span from the fore to the main. *Stay-sail stay Tackles* are composed of double and single blocks; the lower blocks are strapped, with a hook and thimble. *Preventer Backstay Tackles* are composed of double and single blocks, strapped with a hook and thimble, except they are fitted with runners. *Tack Tackle* is composed of a double and single block, strapped with hooks and thimbles. The *Top Tackle* is composed of double and treble blocks. (Pl. 9, figs. 15 and 16). It is strapped with hook and thimble, and hooks to the top-rope pendant; generally iron-bound. *Truss Tackles* are composed of one single or double block, strapped in the truss pendant. *Winding Tackle* is composed of a four-fold and a treble block, or a treble and a double block, strapped with eyes, and toggles to the winding tackle pendant. (Pl. 2, fig. 21). *Yard Tackles* are composed of double and single blocks; the double blocks are spliced into the lower ends of pendants, and the single blocks are strapped with hooks and thimbles. (Pl. 10, figs. 5 and 6).

TIES, for yards, are wormed, parcelled, and served with spunyarn for three-fourths of their length.

TURK'S HEAD. — To make this, take a clove-hitch with a piece of log-line, or house-line, round the rope you intend to work it on, and keep the hitch slack, to allow the other parts to be worked in. Then take one of the bights formed by the clove-hitch, and put it over the other; pass the end under, and up through the bight which is underneath; then cross the bights again, and put the ends round again, under, and up through the bight which is underneath: after this, follow the lead of the other parts, and it will form the Turk's Head, with three parts to each cross. Turk's Heads are generally worked on side-ropes and ladder-ropes.

WHIP. — (See Part I).

WHIP upon WHIP. — (Pl. 6, figs. 12, see Part I).

WHIPPING. — To prevent the unravelling of the end of a rope, take several turns of whipping twine round the end of a rope, and lay one end under the four first turns, and the other end under the four last turns, and haul tight. Another method is, to knot every turn on the contrary side of the rope, hauling it tight, and finishing the last turn with a reef-knot; the latter mode is called *West Country Whipping*.

WORMING (Pl. 5, fig. 2). — Wind a small rope in the contlines of the strands of cables, shrouds, or stays; and spunyarn in those of ropes four inches in circumference, and above. The first end of the worming is securely stopped; it then fills one interval or contline; and, when arrived at the end of the length intended to be served, it is there stopped, then laid back into the second interval; and so on successively, stopping it at the ends. When worming is wanted to be cut without waste, observe this general rule. Once the length of the service multiplied by the number of strands, or intervals, and one-third more added, gives the length of the worming. — *Example:* — Twelve fathoms of service in a four-strand rope, will take sixty-four fathoms of rope for worming; and for a three-strand rope, forty-eight fathoms.

The following articles, and their specific quantities, are required for preparing the rigging in the house

Names of the Articles.	1200 tons.	1000 tons.	800 tons.	600 tons.	500 tons.	450 tons.	400 tons.	300 tons.	200 tons.
Spunyarn................Cwts.	75	70	66	59	35	30	22	20	18
Worn Canvas............Yds.	1050	1000	950	800	620	550	500	450	350
Tar ....Brls.	3½	3½	3	2	2	1½	1	1	1
Tallow ....lbs.	70	50	42	'35	28	28	28	28	28

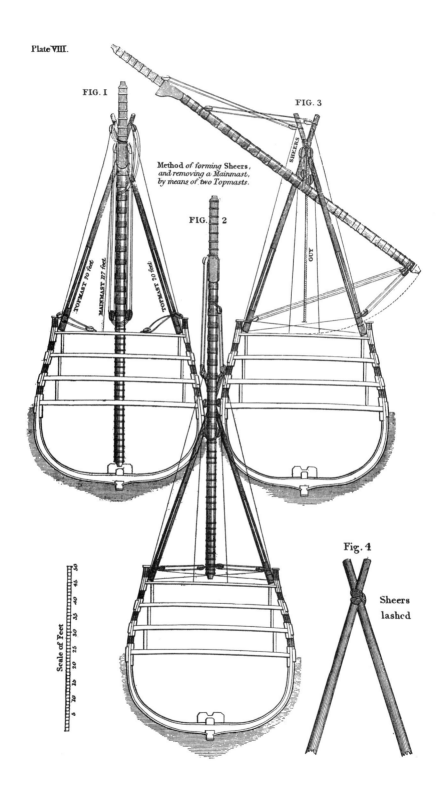

Plate VIII.

FIG. I

FIG. 3

Method of forming Sheers, and removing a Mainmast, by means of two Topmasts.

FIG. 2

TOPMAST 70 feet

MAINMAST 117 feet

TOPMAST 70 feet

SHEERS

GUY

Fig. 4

Sheers lashed

Scale of Feet

A TABLE, showing the comparative strength of Chain Rigging (generally used in steam-vessels) and Hemp Rigging; also Chain and Hemp Cables, and the corresponding weight of each per fathom.

Chain Cables.	Equal to Hempen Cables.	Weight of Chain Cables per fathom.	Weight of Hempen Cables per fathom.	Equal to Tonnage.	Suitable Anchor.
½ in.	4½ or 5 in.	14 lbs.	5 lbs.	20 ,,	1 cwt.
⅝ ,,	5½ ,, 6 ,,	21 ,,	7 ,,	50 ,,	2¾ ,,
11/16 ,,	6½ ,, 7 ,,	26 ,,	9 ,,	65 ,,	3½ ,,
¾ ,,	7½ ,, 8 ,,	29 ,,	12 ,,	70 ,,	4½ ,,
⅞ ,,	8½ 9 or 9½ in.	42 ,,	17 ,,	100 ,,	5¾ ,,
1 ,,	10 or 10½ in.	54 ,,	22 ,,	160 ,,	8 ,,
1⅛ ,,	11 11½ or 12 in.	68 ,,	27 ,,	220 ,,	10½ ,,
1⅜ ,,	14 or 14½ in.	96 ,,	42 ,,	380 ,,	17½ ,,
1½ ,,	15 15½ or 16 in.	133 ,,	48 ,,	480 ,,	21 ,,
1⅝ ,,	16½ 17 ,, 17½ ,,	150 ,,	58 ,,	520 ,,	25 ,,
1¾ ,,	18 18½ ,, 19 ,,	168 ,,	69 ,,	720 ,,	33 ,,
1⅞ ,,	19½ 20 ,, 20½ ,,	190 ,,	82 ,,		
2 ,,	21 21½ ,, 22 ,,	224 ,,	94 ,,		
2⅛ ,,	22½ 23 ,, 23½ ,,	246 ,,	108 ,,		
2¼ ,,	24 24½ ,, 25 ,,	262 ,,	124 ,,		

Chain Rigging.	Equal to Hemp Rigging.	Weight of Chain per fathom.	Chain Rigging.	Equal to Hemp Rigging.	Weight of Chain per fathom.
3/16 in.	1¾ in.	4 lbs.	9/16 in.	4½ in.	20 lbs.
¼ ,,	2 or 2½ ,,	6 ,,	⅝ ,,	5 or 5½ ,,	25 ,,
5/16 ,,	2½ ,, 2¾ ,,	7 ,,	11/16 ,,	6 ,, 6½ ,,	29 ,,
⅜ ,,	3 ,, 3½ ,,	10 ,,	¾ ,,	7 ,, 7½ ,,	36 ,,
7/16 ,,	3¾ ,,	12 ,,	⅞ ,,	8½ ,, 9 ,,	48 ,,
½ ,,	4 ,,	17 ,,	1 ,,	10 ,,	63 ,,

NOTE.—Sailing ships and vessels have a great quantity of chain used, instead of rope; such as the top-sail sheets, bowsprit, gammoning, slings of lower yards, heel-rope to jib-boom, davit guys, back ropes to dolphin striker; and sometimes bobstays, bowsprit shrouds, and top-sail ties.

End of the Second Part

Plate IX.

STANDING RIGGING.

PLATE IX

References on the Plate, delineating the Standing Rigging of a Merchant Ship, of 700 Tons

1 Gammoning.
2 Bobstays.
3 Bowsprit-shrouds.
4 Fore-tackle pendants.
5 Main-tackle pendants.
6 Mizen-burton pendants.
7 Fore-shrouds.
8 Main-shrouds.
9 Mizen-shrouds.
10 Fore-preventer stay.
11 Fore-stay.
12 Main-preventer stay.
13 Main-stay.
14 Mizen-stay.
15 Fore-top-mast burtons and pendants.
16 Main-top-mast burtons and pendants.
17 Fore-top-mast rigging.
18 Main-top-mast rigging.
19 Mizen-top-mast rigging.
20 Fore-top-mast standing backstays.
21 Main-top-mast standing backstays.
22 Mizen-top-mast backstay.
23 Fore-top-mast preventer stay.
24 ———————— stay.
25 Main-top-mast preventer stay.
26 ———————— stay.
27 Mizen-top-mast stay.
28 Fore-top-gallant rigging.
29 Main-top-gallant rigging.
30 Mizen-top-gallant rigging.
31 Fore-top-gallant standing backstay.
32 Main-top-gallant standing backstay.
33 Mizen-top-gallant backstay.
34 Fore-top-gallant stay.

35 Main-top-gallant stay.
36 Mizen-top-gallant stay.
37 Fore royal backstay.
38 Main royal backstay.
39 Mizen royal backstay.
40 Fore royal stay.
41 Main royal stay.
42 Mizen royal stay.
43 Standing jib stay.
44 Flying jib stay.
45 Bowsprit horse.
46 Martingale.
47 Dolphin striker.
48 Fore-stay tackle.
49 Main-stay tackle.
50 Span for tackle.
51 Fore futtock shrouds.
52 Main futtock shrouds.
53 Mizen futtock shrouds.
54 Futtock staves.
55 Bobstay collars.
56 Fore-stay collars.
57 Jib-boom horses.
58 Fore and main runners and tackles.
59 Mizen-burtons.
60 Ensign-staff and halliards.
61 Bowsprit.
62 Fore-mast.
63 Main-mast.
64 Mizen-mast.
65 Jib-boom.
66 Fore-top-mast.
67 Main-top-mast.
68 Mizen-top-mast.
69 Fore-top-gallant-mast.
70 Main-top-gallant-mast.
71 Mizen-top-gallant-mast.
72 Bumpkin.

Plate X.

RUNNING RIGGING

PLATE X

References on the Plate, delineating the Running·Rigging of a Merchant Ship

1 Flying jib-guys.
2 Standing jib-guys.
3 Spritsail lifts.
4 Spritsail braces.
5 Fore-yard tackles.
6 Main-yard tackles.
7 Fore-lifts.
8 Fore-braces.
9 Main-lifts.
10 Main-braces.
11 Cross-jack lifts.
12 Cross-jack braces.
13 Slings of fore-yard.
14 Slings of main-yard.
15 Slings of cross-jack-yard.
16 Fore-top-sail-lifts.
17 ———————— braces.
18 ———————— reef-tackles.
19 Main-top-sail-lifts.
20 ———————— braces.
21 ———————— reef-tackles.
22 Mizen-top-sail-lifts.
23 ———————— braces.
24 Fore-top-gallant-lifts.
25 ———————— braces.
26 ———————— halliards.
27 Main-top-gallant-lifts.
28 ———————— braces.
29 ———————— halliards.
30 Mizen-top-gallant-lifts.
31 ———————— braces.
32 ———————— halliards.
33 Fore-royal-lifts.
34 ———————— braces.

35 Fore-royal halliards.
36 Main-royal-lifts.
37 ———————— braces.
38 ———————— halliards.
39 Signal halliards.
40 Mizen-royal-lifts.
41 ———————— braces.
42 ———————— halliards.
43 Fore-top-sail tie and halliards.
44 Main-top-sail tie and halliards.
45 Mizen-top-sail tie and halliards.
46 Mizen-gaff peak halliards.
47 ———————— throat halliards.
48 ——— vang-pendants and falls.
49 ——— signal halliards.
50 Spanker-boom topping-lift.
51 ———————— quarter guys.
52 ———————— sheet.
53 Spritsail-yard.
54 Fore-yard.
55 Main-yard.
56 Cross-jack-yard.
57 Fore-top-sail-yard.
58 Main-top-sail-yard.
59 Mizen-top-sail-yard.
60 Fore-top-gallant-yard.
61 Main-top-gallant-yard.
62 Mizen-top-gallant-yard.
63 Fore-royal-yard.
64 Main-royal-yard.
65 Mizen-royal-yard.
66 Spanker boom.
67 ——— gaff.

Plate XI.

FORE-AND-AFT SAILS IN A CALM.

PLATE XI

References on the Plate, delineating the Fore-and-Aft Sails of a Merchant Ship in a calm

1 Flying jib.
2 Standing jib.
3 Fore-top-mast-stay-sail.
4 Fore-stay-sail.
5 Main-stay-sail.
6 Main-top-mast-stay-sail.
7 Main-top-gallant-stay-sail.
8 Mizen-stay-sail.
9 Mizen-top-mast-stay-sail.
10 Mizen.
11 Flying jib downhauler.
12 ———— halliards.
13 ———— sheets.
14 ———— stay.
15 Jib downhauler.
16 —— halliards.
17 —— sheets.
18 —— stay.
19 —— outhauler.
20 Fore-top-mast-stay.
21 ———————— stay-sail down-
     hauler.
22 Fore-top-mast halliards.
23 ———————— sheets.
24 Fore-stay-sail-stay.
25 ———————— halliards.
26 ———————— downhauler.

27 Fore-stay-sail-sheets.
28 Main-stay-sail-stay.
29 ———————— halliards.
30 ———————— downhauler.
31 ———————— sheets.
32 Main-top-mast-stay.
33 Stay-sail halliards.
34 ———— downhauler.
35 ———— sheets.
36 Main-top-gallant stay.
37 Stay-sail halliards.
38 ———— downhauler.
39 ———— sheets.
40 Mizen-stay.
41 Stay-sail halliards.
42 ———— downhauler.
43 ———— sheets.
44 Mizen-top-mast-stay.
45 Stay-sail-halliards.
46 ———— downhauler.
47 ———— sheets.
48 Tack of mizen-course.
49 Sheet of mizen course.
50 Throat-brails.
51 Middle-brails.
52 Peak-brails.

Plate XII.

SQUARE SAILS AND DRIVER.

PLATE XII

References on the Plate, delineating the Square-Sails and Driver of a Merchant Ship

 1 Fore-course.
 2 Main-course.
 3 Fore-top-sail.
 4 Main-top-sail.
 5 Mizen-top-sail.
 6 Fore-top-gallant-sail.
 7 Main-top-gallant-sail.
 8 Mizen-top-gallant-sail.
 9 Fore-royal.
10 Main-royal.
11 Mizen-royal.
12 Driver.
13 Fore-lower-studding sails.
14 Main-lower-studding-sails.
15 Fore-top-mast-studding-sails.
16 Main-top-mast-studding-sails.
17 Fore-top-gallant-studding-sails.
18 Main-top-gallant-studding-sails.
19 Fore-sheets.
20 —— tacks.
21 —— leech-lines.
22 —— bunt-lines.
23 —— bowlines.

24 Fore-bowline-bridles.
25 Main-sheets.
26 —— tacks.
27 —— leech-lines.
28 —— bunt-lines.
29 —— bowlines.
30 —— bowline-bridles.
31 Fore-top-sail-bunt-lines.
32 ———————— bowlines.
33 ———————— bowline-bridles.
34 Main-top-sail-bunt-lines.
35 ———————— bowlines.
36 ———————— bowline-bridles.
37 Mizen-top-sail-bunt-lines.
38 ———————— bowlines.
39 ———————— bowline-bridles.
40 Fore-top-gallant-bunt-lines.
41 ———————— bowlines.
42 ———————— bowline-bridles.
43 Main-top-gallant-bunt-lines.
44 ———————— bowlines.
45 ———————— bowline-bridles.
46 Mizen-top-gallant-bowlines.

N. B. — For the ropes that appear to windward of the sails, see Plate XIII. (a Barque).

Plate XIII.

A BARQUE.

PLATE XIII

References on the Plate, delineating the Sails and Running Rigging of a Barque

1 Flying jib.
2 Standing-jib.
3 Fore-top-mast-stay-sail.
4 Fore-sail.
5 Fore-top-sail.
6 Fore-top-gallant-sail.
7 Fore-royal.
8 Main-sail.
9 Main-top-sail.
10 Main-top-gallant-sail.
11 Main-royal.
12 Main-stay-sail.
13 Main-try-sail.
14 Mizen.
15 Gaff-top-sail.
16 Fore-sheet.
17 Fore-tack.
18 ———— clue-garnets.
19 ———— bowlines.
20 Fore-top-sail-sheets.
21 ———— clue-lines.
22 ———— reef-tackles.
23 ———— bowlines.
24 Fore-top-gallant-sheet.
25 ———————— clue-lines.
26 Fore-royal-sheets.

27 Fore-royal clue-lines.
28 Main-tack.
29 —— sheet.
30 —— clue-garnet.
31 Main-top-sail-sheets.
32 ———————— clue-lines.
33 ———————— reef-tackles.
34 ———————— bowlines.
35 Main-top-gallant-sheets.
36 ———————— clue-lines.
37 ———————— bowlines.
38 Main-royal-sheets.
39 ———— clue-lines.
40 Main-stay-sail-sheets.
41 Main-try-sail-sheets.
42 ———— brails.
43 ———— tripping-line.
44 Mizen-peak-halliards.
45 ———— downhauler.
46 Mizen-throat-halliards.
47 Boom-sheet.
48 ———— topping-lift.
49 ———— guys.
50 Gaff-top-sail-sheet.
51 ———— halliards.
52 ———— downhauler.

N. B. — For the ropes that appear to leeward of the sails, see Plate XII. (Square-Sails and Driver).

Plate XIV.

A CUTTER with all SAILS.

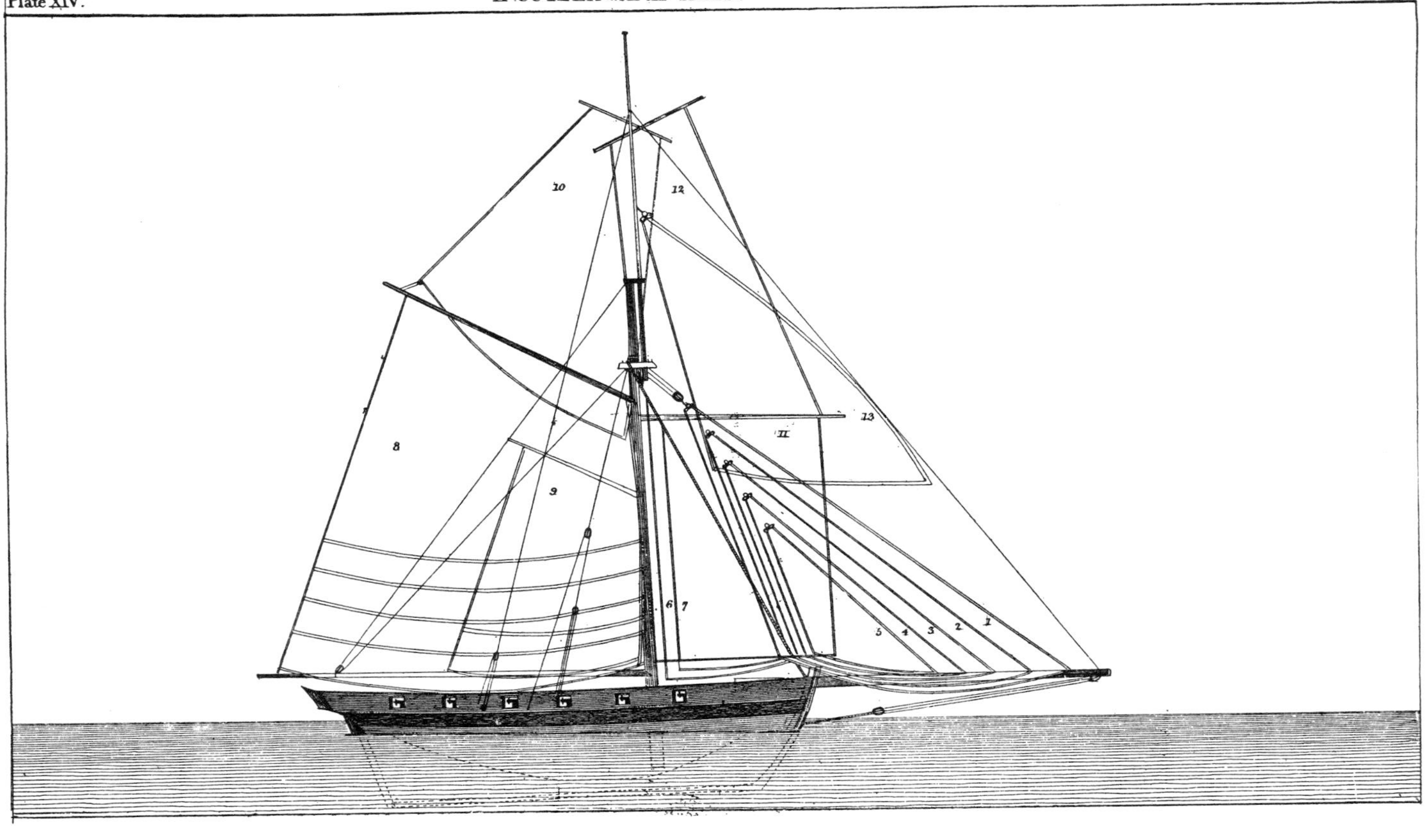

PLATE XIV

References on the Plate, delineating the Sails of a Cutter

1 Main jib.
2 Second jib.
3 Third jib.
4 Storm jib.
5 Spitfire jib.
6 Fore-sail.
7 Storm-fore-sail.
8 Main-sail.
9 Storm-try-sail.
10 Gaff-top-sail.
11 Square-sail.
12 Half-top-sail.
13 Jib top-sail.

THE ART OF RIGGING

PART III

PROGRESSIVE METHOD OF RIGGING SHIPS

WE now presume that the Reader, by his perusal of the two fore-going parts, has made himself so well acquainted with the contents of the engravings, as to render many references to them unneces-sary. We have, therefore, in this part, generally avoided a repeti-tion of them; as, otherwise, they would have disturbed, very considerably, the connexion of the description.

THERE is no one undeviating mode which is pursued in the pro-gressive rigging of ships. It is an operation which must at all times depend upon the time allotted for its performance, and the neces-sity for immediate fitting. The nature of it, however, is such, that many parts may be advancing at the same time; but the usual method, where extreme expedition is not required, is the follow-ing: —

First, rig the bowsprit; then get the lower rigging over the masts; then the top-masts up, and their rigging. Next, rig the jib-boom, spritsail-yard, and whiskers; and get on board and rig the fore, main, and cross-jack yards; then the top-sail-yards; get up the top-gallant-masts, with their rigging and yards, and the flying jib-boom.

RIGGING THE BOWSPRIT. (Pl. 9, fig. 61)

Horses. — The outer ends are spliced round a thimble in an eye-bolt on each side of the upper part of the bowsprit-cap. The inner ends have a thimble seized in, that sets up to the eye-bolt in the timber-head on each side of the stem, by a laniard, passed several times alternately through the thimble and eye-bolt, and set tight by hand: the turns are then frapped together, and the ends hitched.

Gammoning. — Some large ships have two gammonings, of 9 or 11 turns each. The rope is passed over the bowsprit, and through a hole cut in the knee of the head, alternately. The first end is whipt and passed through the hole, and over the bowsprit, with a round-turn, then clinched round the bowsprit close against the cleats; the other end passes through the fore part of the hole, taking care to cross every turn and keep each turn forward on the bowsprit and aft in the hole, and every turn is hove tight and nippered. A selvagee, or lashing, is put round the cutwater, to which a block is hooked abreast of the hawse-hole, through which hawse-hole a pendant is led through the block, with an eye in its outer end, to which the gammoning is toggled every turn, and by which means it is hove taut, either by the capstan, or by clapping a purchase on it; you may have a weight attached to the bowsprit end, but should not be generally used. When all the turns are passed, and hove tight, they are frapped together in the middle, by as many cross-turns as are passed over the bowsprit, each turn hove tight; the end of the gammoning rope is then whipt, and seized to one of the turns. The frapping increases the tension, and adds to the security acquired by the purchase.

The first or *Inner Bobstay Collar* is lashed upon the upper side, two-thirds out, with eight or ten turns, each turn passing, alternately, through the eyes, and hove tight by a heaver.

Fore-Stay Collar is now generally fitted as a double strap round the bowsprit, the bight reeving through its own part, into which part a dead-eye is seized, to reeve the laniard for setting up the fore-stay.

The Middle Bobstay Collar is lashed the same as the inner bobstay collar.

The two Bowsprit Shroud Collars are lashed upon each side of the bowsprit, as the bobstay collar; but the heart of each is to be kept on the opposite side.

The Fore Spring-stay Collar is to be lashed the same as the fore-stay collar.

The outer Bobstay Collar is lashed the same as the others.

Blocks for the fore-bowlines are lashed one on each side of the fore-stay collar.

Blocks for the fore-top-bowlines are seized, one on each side, to an eye-bolt in the bowsprit-cap, or occasionally lead through a sheave-hole in the bees.

Spans for the spritsail-lifts are hitched round the bowsprit-cap, under the jib-boom.

Strap for the standing-lifts (seldom used) has a thimble spliced in each end, and hitches round the bowsprit with the bees. When the rigging of the bowsprit is thus far completed, the bobstays and shrouds are set up as follows: —

Bobstays. — Ships have two or three pairs of bobstays, according to their size; they are fixed by passing one end through the hole bored through the knee of the head (merchant-ships that have no knee, have large triangular bolts driven through the stem, and clinched on a plate of iron inside); the ends are then spliced together, to make it two-fold, or like the link of a chain. A heart, or dead-eye, is seized in the bight, with a splice at the arse of the heart, the same as the collar; a laniard then passes through, and connects with the heart, or dead-eye, in the collar under the bowsprit, and sets up tight, with luff-tackle upon luff, and leads in upon the forecastle. The use of the bobstay is to draw down and keep steady the bowsprit, to counteract the force of the stays of the foremast, which draw it upwards.

Shrouds hook to an eye-bolt on each side of the bow; the foremost end has a heart, or dead-eye, spliced in: the shrouds are then set tight as the bobstays. The shrouds are to secure the bowsprit, as the fore-mast and the upper part of the main-mast are stayed and supported by the bowsprit. It also supports the bowsprit when the ship is pitching or rolling heavily.

RIGGING the SPRITSAIL-YARD. (Pl. 10, fig. 53)

Horses or *Foot-Ropes* (seldom used). — The eye in the outer end is put over the yard-arm on each side, and stops against the cleats; the other end has an eye spliced in it, and seized to the yard about three feet from the slings on the opposite side. The horses hang three feet below the yard. To keep horses more parallel to the yard, they are suspended, at proper distances, by ropes, called

Stirrups, two or three on each side of the slings, having an eye spliced in their lower ends. They hang three feet below the yard, through which the horse reeves. The upper ends are open or plaited, to lie flat to the yard, and are nailed.

Brace Blocks are strapped, and go over the yard-arm, and the brace reeves through the single-block made fast under the foretop, and then leads down to the breast-work of the forecastle; the standing part is made fast to the stay-collar.

Lifts (seldom used) have an eye the size of the yard-arm; after which it reeves through the single block in the span at the cap, and leads in upon the forecastle; they are used to keep the yard level, or to raise one yard-arm higher than the other. Several straps, with thimbles for the jib-guys to reeve through, are seized on, according to the number of guys.

Slings. — One end has an eye, and goes round the yard close within the cleats in the middle, and seizes, with a quarter-seizing, close to the yard; the other end goes over the bowsprit before the saddle, and under the yard, then over the bowsprit again, and an eye is spliced in the end, that comes close to the other eye, and lashes; — now generally chain or iron strap.

RIGGING THE FORE, MAIN, AND MIZEN MASTS
(Pl. 9, figs. 62, 63, 64)

Girtline Blocks, before the mast is in its place, are lashed, one round the mast-head, above the stop of the cap, and one round the trestle-trees, in the score of the cross-trees. This latter block is, when the mast is stepped, shifted opposite the other. The girtlines that reeve through them lead down upon the deck, for hoisting the rigging, tops, and cross-trees, and the persons employed to place the rigging, over the mast-head.

Bolsters, on the trestle-trees, are clothed with old canvas, several times doubled, and tarred.

Lower Tackle Pendants are placed over the mast-head, and fixed, that the thimbles (to which is lashed the block for the runner), may hang one on each side of the mast; but burtons are used to the mizen-mast.

Shrouds are hoisted over the mast-head. The first pair leads down on the starboard side forward, the next pair forward on the port side; then the second pair on the starboard side, and the second on the port side; and so on, alternately, till the whole are fixed. By this method the yards are braced to a greater obliquity when the sails are close-hauled, which could not be the case if the foremost shrouds were fitted last on the mast-head.

Swifters are swayed over the mast-head, next above the shrouds, and are fixed on the starboard and port sides of the mast. They are extended from the mast-head to the starboard and port sides of the ship, to support the masts, and enable them to carry sail, &c.

The Stay is lashed round the mast-head, and supports the mast on the fore-part, by extending from its upper end towards the fore-part of the ship.

The Preventer Stay is next lashed round the mast-head, the same as the former.

The Cross-Trees are then hoisted into their places, and bolted in the trestle-trees, which are fore-locked underneath.

The Top is next got over the mast-head, by the girtlines. Four holes are bored through; one in the middle of the square hole on each side, and two on the fore-part, one on each side of the middle of the top, except the mizen-top, which is bored in the after-part. The top is hoisted on board by the girtlines, and placed up against the aft-side of the mast, except the mizen, which is placed on the fore-side. The girtline is then made fast to the top, for hoisting it over the mast-head, as follows: — Reeve the end of each girtline through the hole by the middle of the square hole, and take a round-turn round the sides of the top; make it fast to the standing part with two half-hitches, and stop it with spunyarn through the midship-holes in the fore-part, except the mizen-top, which is stopped at the aft-part. The girtline at the next mast-head is made fast to the aft-part of the main and fore-top, and fore-part of the mizen-top. The top is then hoisted by its girtlines over the mast-head, and guyed clear of the trestle-trees by the girtline from the next mast-head. When it bears against the mast-head, the stops are cut, and the top is swayed up till it goes over the mast-head, and falls to its berth. Large tops are made in two parts, by which they are more easily hoisted into their places.

Forestays are *thus* set up for sea: — The lower pendants are frapped together abaft the fore-mast; and the lashing block being lashed to them, the runners are rove through them, and the ends taken forward, and passed round the bowsprit with a round-turn, and hitched and seized. The falls being rove, the lower (a single block) is hooked to the knight-heads, and the fall led through a leading block, for the people to haul upon; the shrouds and back-stays being slackened as necessary: haul away on the runners, until the mast is far enough forward. The fore-stay has a heart turned in the lower end, with a throat-seizing and two round-seizings above, and the end of the stay capped with canvas; then set up with a laniard that reeves alternately through the heart in the stay, and the heart in the fore-stay collar on the bowsprit, and are greased, that the strain may be immediately given to all the turns at once. The laniard is then strained tight by the tackles, thus: — The upper or single block of a luff-tackle is hooked to a

selvagee fastened round the stay, and the lower block is hooked
with a cat's-paw to the laniard; then the lower block of the fore-
tackle is hooked with a cat's-paw to the fall of the other tackle. The
fall leads upon the deck, and is hauled upon; then two of the turns
are racked together with spunyarn, to prevent their coming up,
whilst more turns are taken, and hove on as before, till the laniard
is expended; the end is then well secured.

The Preventer Stay sets up the same as the fore-stay.

The Main-Stay sets up as the fore-stay, to a heart in the stem,
or otherwise passes over a cross-piece before the fore-mast, and
back again, when it is seized to its own part.

The Main-Spring-Stay sets up the same as the main-stay.

Main Pendants are frapped together abaft the main-mast, and
the runners made fast round the bitts, similar to the fore-mast;
the tackles hook to the eye-bolts in the decks, and the falls lead aft.

Mizen Burtons are brought to the fore-brace bitts, as the main
runners are the fore bitts.

The Mizen-Stay, if only one, leads down from the mast-head, and
generally has a tongue in the lower end, and a thimble in each leg,
and sets up on each side of the main-mast, to eye-bolts in the deck.

Dead-Eyes are turned into the lower end of the shrouds, according to the lay of the rope, with a throat-seizing clapped on close to
the dead-eye, and above that a round-seizing, crossed, and the end
of the shroud whipt with spunyarn, capped with canvas, and seized.

Laniards are rove through the dead-eyes: the end of the laniard
is thrust through the hole of the upper dead-eye nearest to the
end, and stopped with a wall knot, to prevent its slipping; the
other end is passed through the hole of the lower dead-eye, and,
returning upwards, is rove through the middle hole in the upper
dead-eye, and next through the middle hole of the lower dead-eye,
and finally, through the foremost hole in both dead-eyes; the masts
being stayed by runners and tackles, except when stayed and secured for sea, as before described. The end of the laniard, being
directed upwards from the lower dead-eyes, is set up by a runner
and tackle, or a luff-tackle and main-tackle, which hooks in the
runner-pendant; the single block of the luff-tackle is hooked to a
selvagee in the shroud, and the lower double-block hooked to the
laniard with a cat's-paw, and bowsed tight; the fall is then made
fast to the hook of the main-tackle with another cat's-paw; the
main-tackle is then hauled upon, and the laniards well greased, to

make the whole slide with ease through the holes in the dead-eyes, that all the turns may bear an equal proportion of the strain. When the shrouds are set up for a full due (which is, when the mast is stayed forward and the stays all set up), the laniard is first nipped, or stopped, as before observed, and the end passed between the throat-seizing and the dead-eye with a hitch, then brought round all the parts, in turns, to expand the laniard, and the end is well stopped to its own part with spunyarn. It is customary to set up the shrouds the first time with temporary laniards of worn rope and spunyarn seizings; and with the proper laniards and seizings, when set up the last time for sea.

Futtock-Staves are seized along the lower shrouds horizontally, as much below the lower side of the trestle-trees as the cap is above. The number of shrouds that are in the top-mast rigging are then swiftered together, viz.: — A spar is lashed to the outside of the shrouds, about six feet below the futtock-stave; a single block is then lashed round each shroud and spar that are to be swiftered, so that all come in together; the swifting line is then rove through each block from side to side, beginning in the middle, one end leading aft, the other forward; it then crosses, and reeves through two leading-blocks, one on each side of the deck, and is bowsed tight, till the shrouds come in to the length of the catharpin-legs *(if they are used)*, which are seized at each end, round the futtock-stave and shrouds.

Ratlings are fastened horizontally to the shrouds, at distances of about thirteen inches from each other. Small spars, or boats' oars, are seized to the shrouds, about five feet asunder, for the men to stand upon whilst ratling. The ratlings are fastened round each shroud with a clove-hitch, except at the ends, which have an eye spliced in, and seized round the shroud. The fore and aftermost shrouds are left for the first six ratlings, down from the futtock-staves, and likewise the six lower ratlings next to the dead-eyes. The top-mast shrouds are rattled in the same manner.

The Cap is next swayed up into the top by the girtlines.

RIGGING the JIB-BOOM. (Pl. 9, fig. 65)

The *Traveller* is first put over the outer end of the jib-boom; the hook is kept inwards, to hook the jib-stay to.

Horses. — The bight is taken over the jib-boom with a jambing-knot, and rests against the shoulder made in the end of the jib-boom, to prevent its coming in. The inner ends are brought in, and made fast with a round-turn round the jib-boom, close to the cap.

Guys are put over the jib-boom, the same as horses, and the inner ends reeve through a thimble on the quarters of the spritsail-yard, and turn into the strap of a double block, with a throat and round-seizing, which is connected, by its fall, to a single block, that hooks to an eye-bolt near the cat-head, and leads upon the forecastle.

NOTE. — When no spritsail-yard is carried, the jib-boom may be equally secured by guys and outriggers (which article see in Part II, where it is explained).

Martingale has an eye spliced in each end, one of which is placed over the jib-boom, and the other over the dolphin-striker.

Back Ropes have a horse-shoe in the bight, which goes over the dolphin-striker, and sets up in board with a tackle. (Back ropes are generally chain).

RIGGING THE TOP-MASTS. (Pl. 9, figs. 66, 67, 68)

The Girtlines are now taken down from the mast-head, and one of the top-blocks is securely lashed round the mast-head below the cap. The end of a hawser then leads up from aft, outside the trestle-trees, and reeves through the top-block at the mast-head; then leads down inside the fore-part of the trestle-trees, and reeves through the sheave-hole in the heel of the top-mast, and taken up to the mast-head again, when it is racked to the top-mast in two or three places, between the heel and the hounds, where it is well stopped with lashing, and enough of the end left to make fast round the mast-head. The other end of the hawser is taken to the capstan, through a snatch-block that is lashed to the bitts at the aft-part of the mast. When the top-mast is hove high enough to enter the trestle-trees, the end of the hawser is made fast round the mast-head, and the rackings are cut, the men in the top being ready to place the cap over the head of the top-mast, and lashing it in a secure manner; the top-mast is then hove high enough for the cap to enter over the lower-mast-head; it is then lowered a little, and the cap entered, the lashing taken off, then beaten down firmly over the mast-head. The cap being fixed firmly over the lower-mast-head, the mast is hung by the up and down tackles, to unreeve the hawser. The top-tackle pendant is then rove through an iron-bound top-block, hooked to an eye-bolt on one side of the cap, then downwards, and rove through a hole with a sheave in the heel of the top-mast, and brought upwards on the other side of the mast, and made fast to an eye-bolt in the cap, on the opposite side of the top-block. To the lower end of the top-tackle pendant is hooked, through the thimble, the block of the top-tackle, connected, by its fall, to a block hooked to an eye-bolt in the deck, and brought to the capstan. The top-mast cross-trees are swayed up with the girtline, and got on the lower-mast-head. In very large ships the top-mast cross-trees are swayed into the top by the girtlines, when the top-mast, having a burton made fast to its upper extremity, is swayed about twenty feet; the lower block of the burton is then hooked to the cross-trees, by which burton it is lifted on to the lower cap; when the top-mast is again lowered below the cap, and the cross-trees drop into place. The top-mast is then swayed up, and the cross-trees placed. When the top-masts pass through the lower cap and cross-trees, the girtline-blocks are lashed to the top-mast-cross-trees, and the girtline rove through, that one part may lead down by the mast, and the other part abaft the top.

Bolsters are clothed as the lower ones.

Bullock Blocks, or *Hanging Blocks.* — Generally fitted with a long strap to go to the mast-head, before the rigging is placed. But there are several ways of fitting them, one of which is, by having a necklace of chain to go over the top-mast head, well covered, and fitted up with shakings, made quite round: and then parcelled, so as to avoid chafing the rigging, with two or three long links on each side, abreast the foremost shroud in the top-mast rigging, to shackle the bullock-blocks to, by which they lay under the rigging, and are readily got down when damaged. The blocks may be iron-bound, fitted like the tie-blocks, and connected with the hanging link by a shackle.

Burton Pendants are triced up by the girtlines, and placed over the top-mast-head, that the thimbles may hang on each side, to hook the burton-tackles in.

Shrouds are swayed and placed over the top-mast-head; the first pair to lead down on the starboard side forward; the next pair on the port side forward; and so on with the other pairs.

Backstays are hoisted and placed over the top-mast-head, similar to the shrouds.

Stays are swayed up and lashed abaft the top-mast-head; the lower ends reeve through the bees on the bowsprit, and set up to eye-bolts in the bows with laniards.

Top-mast Cap is next swayed up by the girtlines, which are previously lashed up the mast-head, and got upon the top-mast-head by the assistance of men, then beaten down firmly. The girtlines are unlashed and got down, and the top-mast hove up and fidded.

Futtock Plates are put through the holes in the edge of the top.

Futtock Shrouds are furnished with iron hooks in the upper ends, that hook to a hole in the lower ends of the futtock-plates; and the lower ends of the futtock shrouds are attached to the lower shrouds, with an eye and seizing round the futtock-staff and shroud, or as (explained in Part II).

When the rigging is thus far completed, it is set up as follows:—
The masts are first stayed by the burton.

Dead-Eyes are turned into the lower end of the top-mast shrouds, as the lower ones are into the lower shrouds.

Laniards are rove through the dead-eye in the shrouds, and the dead-eye in the futtock-plate, as the lower ones, and set up with the top burton-tackles, and runners in large vessels. The top-mast shrouds are to secure the top-masts, and the futtock shrouds receive equal tension, by means of the futtock-plates passing through the top, and connecting with the futtock shrouds below.

Ratlines as the lower shrouds.

The Breast Backstay has a single block turned or spliced into the lower end, through which the runner is rove. One end of the runner is made fast to the chain-plates, abreast the mast, with a half-hitch, and the end seized down, occasionally knotted through. In the other end is spliced a double block, connected, by its fall, to a double block that is strapped with an eye, that passes through the channels, where it is toggled.

After Backstays are set up the same as the shrouds, to a small dead-eye in the after-end of the channel.

Fore Top-mast Stays set up through the bees of the bowsprit, through which the stays pass; then set up with thimbles and laniards to an eye-bolt in the bow, on each side.

Main Top-mast Stay reeves through a single block, and fastened round the fore-mast-head, just above the fore-yard, the stay having a thimble turned in; the lower end leads down between the catharpins and the mast, then sets up with a laniard to an eye-bolt in the deck, close abaft the mast. Sometimes it leads on deck abaft the fore-mast, where it is secured to a bolt in the deck.

Main Top-mast Spring Stay reeves through a thimble or block, seized in the bight of the collar, at the after-part of the fore-mast, close to the lower rigging, and then set up to its own part.

Mizen Top-mast Stay reeves through a thimble seized in the bight of a collar, that lashes at the main-mast-head, or a strap to the collar of the main-stay, and secures to its own part.

When the *Shrouds* are again set up for sea, the masts are steadied by their respective stays, instead of the burtons.

RIGGING the FORE and MAIN YARDS. (Pl. 7, fig. 4)

Fore and *Main Yards* are rigged as follows: — The end of the hawser that hove up the top-mast is made fast round the middle of the yard with a round-turn and two half-hitches; then securely stopped along the yard in several places, and also at the upper yard-arm. As it is hove on board, the lashings are cast off, and the lower tackle of the opposite side is brought on to the quarter of the yard, to lower it easily, as the yard advances on board beyond the middle or slings. The yards are placed square, athwart-ships, before their respective masts.

Jack-Stays. — The jack-stays are first placed over the yard-arms, then rove through eye-bolts, driven into or clamped round the yard, and when the inner ends have thimbles spliced into them, through which a laniard is rove, and they set up to each other amidships; after which a strap, with a thimble to reeve the earing through, is put on.

Horses go over the yard-arms, with an eye in their outer ends, and hang about three feet below the yards. To keep the horses more parallel to the yard, it is suspended, at proper distances, by ropes, called stirrups, through which the horses pass; sometimes two, three, or four on each side of the yard: the upper ends have eyes, and are fastened to the yard by being put over the eye-bolts. The inner ends of the horses have a thimble turned in; they lash to the yard, on the opposite side of the cleats, with a laniard, which passes round the yard and through the thimble.

Yard Tackle Pendants (in large ships) are next put over the yard-arm, with an eye in the lower end, in which is spliced a double block, connected, by its fall, to a single one, strapped with a hook and thimble.

Tricing Blocks for the yard-tackles are fitted as cheeks.

Brace Blocks are next put over the yard-arms; with a strap and two thimbles, through which the brace reeves. (Pl. 7, fig. 4).

Fore Braces reeve through the block in the yard-arm; the standing-parts make fast round the collar of the main-stay, on each side, or into the bibbs of the main-mast. The leading-part leads through a single block in the lower-mast-head; it then leads down, and passes through a sheave in the bitts at the fore-part of the quarter-deck, and there belays. — Brigs lead the same.

Main Braces. — The standing-part makes fast with a clinch round a bumpkin, projecting from each quarter; the leading-part reeves through the block at the yard-arm, and back through a block which is strapped to the bumpkin; then through the gunwale, and belays round a cleat inside.

Span for *Main Braces* has two legs, with a thimble spliced in the end of each leg, through which reeves the standing and leading-part of the brace, and the span makes fast with a half-hitch, and the end seized up round the mizen-shrouds.

Fore Preventer Braces, in war, are rove through a block lashed round the yard-arm, and through a block in a span, round the bowsprit-cap; they then lead in upon the forecastle, and the standing-part makes fast round the cap. The main-brace reeves through a block on the yard-arm, then through a block strapped into the fore-mast, just above the catharpins; then leads down upon the forecastle: the standing part makes fast to the shrouds, above the block, with a hitch, and the end seized. — Brigs reeve the same.

Top-sail Sheet Blocks (when used) are next put over the yard-arm, strapped with an eye the size of the yard-arm. [See SHEAVES]. (Pl. 2, fig. 9, and Pl. 7, fig. 4).

Lift Blocks are next put over the yard-arm, as the sheet-blocks. The lifts reeve through the block at the cap of the lower mast-head, then lead down abreast the shrouds, and reeve through a block, or the bitts, where they are belayed. (Pl. 7, fig. 4).

Jeers, in a large ship, are large tackles (Pl. 7, fig. 4). The treble-block at the mast-head is hove up close on the fore-side of the top-mast by the top-burton tackles, and lashed round the lower mast-head. The lower block is strapped with a double strap to the size of the yard, with a long and short leg, and lashes to the middle, or slings, within the cleats. The long leg of the strap goes down the aft-side of the yard, and meets the bight of the short leg on the fore-side, and lashes, every turn passing alternately through each bight, rose-fashion. (Pl. 2, figs. 2, 4, 10). The blocks at the mast-head and on the yard, are connected by their falls, which lead upon deck.

A Quarter Block is a single block, strapped double or single, and lashes on each side the middle of the yard; the sheets reeve on their respective sides, and lead down by the mast. (Pl. 7, fig. 5).

Clue Garnet Blocks lash through the eyes upon the yard, the blocks hanging underneath, three or four feet without the middle cleats on each side. (Pl. 7, fig. 4).

Leech Line Blocks are seized to the jack-stay on the yard, one-fourth within the cleats on each yard-arm; the blocks to hang on the fore-part of the yard. In large ships two leech-lines. (Pl. 7, fig. 4).

Bunt-Line Blocks are lashed as the former, between them and the slings of the yard.

Slab-Line Blocks are strapped with a short eye, that seizes to the span of the quarter-blocks underneath the yard.

Truss Pendants. — Two straps are fitted, with large thimbles, on each side the slings of the yard, for reeving the pendants through. The pendants have an eye spliced in the end, and are passed round the yard within the cleats on each side the middle, or slings, and through the eye. The end then passes round the mast, and through the thimble of the strap; thus the starboard end reeves through the port thimble, and the port end through the starboard thimble. In the upper end a block is turned in, which is connected, by its fall, to a cheek in the trestle-trees, on each side the mast, by which the truss-pendant is slackened or tightened, to let the yard move from, or confine it strictly to the mast. Iron trusses are now very much in use in merchant-ships, by which the yard is kept much steadier when at sea.

Slings for lower yards. (See Part II).

RIGGING the CROSS-JACK-YARD. (Pl. 10, fig. 56)

It is hove on board as the other yards and rigged as follows: — *The Horses, Brace Blocks,* and *Lifts,* go over the yard-arm, the same as the other lower yards. Quarter-blocks sometimes double.

Braces, the same as fore and main, reeve through the block at the yard-arm. The standing-part of the starboard brace makes fast to one of the middle shrouds of the main rigging on the port side, with a hitch, and the end stopped; and the leading-part leads down through a block lashed to the same shroud a little below the cathar-pins; it then leads through a truck, or block, and belays to a pin in the ship's side, and the port brace the contrary.

Lifts (Single) go over the yard-arm with an eye, and reeve through a block at the mizen-cap, and the leading-part comes upon deck.

Truss Pendants. — A strap, with a thimble seized in it, is secured to the yard on one side of the slings; and the truss-pendant, which has an eye in one end, is passed round the yard on the other side of the slings, the end of which is rove through the eye, which jambs it to its place. The end is then passed round abaft the mizen-mast, and rove upwards, through the thimble already mentioned, and a single-block spliced into the end; a fall is rove through it and the cheek in the trestle-tree, which trusses it close to the mast.

RIGGING the TOP-SAIL-YARDS. (Pl. 10, fig. 57)

The Top Rope or *Hawser* is fastened to the slings of the yard, and stopped thence to the yard-arm, by which it is hove on board, and placed for rigging as follows: —

First, the *Jackstays;* the earing strap next; then the *Horses,* the same as the lower yards, with the addition of *Flemish Horses,* which have an eye spliced in each end; one eye is spliced in the eye-bolt in the yard-arm, and the other eye is seized round the yard within the arm-cleats.

Brace Blocks are next put on the yard, as on the lower ones. (Pl. 7, fig. 5). The fore-top-sail braces reeve through the block at the yard-arm, and then through a block lashed on each side of the collar of the main-stay, a little above the fore-braces; the standing-part makes fast to the main-top-mast-head. The leading-part leads from the block upon the collar on the stay, the same as the fore-braces. Brigs the same. Sometimes the standing-part of the fore top-sail-brace is made fast to the main-stay; and then, being rove through the brace-block at the yard-arm, is taken to the main-top-mast-head, where it is rove through a span-block for the purpose, from thence on deck.

Main Top-sail Braces reeve through the block at the yard-arm; the standing-part makes fast to the mizen-top-mast-head. The leading-part leads through a block in the span round the mizen-mast below the hounds, and leads down through a sheave-hole or block in the ship's side, and belays there.

Mizen Top-sail Braces reeve through the block at the yard-arm, and cross as the cross-jack braces; but the lead is at the main-mast-head, instead of the shrouds.

Lift Blocks are strapped with an eye to the size of the yard-arm. (Pl. 7, fig. 5). The lift reeves through the lower sheave in the *Sister Block* in the top-mast shrouds, and through the block in the yard-arm. The standing-part is secured round the top-mast-head, and the leading-part leads down the side of the mast, and sets up in the top, or on deck.

Tie Blocks are sometimes fitted with straps, and lashed to the yard, but generally iron-bound, swivel fashion. (Pl. 7, fig. 5).

Top-sail Ties. — Large ships have double ties; the lower end has a single or double block, called the fly-block, spliced for the hal-liards. The upper end is first rove through the bullock-block from aft, then through the tie-block on the yard, and the end taken to the mast-head, so that it can be shortened up, if necessary.

The Fly Block in the lower end of the top-sail-ties, is connected, by their halliards, to a single-block, that is strapped with a long strap (Pl. 10, figs. 43, 44, 45), with a hook and thimble that hooks to a swivel eye-bolt in the channel on each side. The leading-part leads through a block hooked on each side; the foremost ones abaft the forecastle, and the after ones on the quarter-deck.

Clue-Line and *Top-gallant-Sheet* or *Quarter Blocks* are strapped with two lashing-eyes, and lash upon the yards from two to three feet without the slings; the blocks hanging underneath the yard, through which the clue-line and sheet reeves, and leads down upon the deck. (Pl. 7, fig. 5).

Bunt-Line Lizards are spliced round the strap of the top-sail-tie-block upon the yard.

The Yard is next hove up and the

Parral is passed round the aft-side of the mast, and round the yard, to secure the yard to the mast. The parral has an eye spliced in each end, the eyes passing under the yard, and over, till both eyes meet on the upper side, and are seized together. The parts are then brought together by quarter-seizings, abaft the yard. Iron parrals are now commonly used in merchant-ships.

RIGGING THE TOP-GALLANT-MASTS
(Pl. 9, figs. 69, 70, 71)

The Mast-Rope reeves for the top-gallant-mast as it does for the top-mast, observing to stop it to the top-gallant-mast-head, to keep it steady, till it has entered between the trestle-trees; when the end of the mast-rope is made fast to an eye-bolt in the cap. The mast-rope is then swayed upon until the head of the mast is through the cap; then

The Stay is first placed over the top-gallant-mast-head. *Shrouds* next, the same as the top-mast, setting up in the top. *Backstays* next, the same as the top-mast; then the royal-rigging, if royal masts.

The Top-gallant Mast is then swayed up and fidded.

Shrouds are set up as above.

Backstays set up the same as the top-mast-backstays, to a small dead-eye in the aft-part of the channel, or in a stool abaft the channel.

The Fore-top-gallant Stay is rove through a score in the outer end of the jib-boom; then through a sheave-hole in the *dolphin-striker,* when it is led into the bows where it sets up to an eye-bolt by a tackle.

The Main-top-gallant Stay reeves through a sheave in the after-part of the fore-top-mast-cross-trees, has a thimble turned in the end of the stay, and sets up to a thimble in a strap, made fast to the trestle-trees of the fore-mast, with a laniard.

The Mizen-top-gallant Stay is led through a sheave-hole at the main-top-mast-head, as the main-top-gallant-stay is to the fore-top-mast-head.

Royal Masts are rigged as top-gallant-masts, and in some ships as sliding masts, when they go up abaft the top-gallant-masts.

RIGGING the TOP-GALLANT-YARDS
(Pl. 7, fig. 6, and Pl. 10, figs. 60, 61, 62)

The Yards are got on board and rigged with jack-stays, foot-ropes, and horses, over the yard-arm, the same as the top-sail-yards.

Top-gallant Lifts are single, and go over the yard-arm, with an eye spliced in one end; the other end reeves through a thimble in the top-gallant-shrouds, and leads down into the top.

The Tie or *Halliards* reeves through the sheave-hole in the head of the top-gallant-mast, and clinches round the yard in the slings or middle; the lower end of the halliards comes down abaft the mast, upon which any necessary purchase is added.

Fore-top-gallant Braces reeve through the block at the yard-arm. The standing-part makes fast round the main-top-gallant-mast-head, and the leading-part reeves through a block lashed to the collar of the main-top-mast-stay; then leads through a block in the fore-top, and down upon the forecastle.

Main-top-gallant Braces reeve through the block at the yard-arm, and the standing-part makes fast to the collar of the mizen-top-mast-stay; the leading-part reeves through a block on the collar of the stay, as the former does to the main-top-mast-stay, and leads down the mizen-rigging, where it belays. (Sometimes the standing-part is made fast to the mizen-top-gallant-mast-head).

Mizen-top-gallant Braces are single, and go with a splice over the yard-arm. They lead forward to the main-mast, similar to the cross-jack-yard (which see).

Clue-Line and *Royal Sheet,* or *Quarter-Blocks,* are strapped with two lashing-eyes, and lash upon the yard, eighteen inches without the slings. (Pl. 7, fig. 6). The blocks hang under the yard, through which is rove the clue-lines and royal sheets. The leading-part leads down the mast on deck.

The Yard is swayed up, and

The Parral is fixed as the top-sail-yard.

RIGGING THE ROYAL YARDS. (Pl. 10, figs. 63, 64, 65)

They rig as top-gallant-yards, except when set flying; in which case, the halliard reeves through a sheave-hole close up under the truck; the standing-part clinches to the middle of the yard, and the leading-part comes down upon deck, or in the top.

Braces go over the yard-arm with an eye; they lead through the single blocks at the next top-gallant-mast-head aft, or from the mizen forward, and lead down upon deck.

RIGGING THE MIZEN OR SPANKER GAFF
(Pl. 7, fig. 8, and Pl. 10, fig. 67)

Most ships now prefer having the gaff to traverse up and down the mast; therefore a double or single-block, according to the size of it, is strapped in the throat; a chock in the trestle-trees, abaft the mizen-mast, has sheaves on purpose for the throat-halliards, which are rove alternately through. The peak-halliards: — the end of the halliard is taken through the lubber's-hole, rove through a double-block at the mizen-cap, which block hooks to an iron strap over the cap, down through a block in the middle of the gaff, up again through the double-block before described, then through a block at the gaff-end; and the standing-part is either hitched round the head of the mizen-top-mast, or made fast round the neck of the block, at the after-part of the cap.

RIGGING the SPANKER BOOM. (Pl. 10, fig. 66)

The Topping Lifts have hooks spliced in the end, which hook to eye-bolts in the outer part of the boom; the ends are rove through a single-block lashed on each side the mizen-mast-head, or a cheek; and a double-block spliced in each lower end, which connects, by a fall, to a single-block, hooked in an eye-bolt in the mizen channel on each side. In very large ships, or brigs, the lift is snatched to the boom. The standing-part of the fall makes fast to the becket in the arse of the single-block, and the leading-part leads from the double-block, and belays to a cleat on each side of the boom.

Guy Pendants. — They are spliced round the end of the boom. A thimble is spliced in the inner end of the pendants, with a tackle hooked to them on each side, and are used where most wanted.

Boom-Sheet Block is fitted with a double strap, just within the taffrail, through which the boom-sheet is rove to another block in the taffrail.

SETTING up the SHROUDS

Shrouds are set up for sea after the stays, as before mentioned; so also are the top-mast-shrouds and backstays.

FITTING and REEVING the TILLER-ROPES

To prevent wet from going down, over each groove is a small box, fitted with a sliding top, and a hole just sufficient to admit the rope, which traverses backwards and forwards, as the turns of the rope increase or decrease upon the wheel, by the helm being put on either side. Sometimes a leather collar is nailed on the top, and surrounds the rope for three or four inches high. Each end, passing through the holes in the deck is rove through vertical sheaves, so fixed in a chock, one on each side the midships, close up under the deck in the gun-room, as to direct each end into its respective side, where it reeves through a horizontal sheave or block, fixed in a block of wood at the end of the sweep; thence it leads to the tiller-head, at the extremity of which a block is strapped on each side, through which the tiller-ropes are rove, when an iron thimble is turned into each end, and sets up with a laniard to an eye-bolt driven into each side farther aft. When the tiller is worked upon deck, the tiller-rope is stretched, middled, and marked, and placed on the wheel as before; then rove through a swivel-block fastened on each side the middle of the deck under the wheel, and through another that is lashed to an eye-bolt on each side of the ship, then brought into midships, to an eye, on each side of the hoop on the head of the tiller, and is there seized or spliced with a thimble.

End of the Third Part

THE ART OF RIGGING

PART IV

A DESCRIPTION OF REEVING THE RUNNING RIGGING AND BENDING THE SAILS; ALSO THE RIGGING OF BRIGS, YACHTS, AND SMALL VESSELS

REEVING THE GEAR AND BENDING THE FORE-SAIL
(Pl. 12, fig. 1)

The Tack and *Sheet Blocks* are put over the clues, or shackled to it, on each side, and the strap of the clue-garnet block put through the clues; the eyes are brought up on each side, and seized.

Sheets are rove through the sheet-blocks on each side, and the standing-part seized to a thimble, in an eye-bolt, a little before the gangway. The leading-part leads through a sheave-hole a little before the gangway; then leads forward, and belays round a large cleat in the side.

Tacks, when double. — The standing-part is clinched or spliced round the outer end of the bumpkin, and the leading-part leads through a single-block in the clue of the sail, then through a block at the outer end of the bumpkin, and leads in upon the forecastle.

Clue-Garnets reeve through the blocks on each side the yard, then through the block on the clue of the sail. The standing-part is carried up, and made fast round the yard by its block. The leading-part comes upon deck, and reeves through the sheave-hole in the top-sail-sheet bitts, and there belays.

Leech-Lines reeve through the block under the top; then through the block upon the yard, and the standing-part toggles to the leech-cringle, or leads through the leech-cringles up abaft the sail, to the yard; the leading-part then leads through a block, at the aft-part of the top, and comes down upon the forecastle.

Bunt-Lines reeve through a double-block at the aft-part of the top; then through another block under the fore-part of the top, and through the blocks or lizards on the yard, then down on the fore-side of the sail, and toggle or clinch to the cringles in the foot. The hauling-part leads on deck.

Bowlines reeve through a single-block lashed at the collar of the fore-stay, on the bowsprit, the outer part with a thimble spliced in the end, through which thimble the bridle is rove, when the bridle clinches to the cringle on the leech of the sail. The leading-part leads upon the forecastle.

Slab-Lines reeve through a small block, lashed to the span of the quarter-blocks, and the standing-part toggles or clinches with two legs to the middle bunt-line cringles. The leading-part leads to the top-sail-sheet bitts.

Spilling-Lines (when used) reeve through blocks, lashed on each side of the quarter-blocks of the lower yards, then lead down before the sail, return upwards under the foot of the sail, and make fast round the yard with a timber-hitch.

Life-Lines are sometimes used for the preservation of the men, and make fast round the lift, or the strap of the lift-block and jeer, or tie-blocks, in the middle of the yard.

Yard-Ropes are temporary, and only used to get the sail up for bending; they are made fast round the boom-iron at each yard-arm, and one end comes down and makes fast to the first reef-earing. The leading-part leads upon deck.

Earings, one end of which is spliced to the head-cringle, with a long eye; the other end passed over the yard-arm without the rigging, through the cringle, alternately, two or three times, and is passed round the yard within the rigging, and through the cringle, till the earing is expended, and the end made fast with two half-hitches. The outer turns are to stretch the upper edge of the sail tight along the yard, and the inner turns to draw it close.

Reef-Earings the same.

Rope-Bands are rove through the eyelet-holes in the head of the sail, by which it is made fast to the jackstays.

Points are put in the sail, thus: — An over-hand knot is made in the middle of the point, then thrust through the eyelet-hole in the reef-band, and knotted close to the sail on the opposite side. Sometimes they are sewed in; at others, when in two parts, by reeving the ends through the eyelet-hole in the sail, and through the eye of each other, and jambed home with sheaves.

Gaskets go round the jackstays with a running-eye, two at each quarter, and one on each yard-arm, with a bunt-gasket in the middle.

The Fore-sail being ready, lay it athwart the forecastle; reeve the tacks, sheets, clue-garnets, bunt-lines, leech-lines, bowlines, and slab-line; see the rope-bands and earings all complete, then hook the yard-ropes (or small tackles) to the first reef-cringle; run the sail up to the yard, pass the earings, and fasten the sail to the jackstays by the rope-band, then see the gaskets and reef-earings clear.

REEVING THE GEAR AND BENDING THE MAIN-SAIL
(Pl. 12, fig. 2)

Sheet, Tack, and *Clue-Garnet Blocks,* are placed in the clues as for the fore-sail.

Sheets reeve through the sheet-block at the clues. The standing-part is seized to an eye-bolt with a thimble on the quarters. The leading-part leads through a sheave-hole on the same side, on the upper deck, and belays to a large cleat in the ship's side.

Tacks, when double. The standing-part clinches or hooks to an eye-bolt before the chestree, and the leading-part leads through a single-block in the clue of the sail; then leads through the sheave in the chestree on deck, and belays to a kevel in the side.

Clue-Garnets and *Leech-Lines,* as the fore-sail.

Bunt-Lines, as the fore-sail, but lead down the main-stay to the forecastle, in large ships.

Bowlines. — A tackle is fitted on purpose for the bowline, which toggles to the bowline cringle, and the single-block near the fore-mast, by which tackle it is bowsed out.

Slab-Lines,
Spilling-Lines,
Lift-Lines,
Yard-Ropes,
Earings, } the same as the fore-sail.
Rope-Bands,
Points,
Gaskets,
Bending the sail,

REEVING the GEAR and BENDING the SPANKER
(Pl. 12, fig. 12)

Ships, when fitted with the spanker to brail up, have brail-blocks strapped together, and laid over the gaff, and seized together underneath; the throat blocks next the mast, the middle blocks between the throat and peak, the foot-brail blocks about one-third from the tack of the sail, upwards. (Pl. 7, fig. 8).

Vangs are fitted over the gaff-end; have a purchase, which hooks to an eye-bolt in the quarter-piece on each side.

Signal or *Ensign Halliard Blocks* are seized in the eye-bolt at the end of the gaff. (Pl. 7, fig. 8).

Ships or *Brigs* working the gaff on the mast without brails, have a dawnhauler, which is fitted near the outer earing of the sail.

The Spanker being ready to bend, lower the gaff, reeve both the earings, and ride the head of the sail to stretch it; then secure the earings, and reeve the lacing, seize the mast-hoops to the eyelet-holes in the luff of the sail, reeve the brails and outhauler, and hook the tack-tackles.

REEVING the GEAR and BENDING the JIB
(Pl. 11, fig. 2)

The Downhauler reeves through a small block that lashes to the traveller on the jib-boom, then leads up a few of the hanks, and bends to the head of the jib. The leading-part leads in upon the forecastle.

The Halliards reeve through a block at the fore-top-mast-head, from aft on the starboard side, and bend to the head of the sail. The leading-part leads abaft the top to the after-part of the forecastle. Large ships have double halliards.

Pendants and *Sheets*. — The bight of the pendant is lashed to the clue of the sail, and a single-block turned in each end that reeves the sheets, the standing-part of which makes fast to a bolt in the bows, and the leading-part leads through a block on the forecastle, and belays to a cleat.

Stay reeves through the block at the fore-top-mast-head from aft, then through the hanks, and hooks or clinches to the traveller upon the boom; a double-block is then turned into the lower end, and connected, by its fall, to a single-block, strapped to the after-part of the fore-mast trestle-trees, and leads upon deck.

Outhauler reeves through a sheave-hole at the outer end of the jib-boom, and clinches to the span-shackle of the traveller. The other end has a double-block turned in, which connects, with its fall, a single-block hooked to an eye-bolt in the bows, and the fall leads in upon the forecastle.

Inhauler reeves through a small block lashed to the traveller: the standing-part makes fast to an eye-bolt in the side of the bowsprit cap; and the leading part comes in upon the forecastle.

The Jib being ready to bend, haul the jib stay and traveller close in to the bowsprit cap; unhook the jib-stay, and send it in by the jib-halliards and downhauler; reeve the stay through the hanks (which are already seized to the head of the sail), bend the halliards, put stops on the sail, and haul it out to the traveller; hook the stay, lash the tack and the jib pendants, see the sheets rove, then haul the traveller out to the jib-boom-end (if required), and set the stay up.

REEVING the GEAR and BENDING the FORE-TOP-MAST-STAY-SAIL. (Pl. 11, fig. 3)

The Stay being secured, the hanks for the sail are rove previous to its being set up.

Downhauler the same as the jib.

Halliards reeve through a block at the fore-top-mast-head on the port side, and bend to the head of the sail. The leading-part leads abaft the top to the forecastle.

Pendants and *Sheets,* as the jib.

The Fore-top-mast-stay-sail being ready to bend, the halliards brought on the forecastle, also the downhaul, they are bent to the sail to haul it into the netting; a few stops are put round it, the hanks are then seized to the eyelet-holes in the head of the sail, the tack lashed, and the halliards, downhaul, and sheets bent.

REEVING the GEAR and BENDING the FORE-TOP-SAIL (Pl. 12, fig. 3)

Sheets reeve through the quarter-block, then through the sheavehole in the yard-arm, thence through the block at the clue of the sail; the end is then taken and clinched over the yard-arm. The hauling-part is led to the top-sail-sheet bitts, and belayed there.

Clue-Lines. — The straps of the blocks are passed through the clues of the sail, and brought round the clue to the fore-part, and securely seized. The clue-lines are passed the same as the clue-garnets of the courses, except that they are rove in the fore-most sheave of the quarter-blocks of the top-sail-yard.

Bunt-Lines reeve through a lizard made fast to the tie-block, come down on the fore-side of the sail, and toggles or clinches through the cringles in the foot. The leading-part reeves through a single-block, close under the top-mast cross-trees, leads down through a hole in the top, on to the forecastle.

Bowlines reeve through the blocks or cheeks at the bowsprit outer end. The outer part reeves on the lower bowline-bridle, with a thimble, as the fore-sail. The leading-part comes on the forecastle.

Reef Tackles reeve through the upper sheave in the sister-block in the top-mast shrouds, thence through the sheave-hole in the yard-arm, and through a single-block, which is strapped with an eye and thimble for the reef pendant to reeve through; and the end secures to the yard-arm. The leading-part comes on deck.

Reef Earings reeve through their bights in each reef-cringle, hitch to the next cringle above, and to the head of the sail, till used.

Spilling-Lines (when used in bad weather) have two legs, which are each made fast with a timber-hitch round the quarter of the top-sail-yard, then lead down on the aft-side, return upwards under the foot of the sail, and reeve through a block on the forecastle, lashed to the tie-block on the yard, and then lead upon deck abaft the mast.

Life-Lines,
Earings, (head)
Rope-Bands, } as the fore-sail.
Points,
Gaskets,

The Fore-top-sail being ready, sway it into the top by the sail-tackle; lay it athwart the top, see it clear of turns: reeve the sheets, clue-lines, and reef-tackles, toggle or clinch the bunt-lines and bowlines, take the head earing on the yard, haul up the clue-lines, buntlines, and reef-tackles, then bend the sail.

REEVING THE GEAR AND BENDING THE MAIN-TOP-SAIL
(Pl. 12, fig. 4)

Sheets,
Clue-Lines,
Bunt-Lines,
Reef-Tackles,
Reef-Earings,
Spilling-Lines, } as the fore-top-sail.
Life-Lines,
Earings, (head)
Rope-Bands,
Points,
Gaskets,

Bowlines reeve through blocks at the fore-mast-head; the outer part leads on the lower bowline-bridle, with a thimble, as the fore-top-sail. The leading-part comes down through the square hole of the top, reeves through a sheave-hole in the bitts upon the fore-castle, and there belays.

Main-top-sail being ready, is swayed up in the top, and bent, as the fore-top-sail.

REEVING THE GEAR AND BENDING THE MIZEN-TOP-SAIL
(Pl. 12, fig. 5)

Sheets, when single, reeve through the quarter-block, thence through the sheave-hole at the cross-jack-yard-arm, shackled or bent to the clue of the sail. The hauling-part leads from the quarter-blocks, down on the deck.

Bowlines bend as the fore-top-sail, and reeve through a block seized to the main-shrouds on the opposite side; they lead down on the quarter-deck, and belay.

Sheets,
Clue-Lines,
Bunt-Lines,
Reef-Tackles,
Reef-Earings,
Spilling-Lines, } as the fore-top-sail.
Life-Lines,
Earings, (head)
Rope-Bands,
Points,
Gaskets,

The Mizen-top-sail being ready, is swayed up into the top, and bent as the fore-top-sail.

REEVING THE GEAR AND BENDING THE FORE-TOP-GALLANT-SAIL. (Pl. 12, fig. 6)

Sheets are taken from the deck, through the hole in the top, led through the after-sheave in the quarter-block of the top-sail yard; from thence through the sheave-hole in the yard-arm, when it is bent or toggled to the clue of the sail.

Clue-Lines are bent to the clues of the sail, and lead upon deck, as the fore-top-sail.

Bunt-Lines reeve through a block at the top-gallant-mast-head, then through a lizard made fast to the tie, close down to the yard, and bent, with legs, to the cringles in the foot of the sail. The leading-part comes on deck.

Bowlines reeve through thimbles or blocks at the jib-boom end, and fasten to the sail as the top-sails, with a toggle. The leading-part comes upon the forecastle, and belays.

Halliards reeve through a sheave-hole in the mast-head, and bend to the middle of the yard. The after-part comes down abaft the mast on deck; if necessary, a tackle is formed with its end.

The Fore-top-gallant-sail is bent to the yard on deck, when the fore-part of the halliards is bent to the middle of the yard; it is then swayed up, and the brace-blocks and lifts rigged; the yard is then crossed, and the parral lashing secured, when the sheets and clue-lines are bent, and the bowlines and bunt-lines toggled or clinched.

REEVING the GEAR and BENDING the MAIN-TOP-GALLANT-SAIL. (Pl. 12, fig. 7)

The whole is performed as the fore-top-gallant-sail, except that the bowlines reeve through the sheave-holes in the after-part of the fore-top-mast cross-trees, and lead on the forecastle.

REEVING the GEAR and BENDING the MIZEN-TOP-GALLANT-SAIL. (Pl. 12, fig. 8)

The whole is performed as the fore-top-gallant-sail; the bowlines reeving through the sheave-holes in the aft-part of the main-top-mast cross-trees.

REEVING the GEAR and BENDING the ROYALS (Pl. 12, figs. 9, 10, 11)

Royals are sometimes set flying; but when rigged aloft, they are rigged and set as top-gallant-sails.*

REEVING the GEAR and BENDING the MAIN-STAY-SAIL. (Pl. 11, fig. 5)

Stay. — The upper end clinches round the main-mast-head, and the lower end sets up to a bolt abaft the fore-mast, or a strap round the fore-mast.

Halliards reeve through a single-block, bent to the head of the sail. The standing-part makes fast round the main-mast-head, or stay; and the leading-part reeves through a block lashed to the rigging under the main-top, and leads down abaft the mast, to a single-block, hooked to an eye-bolt in the side, abaft the main-mast.

Downhauler reeves through a single-block seized to the tack, then up through the hanks, and bent to the head of the sail.

The Tack is spliced into the tack of the sail, and lashes the tack of the sail to the bolt in the deck, or secures it to the strap round the fore-mast.

Sheets. — A luff-tackle is generally used to haul it aft.

The Main-stay-sail being ready fitted with grommets, is taken abaft the fore-mast, where the grommets are secured to the stay; reeve the halliards and downhaul, lash the tack, and fit the sheets.

*The before mentioned sails of a ship are generally set immediately they are bent, to see they are clear and complete.

REEVING THE GEAR AND BENDING THE FORE-STAY-SAIL. (Pl. 11, fig. 4)

The Fore-Spring-Stay is occasionally used for this sail, particularly in merchant-ships; but in men-of-war a stay is fitted on purpose, similar to the main-stay-sail-stay; it is clinched round the head of the fore-mast, and the lower end leads through a clump-block, which is strapped on the bowsprit, just outside the knight-heads: it then leads inboard, and sets up with a tackle.

Halliards reeve through a block, under the fore-top, and then through a single-block in the head of the sail. The standing-part is made fast to the stay under the top; the leading-part comes down on the forecastle.

Downhauler reeves through a block at the tack of the sail, then leads up through the hanks, and bends to the head of the sail, and the leading-part comes down upon the forecastle.

Sheets. — A luff-tackle is used.

The Fore-stay-sail, being ready fitted with grommets, is bent as the main-stay-sail.

REEVING THE GEAR AND BENDING THE MAIN-TOP-MAST-STAY-SAIL. (Pl. 11, fig. 6)

Halliards reeve from the aft-side through a block at the main-top-mast-head on the port side, and come down and bend to the head of the sail. The leading-part leads through a block in the midships, and belays there.

Downhauler leads through a block abaft the fore-mast: it is then carried up and rove through another block seized to the top-mast-spring-stay, then upwards through the hanks, and bent to the head of the sail.

Tack is lashed to the stay.

Sheets are double; the bight is secured to the clue of the sail, and the hauling-part leads through a block at the gangway.

Brails are sometimes fitted.

The Main-top-mast-stay-sail being ready, trice it up to the main-top-mast-spring-stay, under the fore-top, seize the eyelet-holes in the head of the sail to the hanks, reeve the halliards, downhaul, and sheets, and lash the tack.

REEVING the GEAR and BENDING the MAIN-TOP-GALLANT-STAY-SAIL. (Pl. 11, fig. 7)

Stay. — The upper end goes on the main-top-gallant-mast-head, and the lower end reeves through a sheave in the fore-top-mast cross-trees, leading down to the fore-top, where it is set up; the hanks are rove on the stay, except when you have a stay on purpose travelling.

Halliards reeve through a sheave-hole, or block, close up to the main-top-gallant rigging; one end bends to the head of the sail, and the leading-part comes down upon deck abaft the main-mast.

Downhauler, Tacks, and *Sheets,* the same as main-top-mast-stay-sail.

The Main-top-gallant-stay-sail being ready, trice it up into the fore-top-mast cross-trees, abaft the mast, and bend it as the main-top-mast-stay-sail.

REEVING the GEAR and BENDING the MIZEN-STAY-SAIL. (Pl. 11, fig. 8)

Stay. — The upper end clinches round the mizen-mast above the rigging, and the lower end sets up to a strap on the main-mast, a few feet above the deck.

Halliards. — The leading-part is rove through a block under the mizen-top, and then on deck, the other end is made fast to the head of the sail.

Downhauler,
Tack,   } as the main-stay-sail.
Sheet,

The Mizen-stay-sail being ready, is bent as the main-stay-sail.

REEVING the GEAR and BENDING the MIZEN-TOP-MAST-STAY-SAIL. (Pl. 11, fig. 9)

Halliards reeve through a block at the mizen-top-mast-head; one end bends to the head of the sail, and the other end leads down upon deck abaft the mast.

Downhauler leads through a block in the main-top, then through the hanks, and bends to the head of the sail; the other end leads down abaft the main-mast.

Tack and *Sheet* as main-top-mast-stay-sail.

The Mizen-top-mast-stay-sail being ready, trice it up in the main-top, and bend it as the main-top-mast-stay-sail.

Note. — Very few ships carry any other kind of stay-sails than the fore, main, and mizen-stay-sails, which are used in bad weather.

REEVING THE GEAR AND BENDING THE LOWER STUDDING-SAILS. (Pl. 12, figs. 13 and 14)

Outer-Halliards reeve through a span-block, from the top-mast-head, and through a block at the top-mast-studding-sail boom-end, then bend to the studding-sail-yard; the hauling-part leads upon deck.

Inner-Halliards bend to the upper inner-cringle of the sail, then reeve through a block made fast to the lower cap, or under the top, and lead on deck.

Tacks bend to the outer clue or tack on the foot of the sail, and reeve through a block at the outer part of the boom: they are carried aft, and lead through a block in the waist, and belay there.

Sheets are double; the bight is put over and the ends through the inner clue on the foot of the sail: one leads forward, and the other aft.

Tripping-Line is rove through a block under the top, then through an eyelet-hole in the centre of the sail, then bends to the tack. The hauling-part leads on the forecastle.

The Lower studding-sail being bent to the yard with nettles, bend the outer and inner halliards and tack, and reeve the tripping-line, when it is ready for setting.

The Lower studding-sail-booms rig as follows, viz.:—The goose-neck in the inner end of booms, hooks to an eye-bolt in the ship's side, abreast the mast, with a fore-lock to keep it in its place; an iron strap goes over its outer end, and secures a few feet in, with eyes for the guys and martingale, all of which are spliced in, and lead to their respective places; a single block is strapped close to the outer end, for the tack.

Note. — Lower studding-sails are set flying occasionally, when the foot of the sail spreads on a yard that rigs with a span, clinched round each yard-arm. A guy is bent to an eye that is crossed in the middle of the span, and leads aft through a sheave-hole in the waist; the sail thus rigged has no tack.

REEVING the GEAR and BENDING the TOP-MAST-STUDDING-SAILS. (Pl. 12, figs. 15 and 16)

Halliards reeve through a block in the span over the top-mast-cap, and through the jewel-block (Pl. 7, fig. 5), that is strapped with a thimble through an eye-bolt in the extremities of the top-sail-yards, and bend to the top-mast-studding-sail-yards; the other end leads down upon deck.

Downhauler reeves through a block lashed to the tack of the sail, and through a thimble on the outer leech: it is then made fast to the top-mast-studding-sail-yard, just within the earing, and leads on deck.

Tacks bend to the tack of the sail: they reeve through a block lashed to the outer end of the boom, and then aft through a block in the main rigging, and belays to a cleat.

Sheets, double. — The bight is put through the lower inner clue, and the ends through the bight. The long sheets of the fore-top-mast-studding-sail leads in upon the forecastle, the main leads in the gangways; the short sheets make fast to the lower yards.

The Top-mast studding-sail being bent to the yard, bend the halliards and tack; see the downhaul and sheets clear. The foot is spread upon the boom that sides out from the extremities of the lower yard.

The Booms are run out by tackles. The strap of one block makes fast to the heel of the boom, and the outer block to the boom-iron, and the fall leads along the yard. They are run in by the same tackles, reversing the outer block to the slings of the yard.

REEVING the GEAR and BENDING the TOP-GALLANT-STUDDING-SAIL. (Pl. 12, figs. 17 and 18)

Halliards reeve through a span-block at the head of the top-gallant-mast, then through a jewel-block (Pl. 7, fig. 6), strapped with a thimble through an eye-bolt at the extremity of the top-gallant-yard, and bend to the top-gallant-studding-sail-yard; the other end leads down the mast into the top, or deck.

Downhauler makes fast to the outer yard-arm within the earing, or to the tack, with a block, to the inner yard-arm, and leads into the top.

Tack bends to the tack of the sail, and reeves through a block at the outer end of the boom, and leads aft; the tack of the fore-top-gallant-studding-sail to the main-chains; the main to the quarter-piece. Sometimes they are led into the tops.

Sheets, double. — The bight is put through the lower inner clue of the sail, and the end passed through the bight; one end makes fast to the quarter of the top-sail-yard, and the other end leads into the top, and belays there.

The Top-gallant studding-sail being bent to the yard, bend the halliards and tack, and see the downhauler and sheets clear.

FITTING and SPREADING the AWNING

Awnings are fitted with middle ridge-ropes, to which they are generally sewed; the after-end of the ridge-ropes are secured, and the fore-end is led through rollers, fitted to the hoop of the mast, for that purpose, to which a tackle is hooked to set them up. The sides of the awning have stops fitted, to set up to the side or ridge-ropes, which go fore and aft outside the rigging; being secured astern, are set up tight forward by a luff-tackle. The ends of the awning are laced together by lacings, through eyelet-holes made for that purpose. Large awnings have a crow-foot in the middle, to keep them up. (See Awning, Part I).

Plate XV

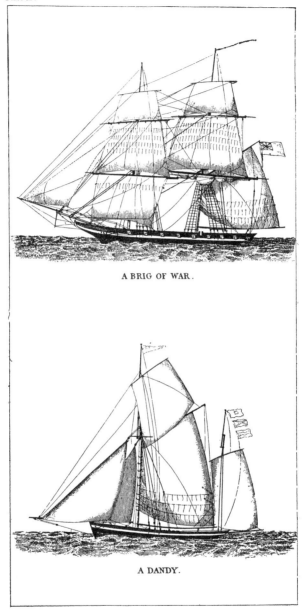

A BRIG OF WAR.

A DANDY.

DESCRIPTION OF THE RIGGING OF BRIGS, YACHTS, AND SMALL VESSELS

RIGGING a BRIG

The rigging of a brig is little different from the fore and main-masts of a ship, the braces of the yards on the main-mast leading forward. The after main-shrouds must be served from the mast-head to the dead-eyes, to prevent its being chafed by the main-boom and gaff. The after-backstays are sometimes fitted with tackles, that they may be slackened when the main-sail-boom is bowsed forward by the pendant and tackle.

RIGGING a BRIGANTINE

A Brigantine is a vessel rigged as a brig on the fore-mast, and as a schooner on the main-mast.

RIGGING a SCHOONER

Schooners have two masts and a bowsprit: the masts rake aft, but the bowsprit lies nearly horizontal; also a jib-boom, and top-masts. On the bowsprit and jib-boom are set stay-sails and jibs: on the fore-mast a square sail; and, abaft the fore-mast, a gaff-fore-sail; and on the top-mast, a gaff-top-sail, and sometimes a square-top-sail. Abaft the main-mast is set a boom-main-sail, and above it a gaff-top-sail. The main-stay leads to the head of the fore-mast, by which means, the sail abaft the fore-mast is not obstructed when the vessel goes about, as the peak passes under the stay. There is also two jumper-stays, which set up to an eye-bolt in the deck, just at the after-part of the fore-rigging, so that the weather one is always kept taut.

RIGGING a KETCH

A Ketch is a vessel with two masts; the main-mast has a top-mast and top-gallant-mast, on which is set a main-sail, top-sail, and top-gallant-sail, similar to a ship's; and sometimes, abaft the main-mast, is a large gaff-sail, called a wing-sail. The mizen-mast has a top-mast, and occasionally carries a top-sail; and, abaft the mast, a gaff-sail, like a ship's spanker. The bowsprit is long, nearly horizontal, with a jib and flying jib-boom, upon which the head-sails are set.

RIGGING A CUTTER

A Cutter has one mast; the stay generally leads through the stem, with a number of shrouds, corresponding to the size of the vessel: also a top-mast and bowsprit. On the mast is set a boom-main-sail and square-sail; on the top-mast a gaff-top-sail, and half-top-sail; a fore-sail on the fore-stay, and jib on the bowsprit, and occasionally a jib-top-sail.

RIGGING A LUGGER

A Lugger is a vessel with two or three masts, and a bowsprit nearly horizontal.

On the bowsprit is set the jib; lug-sails hang obliquely to the masts, their yards being slung at one-third of their length, one on each lower-mast and top-mast. The mizen is set to a boom over the stern: it seldom has a top-sail.

The masts are supported by stays and shrouds; the yards having halliards, lifts, and braces. To the lower clue of the sail is a sheet, and to the weather clue a tack, which is shifted as the vessel goes about.

In blowing weather they have small lug-sails, the tack of which hooks to the mast.

RIGGING OF SLOOPS AND SMACKS

Sloops and *Smacks* are vessels with one mast, and rigged as cutters, but much lighter. Some sloops have a square top-sail and top-gallant sail; the top-sail-yard traversing the heel of the top-mast, below the cap: the top-gallant-sail set flying on the top-mast.

RIGGING OF HOYS AND LIGHTERS

Hoys and *Lighters* are vessels with one mast, and sometimes a bowsprit; abaft the mast is a gaff-main-sail (sometimes a boom); before it a fore-sail, set on the fore-stay, and a jib on the bowsprit. The rigging they have is similar to sloops.

Plate XVI

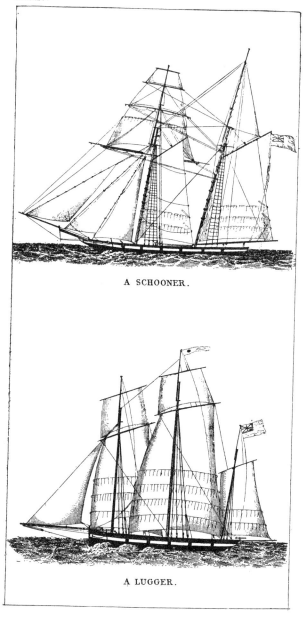

A SCHOONER.

A LUGGER.

RIGGING of BOATS

They are rigged quite as to taste, with lugs, lateens, sprits, or gaff-sails, and as schooners, or cutters.

RIGGING CUTTERS OR VESSELS WITH ONE MAST

RIGGING the MAST

Girtline-Blocks are lashed at the mast-head.

Pendants or *Tackles* are wormed, and served their whole length; then spliced and doubled, and the bight seized to the size of the mast-head, and a single-block seized in the lower bights; the splice to be at the mast-head.

Runners and *Tackles* are fitted with a hook and thimble, spliced at one end, and served over; and reeve through the block in the pendants, and spliced in the long tackle-block.

Falls of *Tackles* reeve through the upper sheave of the long tackle-block, and through a single-block with a long strap, that has a hook and thimble spliced in it, and hooks to an eye-bolt in the side. The fall is then taken upwards, and rove through the lower sheave of the long tackle-block, and down again to the becket in the arse of a single-block, where it is spliced.

Shrouds, as many pairs as are necessary, are fitted and put over the mast-head, similar to those in ships. They are wormed throughout.

The Stay is fitted and got over the mast-head, similar to that in ships; only wormed its whole length. It is rove through the stem, and secured to the knee of the pall-bitts.

RIGGING the BOWSPRIT

The Shrouds are fitted with a hook and thimble, spliced at one end, that hook to an eye on each side of a hoop, driven on the end of the bowsprit. The inner end has a block spliced in, and sets up by a fall, which is led through a block hooked in the bow; the fall leads through the wash streak to a cleat inboard.

Jib Tack is spliced into the traveller, reeves through the sheave-hole at the end of the bowsprit, and a block spliced into the inner end; a whip is rove through the block, which leads inboard, to haul the traveller out with.

Halliards reeve through the block in the head of the sail, and through the block on each side the mast-head. One end has a treble-block spliced or turned in, and connects its fall to a double block, that hooks to an eye-bolt in the deck on one side, and the other end belays to an eye-bolt opposite.

Sheets are either single or with blocks and falls, and lead through the wash streak, and belay to the windlass bitts; the double sheets have two blocks lashed to the clue of the sail, and connect, by their fall, to a block, hooked to an eye-bolt near the cat-head, on each side. The falls lead in upon deck.

Downhaulers make fast to the head of the sail, and lead upon deck.

Inhauler. — A span is seized on to each quarter of the traveller, and a single part from the bight leads inboard.

Heel-Rope is hooked to an eye-bolt in the bow, then rove through a sheave-hole in the heel of the bowsprit, and leads through a block hooked in the knight-heads; and the leading-part is brought to the windlass.

RIGGING THE FORE-SAIL

The Fore-sail bends with hanks to the stay.

Halliards. — The standing-part splices into the arse of the leading-block at the mast-head, then reeve through the block which hooks to the head of the sail, and through the block at the mast-head; the leading-part comes down upon deck.

Downhauler reeves through the hanks, and bends at the head of the sail, then reeves through a leading-block, made fast to the stay at the foot of the sail, and belays to a cleat inboard.

Tack-Tackles. — A pendant, with a hook in one end, which hooks to the tack of the sail, is rove through the sheave-hole in the stem, then a thimble is spliced into it, to which a tackle is hooked, to set it up.

Bowlines. — A hook is spliced in one end, that hooks to the clue; then reeves through a block, lashed to the shrouds on each side, and through a cringle in the leech of the sail, and belays round a pin in the shroud-rack. They are only used when the fore-sheet travels on a horse.

Sheets reeve through a block made fast to the horse with a thimble, or sometimes in a dead-eye, iron-bound, and through a block at the clue, and so on, alternately, between the strap of the block

Plate XVII

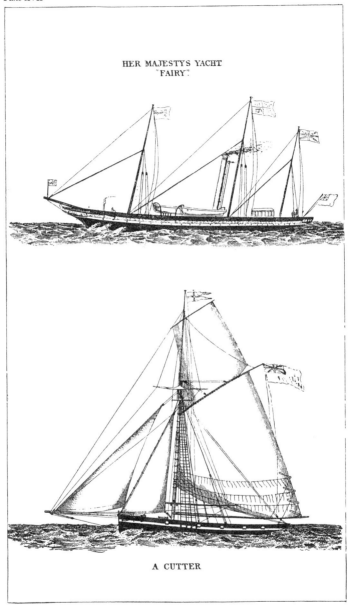

HER MAJESTY'S YACHT
"FAIRY".

A CUTTER

and the seizing of the dead-eye; then through the thimble of the clue, until the whole sheet is expended; then frapped together and hitched. Cutters generally work their fore-sheets hooked in the sides.

RIGGING the BOOM

Topping-Lifts are rove through the upper block, hooked to an eye-bolt in the boom, or led down and rove through a block at the boom-end, when the standing-part clinches round the mast-head, or hooks to an eye-bolt; the leading-part comes down, and has a double block spliced or turned in, that connects, by its fall, to a single block, and hooks to an eye-bolt in the after-part of the channels, and belays to a pin in the shroud-rack. Sometimes it has the addition of a runner, and sometimes is rigged as the driver-boom in ships.

Sheets reeve through a double or treble-block, strapped round the boom, just within the taffrail, and through another double-block, strapped to a bolt in the stern: and belays round a large cleat.

Tack-Tackle. — The double-block is fastened to the tack of the sail, and connects, with its fall, to a single-block, hooked to an eye-bolt in the deck.

Reef-Pendants. — Three or four in number, with a knot in the end, reeve through bolts in the outer end of the boom, then through its respective reef-cringle on the after-leech; and through a sheave-hole in the boom. When a reef is to be taken in, it is hooked to a tackle to haul down the leech of the sail; and afterwards secured to the boom.

Guy Pendants have a hook and thimble, that hook in the thimble of a strap on the boom, just inside the main-sheet-block. In the inner end of the pendant is a thimble, to which is hooked a luff-tackle. Its single block is hooked forward to a timber-head or eye-bolt, and the fall leads inboard.

Peak-Halliards. — Two spans or straps are fitted on the gaff, one outside the other with a thimble, to which straps the peak-halliard blocks hook. Then the halliards are rove through the upper block in the mast-head, to the outer span-block, then to the second block at the mast-head, back to the inner span-block, and then to the lower block at the mast-head, when it comes on deck. The hauling-part is in the lower block, and the purchase-part in the upper block.

Main-Halliards. — If fitted with two iron-bound double-blocks, the upper one hooking into the eye-bolt at the mast-head below the peak-halliards, and the other block hooking into the thimble at the jaws of the gaff. The halliards are rove alternately through these, and there is a becket in the upper block, for the end of the halliards to be spliced into.

Peak-Downhauler reeves through a small block, strapped round the thimble, in the eye-bolt at the outer end of the gaff, and belays round a cleat under the boom.

Throat-Downhauler reeves through a block at the neck of the sail, and leads down the mast.

RIGGING the TOP-MAST

Shrouds are fitted and put over the mast-head as ship's top-gallant-mast rigging, and rove through the holes at the end of the cross-trees; then come down, and set up with a thimble in the chains, or with a gun-tackle purchase.

Stay splices with an eye the size of the mast-head; the lower end reeves through a block hooked in the outer iron on the bowsprit-end, and leads inboard.

Standing-Backstays. — If one pair, they go over the mast-head with a cut-splice; if two pairs, with eyes seized, and in the lower end is a thimble, and set up with a gun-tackle purchase hooked to the chains.

RIGGING the SQUARE-SAILS

Quarter-Block is strapped with a double strap, having a long and short leg, and is fixed in the middle of the yard between the cleats; the long leg comes up the aft-side of the yard, and meets the bight of the short leg on the fore-side, and then lashes through the bights.

Straps, with a thimble seized in the bight, are spliced or lashed through eyes round the middle of the yard; the thimble in one strap is fixed on the aft-side of the yard, the other thimble on the upper-side of the yard.

Brace-Blocks, as ship's after-brace-blocks, go over the yard-arm with an eye, or hook to eye-bolts in the yard-arm.

Fore-Braces hook to the yard-arm, and reeve through a block seized on the bowsprit shrouds; the leading-part comes in upon deck.

After-Braces lead in upon the quarter-deck through a snatch-block or a sheave-hole in the side; and belay to a cleat or timber-head.

Lifts reeve through a span-block round the cap or mast-head, and lead down upon deck.

Tackles or *Halliards* for swaying up the yard, are either treble or double, according to the size of the vessel. The upper block hooks to an eye-bolt in the cap, the lower block hooks to the thimble in the strap, on the middle of the yard; the fall reeves through the sheave-hole in the top-sail-sheet bitts, and leads aft.

Jack-stay hooks to a bolt in the fore-part of the mast, and sets up with two thimbles below.

RIGGING THE MAIN-SAIL

The Main-Sail bends at the head to the gaff with earings and lacing, as the ship's spanker; and is seized to the hoops round the mast, through the hole in the foremost leech.

Throat-Downhauler. — The block hooks to the eye-bolt under the throat of the gaff, and connects, by its fall, to a single block, hooked to a bolt in the deck.

Tricing-Line is fitted as a gun-tackle purchase, with a long pend-ant to hook to an eye-bolt under the mast-head, or otherwise to the second shroud in the rigging; the lower block makes fast to the tack of the sail.

Sheet-Rope, or *Boom-Earing,* is generally fitted with a traveller over the boom, and a sheave-hole in the boom; and through which the outhaul is rove, and led in along the boom, where it sets up. The clue of the sail is shackled to the traveller.

RIGGING THE TRY-SAIL OR STORM MAIN-SAIL

This sail bends to the try-sail-gaff, and may be rigged with the same materials as the main-gaff, with sheets, and no boom, like a ship's mizen, and lacing to the mast.

RIGGING THE GAFF-TOP-SAIL

The Gaff-Top-Sail is bent to a yard.

Halliards reeve through the fore-part of the sheave-hole at the mast-head, then through the traveller, and bend to one-third of the yard, from forward; the leading-part comes down upon deck.

Tack makes fast to the tack of the sail, and leads on deck.

Sheet reeves through a block seized at the peak of the main-sail, or a sheave-hole, and bends to the clue of the sail, and leads through another block in the jaws of the gaff, and then on deck.

RIGGING THE HALF-TOP-SAIL

The Sail is bent to a yard, and the halliards reeve through a sheave-hole above the top-mast-rigging, and bent about the middle of the yard. The sheets reeve through the sheave-hole in the square-sail-yard-arm, and in through the quarter-blocks, then down on deck.

RIGGING THE RINGTAIL-SAIL

The Ringtail-Sail is similar to a top-mast-studding-sail, and bends to a small yard on the head, and hoisted by the peak-down-hauler, which serves for halliards. The foot is extended on a spar, or small boom, lashed to the outer end of the main-boom, generally fitted as a top-mast-studding-sail-boom.

RIGGING THE MIZEN OF A YAWL OR DANDY

The Mizen is set on a small mast at the stern. It bends to a yard, and is hoisted by halliards rove through the mast-head with a traveller, and is spread by a sheet at the foot to an outrigger over the stern. The tack hooks to the mast.

End of the Fourth Part

THE ART OF RIGGING

PART V

TABLES OF THE QUANTITIES AND DIMEN-SIONS OF THE STANDING AND RUNNING RIGGING OF

SHIPS	BRIGS
From 1,250 to 300 Tons;	Of 200 Tons;
FORE-AND-AFT SCHOON-ERS	CUTTER-YACHTS,
From 120 to 200 Tons;	From 30 to 90 Tons.

WITH THE SPECIES, SIZE, AND NUMBER OF BLOCKS, HEARTS, DEAD-EYES, &c.

Explanations of the Abbreviations in the following Tables

SHIPS AND BRIGS

C. ....Clump-block.
D. ....Double-block.
D.E. ....Dead-Eye.
H. ....Heart.
H.&T. ....Hook and Thimble, where room, or*
* ....Hook and Thimble.
I.-bd. ....Iron-bound.

Pl.D.E. ....Plates with Dead-Eyes.
S. ....Single-block.
Sis. ....Sister-block.
St.-bd. ....Strap-bound-block.
T. ....Thimble.
Tr. ....Treble-block.

FORE-AND-AFT SCHOONERS AND CUTTER-YACHTS

I.B.S. ....Iron-bound Single-block
I.B.S.C. ....Iron-bound Single Clump-block.
I.B.D. ....Iron-bound Double-block.

I.B.D.C. ....Iron-bound Double Clump-block.
Double ....Double-block.
Single ....Single-block.

NOTE. — The blocks are only described as *single*, *double*, or *treble*, as the case may be; as every person with a knowledge of rigging will be readily aware where it is necessary to have the common block, or a thin long or double-scored block.

	SHIPS.													
BOWSPRIT, SPRITSAIL-YARD, AND JIB.	1250 Tons.					1000 Tons.					800 Tons.			
	Size in Inches.	Length in Fathoms.	Blocks, &c.			Size in Inches.	Length in Fathoms.	Blocks, &c.			Size in Inches.	Length in Fathoms.	Blocks,	
			Species.	Sz.inIn.	Number			Species.	Sz.inIn.	Number			Species.	Sz.inIn.
BOWSPRIT.														
Gammoning*	7	120	...	·7	1	7	100	...	...	...	6½	96	...	...
Shrouds	7	32	H.	10	4	6½	30	H.	10	4	6½	15	H.	
Collars	6	11	H.	10	4	5	10	H.	10	4	5	5	H.	
Seizings	1½	16	...	...	...	1½	15	...	...	...	1	8	...	
Lashings	2	10	...	...	...	2	10	...	...	...	1¾	10	...	
Laniards	3	17	...	...	...	3	16	...	...	...	2½	10	...	
Bobstays	9	32	H.	12	3	8½	30	H.	12	3	8	26	H.	
Collars	9	8	H.	12	3	9	8	H.	12	3	8	8	H.	
Seizings	2	25	...	...	...	2	24	...	...	...	1½	23	...	
Lashings	2½	9	...	...	...	2½	9	...	...	...	2	9	...	
Laniards	4½	10	...	...	...	4	10	...	...	...	4	9	...	
Man-ropes	4½	18	T.	...	4	4	17	T.	...	4	3½	16	T.	
Laniards	2	6	...	...	...	2	6	...	...	...	1½	6	...	
Stirrups	2½	3	T.	...	2	2½	2½	T.	...	2	2	2½	T.	
SPRITSAIL-YARD, at Night-Heads.														
Foot-ropes	3½	13	...	...	...	3	12	...	...	...	3	11	...	
Laniards	2	5	...	...	...	2	5	...	...	...	1½	5	...	
Stirrups	2½	3	T.	...	2	2½	3	T.	...	2	2½	2½	T.	
If chain or an iron strap is not used ⎰ Slings ... ⎱ Laniards	4½ / 2	6 / 4	...	...	...	4 / 2	6 / 4	...	...	...	3½ / 2	5 / 3½	...	
Cathead Strap	4	3	T.	...	4	4	3	T.	...	4	3½	3	T.	
Laniards	2	5	...	...	...	2	5	...	...	...	2	4	...	
JIB.														
Foot-ropes	3½	17	...	...	...	3	16	...	...	...	3	15	...	
Guys, single	5¾	30	...	...	...	5	28	...	...	...	4½	26	...	
Falls	3	25	D.	9	4	3	24	D.	9	4	2¾	22	D.	
Strapping	3	3	H.&T.	...	2	3	3	H.&T.	...	2	2¾	2½	H.&T.	
Seizings	¾	6	...	...	...	¾	6	...	...	...	¾	6	...	
Martingale	7½	10	...	...	...	7	9	...	...	...	6½	8½	...	
Back-ropes	5	13	...	...	...	4½	12	...	...	...	4	11	...	
Falls	2½	10	{D. / S.*	8 / 8	2 / 2	2½	10	{D. / S.*	8 / 8	2 / 2	2	10	{D. / S.*	
Seizings ... Marline	—	—	...	...	...	—	—	...	...	...	—	—	...	
Heel-strap	4½	6	...	...	...	4	6	...	...	...	3½	6	...	
Frapping	2¼	2	...	...	...	2	2	...	...	...	1½	2	...	
Stay and Strapping	6	30	C.	12	1	5½	28	C.	11	1	5	26	C.	
Seizings	1½	3	...	...	...	1½	3	...	...	...	1½	3	...	
Tackle-fall and Strapping	3	32	{D. / S.*	9 / 9	1 / 1	3	28	{D. / S.*	9 / 9	1 / 1	2½	26	{D. / S.*	
Seizings ... Marline	—	—	...	...	...	—	—	...	...	...	—	—	...	
Halliards	3½	36	S.	10	1	3¼	34	S.	10	1	3	32	S.	
Tack-lashing and Lacing	1	8	...	...	...	1	7	...	...	...	1	6	...	
Downhauller and Strapping	2½	34	S.	8	1	2½	32	S.	8	1	2¼	30	S.	
Outhauller	4	12	...	...	...	4	11	...	...	...	4	11	...	

* The Gammoning cannot be given the exact length, as it depends on the angle of the bowsprit.

														BRIG.				
600 Tons.				450 Tons.					300 Tons.					200 Tons.				
Length in Fathoms.	*Blocks, &c.*			Size in Inches.	Length in Fathoms.	*Blocks, &c.*			Size in Inches.	Length in Fathoms.	*Blocks, &c.*			Size in Inches.	Length in Fathoms.	*Blocks, &c.*		
	Species.	Sz. in In.	Number			Species.	Sz. in In.	Number			Species.	Sz. in In.	Number			Species.	Sz. in In.	Number
70	...	...	...	5	60	...	...	...	4½	45	...	...	...	4	30	...	...	...
12	H.	8	2	5	10	H.	7	2	4½	10	H.	6	2	4½	9	T.	...	2
5	H.	8	2	4	4	H.	7	2	4	4	H.	6	2	3½	3	T.	...	2
7	...	...	...	1	6	...	...	...	1	6	...	...	...	¾	5	...	...	...
7	...	...	...	1½	6	...	...	...	1¼	6	...	...	...	1¼	5	...	...	...
10	...	...	...	2½	10	...	...	...	2	10	...	...	...	2	7	...	...	...
16	H.	9	2	6	12	H.	8	2	5½	12	H.	7	2	5	10	T.	...	2
5	H.	9	2	6	4	H.	8	2	5½	4	H.	7	2	5	3½	T.	...	2
10	...	...	...	1½	10	...	...	...	1½	10	...	...	...	1	6	...	...	...
6	...	...	...	1½	6	...	...	...	1½	6	...	...	...	1	6	...	...	...
6	...	...	...	3	6	...	...	...	2½	6	...	...	...	2	6	...	...	...
14	T.	...	4	3	13	T.	...	4	3	12	T.	...	4	2½	11	T.	...	4
6	...	...	...	1¼	6	...	...	...	1	6	...	...	...	1	6	...	...	...
2	T.	...	2	2	2	T.	...	2	2	1½	T.	...	2	2	1½	T.	...	2
10	...	...	...	2½	9	...	...	...	—		*Whiskers*	—	—	—	—	—	—	—
5	...	...	...	1½	4	...	...	...	—		*Iron*	—	—	—	—	—	—	—
2½	T.	...	2	2	2	T.	...	2	...	...	...	...	...	...	...	...	...	...
5	...	...	...	3	4½	...	...	...	...	...	...	...	...	...	...	...	...	...
3	...	...	...	2	3	...	...	...	...	...	...	...	...	...	...	...	...	...
3	T.	...	4	2	3	T.	...	4	...	...	...	...	...	...	...	...	...	...
4	...	...	...	1½	4	...	...	...	...	...	...	...	...	...	...	...	...	...
14	...	...	...	2½	13	...	...	...	2½	12	...	...	...	2½	10	...	...	...
24	...	...	...	4	23	...	...	...	4	12	...	...	...	4	22	...	...	...
20	D.	8	4	2	18	D.	7	4	2	15	D.	7	4	2	10	T.	...	4
2½	H. & T.	...	2	2	2	H. & T.	...	2	2	2	H. & T.	...	2	...	...	...	...	...
6	...	...	...	—		*Marline*	—	—	—	—	—	—	—	—	—	—	—	—
8	...	...	...	6	7½	...	...	...	5½	7	...	...	...	4½	6½	...	...	...
10	...	...	...	3½	9	...	...	...	3	8	...	...	...	2½	9	...	...	...
10	D. S.*	7 7	2 2	1¾	10	D. S.*	6 6	2 2	1½	10	D. S.*	6 6	2 2	1½	9	T.	...	2
—	—	—	—	—	—	—	—	—	—	—	—	—	—	—	—	—	—	—
5	...	...	...	3	5	...	...	...	3	4	...	...	...	2½	4	...	...	...
2	...	...	...	1¼	2	...	...	...	1	2	...	...	...	1	2	...	...	...
24	C.	9	1	4	22	C.	8	1	4	22	C.	8	1	3½	18	C.	8	1
3	...	...	...	1¼	3	...	...	...	1	3	...	...	...	1	3	...	...	...
25	D. S.*	8 8	1 1	2	24	D. S.*	7 7	1 1	2	22	D. S.*	7 7	1 1	2	18	D. S.*	7 7	1 1
—	—	—	—	—	—	—	—	—	—	—	—	—	—	—	—	—	—	—
31	S.	9	1	3	30	S.	9	1	2½	30	S.	8	1	2	30	S.	7	1
5½	...	...	...	¾	5	...	...	...	3¼	4½	...	...	...	¾	4	...	...	...
28	S.	7	1	2	27	S.	7	1	2	26	S.	7	1	2	24	S.	7	1
10	...	...	...	3	10	...	...	...	3	9	...	...	...	3	8	...	...	...

JIB (*continued*), FLYING-JIB, FORE-MAST, AND FORE-YARD.	SHIPS. 1250 Tons. Size in Inches.	Length in Fathoms.	Blocks, &c. Species.	Sz. in In.	Number	1000 Tons. Size in Inches.	Length in Fathoms.	Blocks, &c. Species.	Sz. in In.	Number	800 Tons. Size in Inches.	Length in Fathoms.	Blocks, &c. Species.	Sz. in In.
Fall and Strapping	2½	30	S. *	8	2 1	2½	30	S. *	8	2 1	2	28	S. *	
Pendants	5	9	...	...	...	4½	9	...	...	...	4½	9	...	...
Sheets	3	40	S.	9	2	3	38	S.	9	2	2½	36	S.	
FLYING-JIB.														
Foot-ropes	2½	10	...	...	...	2½	9	...	...	...	2	9	...	...
Guys	3½	35	...	...	...	3	34	...	...	...	3	33	...	...
Laniards	2	6	T.	2	2	2	6	...	...	2	2	5	T.	...
Martingale	4	20	...	...	...	4	19	...	...	...	3½	18	...	...
Heel-lashing	1½	4	...	...	...	1½	4	...	...	...	1½	3	...	...
Halliards and Strapping	2½	45	S.	8	1	2½	42	S.	8	1	2½	40	S.	
Tack-lashing and Lacing	¾	5	...	...	...	¾	5	...	...	...	½	4	...	...
Downhauller and Strapping	2	45	S.	7	1	2	43	S.	7	1	2	40	S.	
Sheets	3	42	...	...	...	2½	40	...	...	...	2¼	30	...	...
Stay	4	35	...	...	...	3½	33	...	...	...	3	31	...	...
Tackle-fall and Strapping	2	11	S. *	7	2 1	2	10	S. *	7	2 1	1¾	10	S. *	
Seizings ... *Marline*	—	—	—	—	—	—	—	—	—	—	—	—	—	—
FORE-MAST.														
Pendants	10½	9	T.	...	2	10	9	T.	...	2	9	8	T.	
Runners of Tackles*	...	...	...	...	...	...	...	...	...	...	...	...	...	...
Falls of Tackles	4	170	D.	13	4	4	140	D.	13	4	3½	120	D.	
Strapping	5½	4	* T.	...	2 2	5	3	* T.	... ...	2 2	4½	3	* T.	
Seizings	1	10	...	...	...	1	8	...	...	...	1	8	...	...
Shrouds†	10½	156	D. E.	16	14	10	150	D. E.	16	14	9	140	D. E.	
Seizings: Eye	1¾	40	...	...	...	1¾	40	...	...	...	1½	40	...	...
Seizings: Throat	1½	80	...	...	...	1½	80	...	...	...	1½	75	...	...
Seizings: End	1¼	80	...	...	...	1¼	80	...	...	...	1	70	...	...
Laniards	5	70	...	...	...	5	70	...	...	...	4½	70	...	...
Ratlines	1½	226	...	...	...	1½	210	...	...	...	1¼	190	...	...
Stays‡	16	33	T.	...	2	15	32	T.	...	2	14	28	T.	
Collars	9	10	T.	...	2	8	10	T.	...	2	7	10	T.	
Lashings	2½	9	...	...	...	2½	9	...	...	...	2	9	...	...
Seizings for Stays and Collars	1¾	50	...	...	...	1¾	47	...	...	...	1½	40	...	...
Laniards	5	14	...	...	...	5	14	...	...	...	4½	14	...	...
Catharpins§	...	...	...	...	...	...	...	...	...	...	...	...	...	...
FORE-YARD.														
Slings‖	...	...	...	...	...	...	...	...	...	...	...	...	...	...
Truss Pendants	7½	16	S.	9	2	7	14	S.	8	2	6¾	12	S.	
Falls	3	60	...	...	...	2½	60	...	...	...	2½	55	...	...
Straps	3½	6½	T.	...	2	3½	6	T.	...	2	3½	6	T.	
Jackstay	3½	14	T.	...	2	3½	12	T.	...	2	3	12	T.	
Laniards	1½	2	...	...	...	1½	2	...	...	...	1¼	2	...	...
Foot-ropes	5	15	T.	...	2	4½	14	T.	...	2	4	14	T.	
Laniards	2	6	...	...	...	2	5	...	...	...	2	5	...	...

* Merchant-ships generally use double-blocks, lashing the upper one to the pendants.

† The exact length of the lower shrouds cannot be given, as a great deal depends on the beam of the vessel.

‡ Stays are all formed with a collar, with a lashing abaft the mast.

600 Tons.					450 Tons.					300 Tons.					BRIG. 200 Tons.				
Inches.	Length in Fathoms.	Blocks, &c. Species.	Blocks, &c. Sz. in In.	Blocks, &c. Number	Size in Inches.	Length in Fathoms.	Blocks, &c. Species.	Blocks, &c. Sz. in In.	Blocks, &c. Number	Size in Inches.	Length in Fathoms.	Blocks, &c. Species.	Blocks, &c. Sz. in In.	Blocks, &c. Number	Size in Inches.	Length in Fathoms.	Blocks, &c. Species.	Blocks, &c. Sz. in In.	Blocks, &c. Number
	25	{S. *	7	2 1	2	22	{S. *	7	2 1	2	18	{S. *	7	2 1	2	16	{S. *	7	2 1
	8	...	...	...	4	8	...	...	...	3½	7	...	...	...	3	6	...	...	...
½	34	S.	8	2	2¼	32	S.	8	2	2¼	30	S.	8	2	2	28	S.	7	2
	8	...	...	...	2	8	...	...	...	2	7	...	...	...	2	7	...	...	...
¾	31	...	...	...	2½	30	...	...	...	2½	28	...	...	...	2½	26	...	...	...
½	5	T.	...	2	1½	4	T.	...	2	1½	4	T.	...	2	1½	4	T.	...	2
½	17	...	...	...	3	16	...	...	...	3	15	...	...	...	2¾	13	...	...	...
	3	...	...	1	1	2½	...	...	...	¾	2	...	...	...	¾	2	...	...	...
	38	S.	7	...	2	36	S.	7	1	2	34	S.	7	1	1½	30	S.	6	1
½	4	...	...	...	½	4	...	...	...	½	3	...	...	...	½	3	...	...	...
	38	S.	7	1	1½	36	S.	6	1	1½	34	S.	6	1	1½	32	S.	6	1
	36	...	...	...	2	34	...	...	...	2	32	...	...	...	2	30	...	...	...
	30	...	...	...	2½	28	...	...	...	2½	27	...	...	...	2	25	...	...	...
½	10	{S. *	6	9 1	1½	10	{S. *	6	2 1	1½	10	{S. *	6	2 1	1½	10	{S. *	6	2
—	—	—	—	—	—	—	—	—	—	—	—	—	—	—	—	—	—	—	—
3	7	T.	...	2	7½	6½	T.	...	2	7	6	T.	...	2	6	6	T.	...	2
..	...	...	...	...	...	...	...	...	...	...	...	...	...	...	...	...	...	...	...
3	114	D.	11	4	3	110	D.	11	4	3	100	D.	10	4	3	85	D.	10	4
4	3	{* T.	...	2 2	3	3	{* T.	...	2 2	3	2½	{* T.	...	2 2	3	2½	{* T.	...	2 2
1	7	...	...	...	¾	6	...	...	...	¾	6	...	...	...	¾	6	...	...	...
3	115	D. E.	11	12	7½	100	D. E.	11	10	7	95	D. E.	10	10	6	76	D. E.	8	8
1¼	40	...	...	...	1¼	35	...	...	...	1¼	30	...	...	...	1¼	20	...	...	...
1½	60	...	...	...	1¼	50	...	...	...	1	50	...	...	...	1¼	45	...	...	...
1	60	...	...	...	1	50	...	...	...	1	50	...	...	...	¾	40	...	...	...
4	60	...	...	...	4	50	...	...	...	3½	50	...	...	...	3	40	...	...	...
1¼	160	...	...	...	1¼	140	...	...	...	1	105	...	...	...	1	90	...	...	...
3	28	T.	...	2	12	24	T.	...	2	10	22	T.	...	2	8	18	T.	...	2
6	9	T.	...	2	5	9	T.	...	2	5	9	T.	...	2	4½	8	T.	...	2
2	6	...	...	...	1½	6	...	...	...	1½	6	...	...	...	1	6	...	...	...
1¼	36	...	...	...	1¼	36	...	...	...	1¼	30	...	...	...	1	25	...	...	...
4	14	...	...	...	3½	14	...	...	...	3½	14	...	...	...	3	14	...	...	...
...	...	...	...	...	...	...	...	...	...	...	...	...	...	...	...	...	...	...	...
...	...	...	...	...	...	...	...	...	...	...	...	...	...	...	...	...	...	...	...
6	12	S.	8	2	5	10	S.	7	2	4	9	S.	7	2	3½	7	S.	7	2
2	50	.	...	...	2	45	...	...	...	2	40	...	...	...	2	36	...	...	...
3	6	T.	...	2	3	5	T.	...	2	2½	5	T.	...	2	2	4½	T.	...	2
3	11	T.	...	2	2½	10	T.	...	2	2½	9	T.	...	2	2½	9	T.	...	2
1	2	...	...	...	1	1½	...	...	...	1	1½	...	...	...	1	1½	...	...	...
3½	13	T.	...	2	3	12	T.	...	2	3	11	T.	...	2	3	11	T.	...	2
1½	5	...	...	...	1¼	5	...	...	...	1	5	...	...	...	1	4	...	...	...

§ Catharpins are not used; instead of which, a necklace of two parts, of chain, is secured round the lower-mast, to set the futtock rigging up to.

‖ Slings of lower yard and mast-head are generally of chain, and depend on the girth of the yard, and to where they are led at the mast-head.

SHIPS.

FORE-YARD (continued).	1250 Tons. Size in Inches.	Length in Fathoms.	Blocks, &c. Species.	Sz.inIn	Number	1000 Tons. Size in Inches.	Length in Fathoms.	Blocks, &c. Species.	Sz.inIn	Number	800 Tons. Size in Inches.	Length in Fathoms.	Blocks, & Species.	Sz.inIn
Stirrups	4	14	T.	...	6	3	12	T.	...	6	3	10	T.	...
Clue-garnets	3½	64	St. bd.	11	2	3½	60	St.bd.	11	2	3	55	St. bd.	10
Straps for Yard & Strapping	3½	9½	S.	11	2	3½	8	S.	11	2	3	8	S.	10
Lashing	1¼	10	...	...	...	1¼	10	...	...	...	1	10	...	...
Seizings	¾	10	...	...	...	¾	10	...			¾	10	...	...
Buntlines and Falls	3	95	{D. S.	10 10	4 8	3	84	{D. S.	10 10	4 8	3	80	{D. S.	10
Strapping	3½	12	...			3	12	...			3	11	...	
Seizings	½	30	...			½	30	...			½	30	...	...
Leech-lines	2½	47	S.	8	4	2½	45	S.	8	4	2½	40	S.	8
Strapping	2	2	...			2	2	...			2	2	...	...
Seizings ....Marline	—	—												
Slab-line and Strapping	2	37	S.	7	1	2	30	S.	7	1	4	25	S.	7
Bowlines and Bridles	4½	64	{S. T.	12	2 4	4	60	{S. T.	12	2 4	4	56	{S. T.	12
Strapping	4½	4	...			4	3	...			4	3	...	...
Seizings	1	8	...			1	6	...			1	6	...	...
Lashings	2	10	...			1½	8	...			1½	8	...	...
Earings (4 in No.)	2½	20	...			2	20	...			1½	20	...	...
Sheets (tapered)	5	56	C.	10	2	5	63	C.	10	2	5	60	C.	10
Tacks (tapered)	5	60	C.	10	4	5	58	C.	10	4	5	55	C.	10
Strapping	5	11	...			5	11	...			5	11	...	...
Seizings	1¼	24	...			1¼	24	...			1¼	24	...	...
Braces	4	100	S.	16	4	4	90	S.	16	4	3½	80	S.	14
Strapping {Yard	5	6	T.	...	4	5	6	T.	...	4	4½	6	T.	...
Strapping {Mast	3	12	T.	...	2	3	10	T.	...	2	3	10	T.	...
Seizings	1¼	20	...			1¼	18	...			1¼	18	...	...
Strapping, Quarter-blocks	4	11	D.	16	2	4	10	D.	16	2	4	10	D.	16
Lashing	2½	6	...			2½	6	...			2	5	...	...
Seizings	1¼	6	...			1¼	6	...			1	6	...	...
Lifts	4	100	S.	13	2	4	90	S.	13	2	3½	80	S.	12
Strapping	4½	4	...			4½	3	...			4	3	...	...
Short Span	5	5	C.	13	2	4½	4	C.	13	2	4	4	C.	12
Seizings	¾	12	...			¾	12	...			¾	12	...	...
Jigger-falls and Strapping	2½	35	{D.* S.*	8 8	2 2	2½	30	{D.* S.*	8 8	2 2	2	28	{D.* S.*	7 7
Seizings	½	5	...			½	5	...			½	4	...	...
Fore-stay-sail-stay	6	18	C.	12	1	6	17	C.	12	1	5½	16	C.	11
Halliards	3¼	50	S.	10	2	3	45	S.	9	2	3	42	S.	9
Sheets	3	30	{D.* S.*	10 10	2 2	3	30	{D.* S.*	10 10	2 2	3	28	{D.* S.*	10 10
Tack-lashing	2	4	...			2	4	...			2	4	...	...
Downhauller	2½	30	S.	8	1	2½	28	S.	8	1	2½	24	S.	8
Strapping {Mast-head	3	4	...			3	4	...			3	4	...	...
Strapping {Sheet	2	1	...			2	1	...			2	1	...	...
Seizings ....Marline	—													
Studding-sail Hal- {Outer	3½	80	S.	11	2	3	70	S.	9	2	3	66	S.	9
liard {Inner	3	45	S.	9	4	3	40	S.	9	4	3	35	S.	9
Span for outer Halliard	3½	8	S.	11	2	3½	7	S.	9	2	3½	7	S.	9

														BRIG.				
600 Tons.				450 Tons.					300 Tons.					200 Tons.				
Length in Fathoms.	Blocks, &c.			Size in Inches.	Length in Fathoms.	Blocks, &c.			Size in Inches.	Length in Fathoms.	Blocks, &c.			Size in Inches.	Length in Fathoms.	Blocks, &c.		
	Species.	Sz. in In.	Number			Species.	Sz. in In.	Number			Species.	Sz. in In.	Number			Species.	Sz. in In.	Number
10	T.	...	6	2½	9	T.	...	6	2½	8	T.	...	6	2½	6	T.	...	4
50	St. bd.	10	2	2½	45	St. bd.	9	2	2	40	St. bd.	8	2	2	40	St. bd.	8	2
7	S.	10	2	2½	7	S.	10	2	2	7	S.	8	2	2	7	S.	8	2
9	...	...	...	¾	8	...	...	...	¾	7	...	...	...	¾	6	...	...	...
10	...	...	...	½	10	...	...	...	½	10	...	...	...	½	10	...	...	...
72	D. S.	9 9	4 8	2½	68	D. S.	9 9	4 8	2½	54	D. S.	9 8	2 4	2	52	D. S.	7 7	2 4
10	...	...	...	3	10	...	...	...	2½	10	...	...	...	2½	7	...	...	...
28	...	...	...	—		Marline	—	—	—	—	—	—	—	—	—	—	—	—
35	S.	8	4	2½	33	S.	8	4	2	30	S.	7	4	2	28	S.	7	4
2	...	...	...	2	2	...	...	...	2	2	...	...	...	1½	2	...	...	...
—	—	—	—	—	—	—	—	—	—	—	—	—	—	—	—	—	—	—
20	S.	7	1	2	18	S.	7	1	2	18	S.	7	1	2	16	S.	7	1
50	S. T.	11	2 4	3½	46	S. T.	11	2 4	3	42	S. T.	9	2 4	2½	36	S. T.	8	2 4
3	...	...	...	3½	3	...	...	...	3½	3	...	...	...	2½	2	...	...	...
5	...	...	...	¾	5	...	...	...	½	4	...	...	...	½	4	...	...	...
7	...	...	...	1¼	6	...	...	...	1	6	...	...	...	1	5	...	...	...
18	...	...	...	1¼	18	...	...	...	1¼	17	...	...	...	1¼	16	...	...	...
58	C.	9	2	4¼	55	C.	8	2	4	50	C.	8	2	3	46	C.	7	2
55	C.	10	4	4	50	C.	8	4	4	45	C.	8	4	3½	40	C.	7	4
11	...	...	...	4	10	...	...	...	4	10	...	...	...	3½	9	...	...	...
22	...	...	...	1	22	...	...	...	1	22	...	...	...	¾	18	...	...	...
65	S.	12	4	3	56	S.	10	4	3	50	S.	10	4	2½	60	S.	8	4
5	T.	...	4	4	4	T.	...	4	4	4	T.	...	4	3	3	T.	...	4
9	T.	...	2	2½	9	T.	...	2	2	9	T.	...	2	2	8	T.	...	2
16	...	...	...	¾	14	...	...	...	½	12	...	...	...	½	12	...	...	...
9	D.	14	2	3½	9	D.	14	2	3	8	D.	13	2	2½	6	D.	12	2
5	...	...	...	2	4	...	...	...	2	4	...	...	...	1½	4	...	...	...
5	...	...	..	1	4	...	...	...	¾	4	...	...	...	¾	4	...	...	...
35	...	...	...	4½	30	...	...	...	4	30	...	...	...	4	25	...	...	...
...	...	...	...	...	...	...	...	...	...	...	...	...	...	...	...	...	...	..
3½	C.	10	2	4	3½	C.	9	2	4	3	C.	8	2	4	3	C.	8	2
6	...	...	...	½	6	...	...	...	½	5	...	...	...	½	5	...	...	...
26	D. S.*	7 7	2 2	2	26	D. S.*	7 7	2 2	2	24	D. S.*	7 7	2 2	2	24	D. S.*	7 7	2 2
4	...	...	...	½	4	...	...	...	½	4	...	...	...	½	4	...	...	...
15	C.	11	1	4½	14	C.	10	1	4½	12	C.	10	1	4	12	C.	8	1
35	S.	8	2	2½	33	S.	8	2	3	25	S.	9	1	3	25	S.	9	1
26	D.* S.*	10 10	2 2	3	24	D.* S.*	10 10	2 2	2½	22	D.* S.*	9 9	2 2	2½	22	D.* S.*	9 9	2 2
4	...	...	...	½	4	...	...	...	1¼	4	...	...	...	1¼	4	...	...	...
24	S.	7	1	2	22	S.	7	1	2	20	S.	7	1	2	20	S.	7	1
4	...	...	...	2½	4	...	...	...	2½	4	...	...	...	2½	4	...	...	...
1	...	...	...	2	1	...	...	...	2	1	...	...	...	2	1	...	...	...
—	—	—	—	—	—	—	—	—	—	—	—	—	—	—	—	—	—	—
54	S.	9	2	3	50	S.	9	2	2½	46	S.	8	2	2½	38	S.	8	2
33	S.	9	4	3	30	S.	9	4	2½	26	S.	8	4	2½	25	S.	8	4
6	S.	9	2	3	6	S.	9	2	2½	5	S.	8	2	2½	5	S.	8	2

FORE-YARD (continued), FORE-TOP-MAST AND FORE-TOP-SAIL-YARD.	SHIPS.													
	1250 Tons.					1000 Tons.					800 Tons.		
	Size in Inches.	Length in Fathoms.	Blocks, &c.			Size in Inches.	Length in Fathoms.	Blocks, &c.			Size in Inches.	Length in Fathoms.	Blocks,
			Species.	Sz.inIn.	Number			Species.	Sz.inIn.	Number			Species.
Sheets	3	15	...	...	...	3	14	...	...	...	3	12	...
Tack	3½	60	S.	11	2	3	55	S.	9	2	3	46	S.
Tripping-line	2	30	S.	6	2	2	30	S.	6	2	2	30	S.
Strapping and Tailing.......	3½	12	...	...	...	3½	12	...	...	...	3	12	...
Swinging-boom Guys	3	60	...	...	...	3	50	...	...	...	3	46	...
FORE-TOP-MAST.													
Burton Pendants	5	6	T.	...	2	4½	6	T.	...	2	4	5	T.
Burton Falls and Strapping..	2½	55	{D.* {S.*	9 9	2 2	2½	50	{D.* {S.*	9 9	2 2	2	45	{D.* {S.*
Seizings ....Marline	—	—									—	—	
Shrouds.....................	6½	66	D. E.	10	8	6	55	D. E.	9	8	5½	50	D. E.
Seizings {Eye	1	16	...	...	...	1	12	...	...	...	1	12	...
{Throat.............	1	28	...	...	...	1	25	...	...	...	1	24	...
{End	¾	24	...	...	...	¾	20	...	...	...	¾	20	...
Laniards	3½	32	...	...	...	3	32	...	...	...	2¼	32	...
Ratlines	1	95	...	...	...	1	90	...	...	...	1	80	...
Backstays	7	115	D. E.	10	6	7	110	D. E.	10	6	6½	100	D. E.
Seizings {Eye	1¼	13	...	...	...	1¼	12	...	...	...	1	12	...
{Throat.............	1¼	24	...	...	...	1¼	24	...	...	...	1	24	...
{End	¾	20	...	...	...	¾	24	...	...	...	½	24	...
Laniards	3¼	20	...	...	...	3¼	20	...	...	...	3	20	...
Futtock-shrouds	6½	28	Pl.DE.	9	8	6	26	Pl.DE.	9	8	5½	25	Pl.DE.
Lashings	1½	24	...	...	...	1½	20	...	...	...	1¼	20	...
Ratlines	1	30	...	...	...	1	30	...	...	...	1	30	...
Stays	7½	45	T.	...	2	7	44	T.	...	2	6½	40	T.
Seizings {Throat	1½	6	...	...	...	1½	6	...	...	...	1½	6	...
{End	¾	6	...	...	...	¾	6	...	...	...	¾	6	...
Laniards	3	10	...	...	...	3	10	...	...	...	3	10	...
Stay-sail Halliards	3½	40	S.	9	1	3	36	S.	9	1	3	34	S.
Downhauller	2½	28	S.	8	1	2½	26	S.	8	1	2½	24	S.
Strapping	2½	1	...	...	...	2½	1	...	...	...	2½	1	...
Seizings ....Marline	—	—									—	—	
Pendants	4½	6	S.	6	11	4½	6	S.	11	2	4	6	S.
Sheets	3½	32	...	...	...	3½	32	...	...	...	3½	28	...
Tack-lashing	½	2	...	...	...	½	2	...	...	...	½	2	...
FORE-TOP-SAIL-YARD.													
Tie (if not chain)	5½	40	S.I.bd.	18	1	5	33	S.I.bd.	17	2	4	28	S.I.bd.
Strapping (Bullock Blocks)	5¼	8	S.	18	2	5	6	S.	17	1	4½	4	S.
Lashing	2½	12	...	...	...	2	12	...	...	...	2	10	...
Seizings	1	8	...	...	...	1	6	...	...	...	1	6	...
Halliards	3½	110	{D. {S.*	15 15	2 2	3	100	{D. {S.*	13 13	2 2	3	90	{D. {S.*
Strapping	4½	6	...	...	...	4	4	...	...	...	3½	4	...
Seizings	¾	16	...	...	...	¾	16	...	...	...	½	14	...
Jackstays..................	3	11	T.	...	2	3	10	T.	...	2	2½	10	T.
Laniards ,..................	¾	2	...	...	...	¾	2	...	...	...	¾	2	...
Foot-ropes..................	4	12	...	...	...	3¼	11	...	...	...	3½	11	...

600 Tons.				450 Tons.					300 Tons.					BRIG. 200 Tons.				
Length in Fathoms.	Blocks, &c. Species.	Sz. in In.	Number	Size in Inches.	Length in Fathoms.	Blocks, &c. Species.	Sz. in In.	Number	Size in Inches.	Length in Fathoms.	Blocks, &c. Species.	Sz. in In.	Number	Size in Inches.	Length in Fathoms.	Blocks, &c. Species.	Sz. in In.	Number
12	…	…	…	2½	11	…	…	…	2½	10	…	…	…	2½	10	…	…	…
40	S.	8	2	2½	38	S.	8	2	2½	35	S.	8	2	2¾	30	S.	8	2
26	S.	6	2	2	24	S.	6	2	1½	24	S.	5	2	1½	22	S.	5	2
10	…	…	…	2½	9	…	…	…	2½	9	…	…	…	2½	9	…	…	…
44	…	…	…	2½	40	…	…	…	2½	38	…	…	…	2	35	…	…	…
4½	T.	…	2	…	…	…	…	…	…	…	…	…	…	…	…	…	…	…
43	D.* S.*	7 7	2 2	…	…	…	…	…	…	…	…	…	…	…	…	…	…	…
—	—	—	—	—	—	—	—	—	—	—	—	—	—	—	—	—	—	—
45	D. E.	7	6	4½	42	D. E.	6	6	4	40	D. E.	6	6	4	36	D. E.	6	6
10	…	…	…	¾	8	…	…	…	½	8	…	…	…	½	8	…	…	…
22	…	…	…	¾	20	…	…	…	½	20	…	…	…	½	18	…	…	…
18	…	…	…	½	16	…	…	…	½	16	…	…	…	½	14	…	…	…
24	…	…	…	2	24	…	…	…	2	24	…	…	…	2	24	…	…	…
75	…	…	…	¾	70	…	…	…	¾	65	…	…	…	¾	60	…	…	…
90	D. E.	8	6	5½	60	D. E.	8	4	5½	55	D. E.	8	4	5	55	D. E.	8	4
12	…	…	…	1	8	…	…	…	1	8	…	…	…	1	8	…	…	…
24	…	…	…	1	12	…	…	…	1	12	…	…	…	1	12	…	…	…
24	…	…	…	¾	12	…	…	…	½	12	…	…	…	½	12	…	…	…
20	…	…	…	3	16	…	…	…	3	16	…	…	…	3	16	…	…	…
24	Pl.DE.	7	6	5	21	Pl.DE.	6	6	4½	20	Pl.DE.	6	6	4	20	Pl.DE.	6	6
18	…	…	…	1¼	18	…	…	…	1¼	18	…	…	…	1¼	18	…	…	…
30	…	…	…	¾	26	…	…	…	¾	24	…	…	…	¾	24	…	…	…
40	T.	…	2	5½	36	T.	…	2	5½	34	T.	…	2	5	30	T.	…	2
6	…	…	…	¾	6	…	…	…	¾	6	…	…	…	¾	6	…	…	…
6	…	…	…	½	4	…	…	…	½	4	…	…	…	½	4	…	…	…
9	…	…	…	2½	8	…	…	…	2	8	…	…	…	2	8	…	…	…
30	S.	9	1	2½	30	S.	8	1	2½	28	S.	8	1	2	26	S.	8	1
22	S.	7	1	2	22	S.	7	1	2	20	S.	7	1	1½	18	S.	6	1
1	…	…	…	2	1	…	…	…	2	1	…	…	…	1½	1	…	…	…
—	—	—	—	—	—	—	—	—	—	—	—	—	—	—	—	—	—	—
6	S.	10	2	3½	5	S.	10	2	3½	5	S.	9	2	3	5	S.	9	2
24	…	…	…	3	22	…	…	…	2½	22	…	…	…	2½	22	…	…	…
2	…	…	…	½	1½	…	…	…	½	1½	…	…	…	½	1½	…	…	…
26	S. I. bd.	14	1	4	24	S. I. bd.	14	1	3½	22	S. I. bd.	12	1	3½	20	S. I. bd.	12	1
4	S.	14	2	4	4	S.	14	2	3½	4	S.	12	2	3½	4	S.	12	2
9	…	…	…	1½	9	…	…	…	1½	8	…	…	…	1½	6	…	…	…
6	…	…	…	1	5	…	…	…	¾	5	…	…	…	¾	5	…	…	…
85	D. S.*	13 13	2 2	2½	80	D. S.*	11 11	2 2	2½	75	D. S.*	11 11	2 2	2	60	D. S.*	11 11	2 2
3½	…	…	…	3½	3	…	…	…	3	3	…	…	…	3	3	…	…	…
12	…	…	…	½	10	…	…	…	½	10	…	…	…	½	10	…	…	…
9	T.	…	2	2½	8	T.	…	2	2	8	T.	…	2	2	8	T.	…	2
2	…	…	…	½	2	…	…	…	½	2	…	…	…	½	2	…	…	…
10	…	…	…	3	10	…	…	…	2½	9	…	…	…	2½	9	…	…	…

FORE-TOP-SAIL-YARD (*continued*) AND FORE-TOP-GALLANT-YARD.	SHIPS. 1250 Tons. Size in Inches.	Length in Fathoms.	*Blocks, &c.* Species.	Sz. in In.	Number	1000 Tons. Size in Inches.	Length in Fathoms.	*Blocks, &c.* Species.	Sz. in In.	Number	800 Tons. Size in Inches.	Length in Fathoms.	*Blocks,* Species.	Sz. in In.
Laniards	1½	4	...	...	...	1¼	4	...	...	...	1¼	4	...	..
Stirrups	2½	6	T.	...	4	2	6	T.	...	4	2	6	T.	..
Flemish Horses	3	6	...	...	...	2½	5	...	...	...	2½	4	...	..
Seizings	¾	2	...	...	...	½	2	...	...	...	½	2	...	..
Braces	3½	95	S.	11	4	3	90	S.	10	4	3	80	S.	1
			S.	10	2			S.	9	2			S.	
Strapping, Yard	3	6	T.	...	6	2½	5	T.	...	6	2	4½	T.	..
Strapping, Stay	4	3	...	...	...	4	3	...	...	...	3½	3	...	..
Seizings	1	6	...	...	...	1	5	...	...	...	¾	5	...	
Lifts	4	62	Sis.	14	2	3½	55	Sis.	14	2	3½	50	Sis.	1
Laniards	1½	4	T.	...	2	1½	4	T.	...	2	1¼	4	T.	..
Jiggers	2	25	S.*	7	2	2	20	S.*	7	2	2	20	S.*	
Strapping	2½	2	...	...	...	2½	2	...	...	...	2½	2	...	.
Seizings .... *Marline*	—	—	—	—	—	—	—	—	—	—	—	—	—	—
Parral-rope	4	5	...	...	...	4	4	...	...	...	4	4	...	..
Lashing	1¼	16	...	...	...	1¼	15	...	...	...	1	14	...	.
Clue-lines and Strapping	3½	82	St.bd.	11	2	3½	78	St.bd.	11	2	3	75	St.bd.	1
Seizings .... *Marline*	—	—	—	—	—	—	—	—	—	—	—	—	—	—
Bunt-lines and Strapping	3	68	S.	9	2	3	62	S.	9	2	3	55	S.	
Seizings .... *Marline*	—	—	—	—	—	—	—	—	—	—	—	—	—	—
Span	3	2	T.	...	2	3	2	T.	...	2	3	2	T.	.
Bow-lines and Strapping	3	62	S.	9	2	3	54	S.	9	2	3	48	S.	
Bridles	3	8	T.	...	2	3	6	T.	...	2	3	6	T.	.
Seizings .... *Marline*	—	—	—	—	—	—	—	—	—	—	—	—	—	—
Reef-tackles and Strapping	3½	60	S.	11	2	3	57	S.	9	2	3	55	S.	
			T.		2			T.		2			T.	
Earings	1½	38	...	...	...	1½	36	...	...	...	1½	34	...	.
Sheets (if not chain)	5½	53	C.	12	2	5	50	C.	11	2	5	45	C.	
Strapping, quarter-blocks	3½	6	D.	12	2	3½	6	D.	11	2	3½	6	D.	
Lashing	1½	6	...	...	...	1¼	5	...	...	...	1	5	...	
Seizings	¾	6	...	...	...	¾	6	...	...	...	¾	6	...	
Studding-sail Halliards	3½	90	S.	11	4	3½	80	S.	11	4	3½	75	S.	
Sheets	3½	35	...	...	...	3¼	30	...	...	...	3	25	...	
Tacks	3½	100	S.	11	4	3½	95	S.	11	4	3½	90	S.	
Downhauller	2	55	S.	6	2	2	45	S.	6	2	2	43	S.	
Boom Jiggers	2	75	D.	7	2	2	70	D.	7	2	2	65	D.	
			S.	7	2			S.	7	2			S.	
Heel-lashing	3	7	...	...	...	3	6	...	...	...	3	6	...	
Strapping for all the blocks	3½	18	...	...	...	3½	16	...	...	...	3½	15	...	.
	2½	8	...	...	...	2½	6	..	...	...	2	6	...	.
Seizings	½	10	...	...	...	½	9	...	...	...	½	8	...	.
Boom Brace-pendant	3½	10	S.	6	2	3½	10	S.	6	2	3	9	S.	
Whip	2	50	...	...	...	2	45	...	...	...	2	40	..	
FORE-TOP-GALLANT-MAST.														
Shrouds	4½	50	T.	...	8	4	45	T.	...	8	3½	42	T.	
Laniards	2	12	...	...	...	2	12	...	...		1½	12	...	
Backstays	4½	90	D. E.	6	4	4½	86	D. E.	6	4	4	80	D. E.	

600 Tons.				450 Tons.					300 Tons.					BRIG. 200 Tons.				
Length in Fathoms.	Blocks, &c. Species.	Sz. in In.	Number	Size in Inches.	Length in Fathoms.	Blocks, &c. Species.	Sz. in In.	Number	Size in Inches.	Length in Fathoms.	Blocks, &c. Species.	Sz. in In.	Number	Size in Inches.	Length in Fathoms.	Blocks, &c. Species.	Sz. in In.	Number
4	...	...	...	1	3½	...	...	...	1	3	...	...	...	1	3	...	...	...
6	T.	...	4	2	3	T.	...	2	2	3	T.	...	2	2	3	T.	...	2
4	...	...	...	2	4	...	...	...	2	3	...	...	...	2	3	...	...	...
1½	...	...	...	½	1½	...	...	...	½	1½	...	...	...	½	1½	...	...	...
70	{ S. { S.	10 9	4 2	2½	65	{ S. { S.	9 8	4 2	2½	60	{ S. { S.	9 8	4 2	2¼	58	{ S. { S.	9 8	4 2
4	T.	...	6	2	3½	T.	...	6	2	3½	T.	...	6	2	3	T.	...	6
3	...	...	...	3	3	...	...	...	3	3	...	...	...	3	2	...	...	...
4	...	...	...	½	4	...	...	...	½	4	...	...	...	½	3	...	...	...
45	Sis.	12	2	3	40	Sis.	12	2	3	35	Sis.	12	2	2½	30	Sis.	10	2
4	T.	...	2	1	4	T.	...	2	1	4	T.	...	2	¾	4	T.	...	2
18	S.*	6	2	1¾	16	S.*	6	2	1½	15	S.*	6	2	1½	15	S.*	6	2
1½	...	...	...	2	1½	...	...	...	2	1½	...	...	...	2	1½	...	...	...
—	—	—	—	—	—	—	—	—	—	—	—	—	—	—	—	—	—	—
4	...	...	...	3½	3	...	...	...	3	3	...	...	...	3	3	. .	...	...
12	...	...	...	1	10	...	...	...	1	8	...	...	...	1	8	...	...	...
70	St.bd.	10	2	2½	65	St.bd.	9	2	2¼	60	St. bd.	9	2	2	55	St.bd.	7	2
—	—	—	—	—	—	—	—	—	—	—	—	—	—	—	—	—	—	—
50	S.	8	2	2½	45	S.	8	2	2¼	40	S.	7	2	2	36	S.	7	2
—	—	—	—	—	—	—	—	—	—	—	—	—	—	—	—	—	—	—
2	T.	...	2	2½	2	T.	...	2	2	2	T.	...	2	2	2	T.	...	2
42	S.	9	2	2½	38	S.	8	2	2½	36	S.	8	2	2	38	S.	7	2
6	T.	...	2	2½	6	T.	...	2	2½	6	S.	...	2	2	6	T.	...	2
—	—	—	—	—	—	—	—	—	—	—	—	—	—	—	—	—	—	—
52	{ S. { T.	9	2 2	2½	48	{ S. { T.	8	2 2	2½	45	{ S. { T.	8	2 2	2	42	{ S. { T.	7	2 2
32	...	...	...	1¼	32	...	...	...	1	32	...	...	...	1	32	...	...	...
43	C.	10	2	4½	40	C.	9	2	4	38	C.	8	2	3½	36	C.	7	2
5	D.	10	2	3	5	D.	9	2	2½	5	D.	8	2	2	5	D.	7	2
4	...	...	...	¾	4	...	...	...	¾	4	...	...	...	½	4	...	...	...
6	...	...	...	½	6	...	...	...	½	6	...	...	...	½	6	...	...	...
65	S.	11	4	3	60	S.	10	4	2½	55	S.	10	4	2	50	S.	9	4
22	...	...	...	3	18	...	...	...	2½	16	...	...	...	2	14	...	...	...
75	S.	11	4	3	65	S.	10	4	2½	55	S.	10	4	2	50	S.	9	4
40	S.	5	2	1½	38	S.	5	2	1½	36	S.	5	2	1½	34	S.	5	2
60	{ D. { S.	7 7	2 2	2	55	{ D. { S.	7 7	2 2	...	...	...	...	...	...	...	...	...	...
5	...	...	...	2½	5	...	...	...	2	4	...	...	...	2	4	...	...	...
15	...	...	...	3	12	...	...	...	3	11	...	...	...	2½	10	...	...	...
6	. .	...	...	2	5	...	...	...	2	5	...	...	...	1½	5	...	...	...
7	...	...	...	½	7	...	...	...	½	6	...	...	...	—	*Marline*		—	—
8	S.	6	2	3	7	S.	6	2	2½	6	S.	6	2	2½	6	S.	6	2
38	...	...	...	2	34	...	...	...	2	30	...	...	...	2	30	...	...	...
40	T.	...	8	3	36	T.	...	8	3	34	T.	...	8	2½	32	T.	...	8
12	...	...	...	1¼	10	...	...	...	1	10	...	...	...	1	9	...	...	...
75	D. E.	6	4	3	70	T.	...	4	3	65	T.	...	4	2½	65	T.	...	4

FORE-TOP-GALLANT-MAST (*continued*), FORE-TOP-GALLANT-YARD, AND FORE-ROYAL-YARD.	SHIPS.												
	1250 Tons.					1000 Tons.					800 Tons.		
	Size in Inches.	Length in Fathoms.	*Blocks, &c.* Species.	Sz. in In.	Number	Size in Inches.	Length in Fathoms.	*Blocks, &c.* Species.	Sz. in In.	Number	Size in Inches.	Length in Fathoms.	*Blocks,* Species.
Seizings	¾	6	...	...	...	¾	6	...	...	...	½	6	...
Laniards	2	12	...	...	...	2	12	...	...	...	2	12	...
Stay	4½	34	...	...	...	4	30	...	...	...	3½	28	...
Tackle-fall and Strapping	2¼	17	D. S.*	7 7	1 1	2¼	17	D. S.*	7 7	1 1	2¼	17	D. S.*
Seizings .... *Marline*	—	—	—	—	—	—	—	—	—	—	—	—	—
Royal-stay	2½	38	...	...	...	2½	33	...	...	...	2¼	30	...
Backstays	2½	105	T.	...	4	2½	92	T.	...	4	2¼	92	T.
Laniards	1	6	...	...	...	1	6	...	...	...	1	6	...
FORE-TOP-GALLANT-YARD.													
Halliards and Strapping	3½	54	D. S.*	11 11	1 1	3½	46	D. S.*	11 11	1 1	3	40	D. S.*
Jackstay	2	8	T.	...	2	2	7	T.	...	2	1½	7	T.
Laniards	¾	2	...	...	...	¾	2	...	...	...	¾	2	...
Foot-ropes	2½	9	...	...	...	2½	8	...	...	...	2½	8	...
Laniards .... *Marline*	—	—	—	—	—	—	—	—	—	—	—	—	—
Braces and Strapping	2½	100	S.	6	6	2¼	90	S.	6	6	2¼	85	S.
Seizings .... *Marline*	—	—	—	—	—	—	—	—	—	—	—	—	—
Lifts	3	54	T.	...	2	3	50	T.	...	2	2½	45	T.
Laniards	1½	3	T.	...	2	1¼	3	T.	...	2	1	3	T.
Parral-ropes	2	2	...	...	...	2	2	...	...	...	2	2	...
Seizings	1	1	...	...	...	¾	1	...	...	...	½	1	...
Clue-lines	2	80	S.	6	2	2	75	S.	6	2	2	70	S.
Strapg. for quarter-blocks.	2	2½	D.	6	2	2	2½	D.	6	2	2	2½	D.
Lashing	1	3	...	...	...	1	3	...	...	...	1	2½	...
Seizings .... *Marline*	—	—	—	—	—	—	—	—	—	—	—	—	—
Bow-lines and Strapping	2	74	S.	6	2	2	68	S.	6	2	2	62	S.
Bridles	2	3	T.	...	2	2	3	T.	...	2	2	3	T.
Seizings .... *Marline*	—	—	—	—	—	—	—	—	—	—	—	—	—
Sheets	4	54	...	...	...	3¾	50	...	...	...	3½	46	...
Earings	1¼	3	...	...	...	1	3	...	...	...	¾	2½	...
Studg. sail Halliards & Strapg.	2½	76	S.	7	4	2½	72	S.	7	4	2	68	S.
Sheets	2	40	...	...	...	2	36	...	...	...	2	34	...
Tacks and Strapping	2	57	S.	6	2	2	52	S.	6	2	2	48	S.
Downhauller & Strapping	1½	47	S.	5	2	1½	42	S.	5	2	1½	40	S.
Seizings .... *Marline*	—	—	—	—	—	—	—	—	—	—	—	—	—
FORE-ROYAL-YARD.													
Halliards	2½	62	...	...	...	2½	58	...	...	...	2½	55	...
Jack-stay	¾	6	T.	...	2	¾	5½	T.	...	2	¾	5	T.
Laniards .... *Marline*	—	—	—	—	—	—	—	—	—	—	—	—	—
Foot-ropes	1	7	...	...	...	1	6	...	...	...	1	6	...
Braces and Strapping	2	80	S.	5	2	2	76	S.	5	2	2	72	S.
Lifts	2	27	T.	...	2	2	25	T.	...	2	2	22	T.
Parral-lashing	1	1	...	...	...	1	1	...	...	...	1	1	...
Clue-lines and Strapping	1	76	S.	4	2	1	72	S.	4	2	1	68	S.
Bow-lines	1	72	T.	...	2	1	70	T.	...	2	1	65	T.
Sheets	2¼	76	...	...	...	2¼	72	...	...	...	2¼	65	...

														BRIG.				
600 Tons.				450 Tons.					300 Tons.					200 Tons.				
Length in Fathoms.	Blocks, &c.			Size in Inches.	Length in Fathoms.	Blocks, &c.			Size in Inches.	Length in Fathoms.	Blocks, &c.			Size in Inches.	Length in Fathoms.	Blocks, &c.		
	Species.	Sz. in In.	Number			Species.	Sz. in In.	Number			Species.	Sz. in In.	Number			Species.	Sz. in In.	Number
6	...	...	...	—		*Marline*	—	—	—	—	—	—	—	—	—	—	—	—
12	...	...	...	1½	10	...	...	...	1¼	10	...	...	...	1¼	8	...	...	...
26	...	...	...	3¼	26	...	...	...	3	24	...	...	...	2½	24	...	...	...
15	D. S.*	6 6	1 1	2	14	D. S.*	6 6	1 1	1½	5	T.	...	1	1½	5	T.	...	1
28	...	...	...	2	27	...	...	...	2	26	...	...	...	1½	25	...	...	...
86	T.	...	4	2	82	T.	...	4	2	76	T.	...	4	1½	76	T.	...	4
6	...	...	...	¾	6	...	...	...	½	6	...	...	...	½	6	...	...	...
38	D. S.*	9 9	1 1	2½	36	D. S.*	7 7	1 1	2½	32	D. S.*	7 7	1 1	2¼	30	D. S.*	7 7	1 1
6	T.	...	2	1¼	6	T.	...	2	1¼	5	T.	...	2	1	5	T.	...	2
2	...	...	...	½	2	...	...	...	½	2	...	...	...	½	2	...	...	...
7	...	...	...	2	7	...	...	...	2	6	...	...	...	2	6	...	...	...
80	S.	6	6	2	65	S.	6	4	1½	58	S.	6	4	1¼	55	S.	6	4
40	T.	...	2	2¼	36	T.	...	2	2¼	32	T.	...	2	2	30	T.	...	2
3	T.	...	2	¾	3	T.	...	2	¾	2	T.	...	2	¾	2	T.	...	2
2	...	...	...	1½	1½	...	...	...	1	1½	...	...	...	1	1½	...	...	...
1	...	...	...	½	1	...	...	...	—		*Marline*	—	—	—	—	—	—	—
65	S.	6	2	2	50	...	...	...	1½	45	...	...	...	1¼	45	...	...	...
2½	D.	6	2	2	1½	D.	6	2	2	1½	D.	6	2	2	1½	D.	6	2
2	...	...	...	1	2	...	...	...	¾	2	...	...	...	¾	2	...	...	...
60	S.	5	2	1½	55	S.	5	2	1½	48	S.	5	2	1½	48	S.	5	2
2½	T.	...	2	1½	2½	T.	...	2	1½	2	T.	...	2	1½	2	T.	...	2
40	...	...	...	2½	38	...	...	...	2½	36	...	...	...	2	36	...	...	...
2	...	...	...	¾	2	...	...	...	¾	2	...	...	...	¾	2	...	...	...
65	S.	6	4	2	62	S.	6	4	1½	55	S.	6	4	1¼	50	S.	6	4
30	...	...	...	2	26	...	...	...	2	24	...	...	...	2	24	...	...	...
44	S.	6	2	2	38	S.	6	2	2	36	S.	6	2	2	36	S.	6	2
...	...	...	...	...	...	...	...	...	...	...	...	...	...	...	...	...	...	...
50	...	...	...	2	45	...	...	...	2	40	...	...	...	1½	40	...	...	...
4½	T.	...	2	½	4	T.	...	2	½	4	T.	...	2	½	4	T.	...	2
5	...	...	...	1	5	...	...	...	1	5	...	...	...	1	5	...	...	...
68	S.	5	2	1½	62	S.	4	2	1	60	S.	4	2	1	60	S.	4	2
20	T.	...	2	1½	20	T.	...	2	1½	20	T.	...	2	1½	20	T.	...	2
1	...	...	...	¾	1	...	...	...	½	1	...	...	...	½	1	...	...	...
64	S.	4	2	1	60	S.	4	2	1	56	S.	4	2	1	56	S.	4	2
60	T.	...	2	¾	55	T.	...	2	¾	50	T.	...	2	¾	50	T.	...	2
60	...	...	...	2	54	...	...	...	1½	48	...	...	...	1¼	48	...	...	...

FORE-ROYAL-YARD (continued), MAIN-MAST, AND MAIN-YARD.	SHIPS. 1250 Tons.					1000 Tons.					800 Tons.			
	Size in Inches.	Length in Fathoms.	Blocks, &c. Species.	Sz. in In.	Number	Size in Inches.	Length in Fathoms.	Blocks, &c. Species.	Sz. in In.	Number	Size in Inches.	Length in Fathoms.	Blocks, &c. Species.	Sz. in In.
Earings	½	1	...	...	...	½	1	...	...	...	½	1	...	..
Seizings ... *Marline*	—	—	—	—	—	—	—	—	—	—	—	—	—	—
MAIN-MAST.														
Pendants	10½	9	T.	...	2	10	9	T.	...	2	9	8	T.	..
Runners of Tackles*	...	...	...	...	...	...	...	...	...	...	...	...	...	..
Falls of Tackles	4	190	D.	13	4	4	160	D.	13	4	3½	150	D.	1
Strapping	5½	4	* / T.	... / ...	2 / 2	5	3½	* / T.	... / ...	2 / 2	4½	3	* / T.	.. / .
Seizings	1	10	...	...	...	1	8	...	...	...	1	8	...	..
Shrouds	10½	160	D. E.	16	14	10	156	D. E.	16	14	9½	146	D. E.	1
Seizings: Eye	1¾	40	...	...	...	1¾	40	...	...	...	1¼	40	...	..
Seizings: Throat	1½	80	...	...	...	1½	80	...	...	...	1½	75	...	..
Seizings: End	1¼	80	...	...	...	1¼	80	...	...	...	1	70	...	..
Laniards	5	70	...	...	...	5	70	...	...	...	4½	70	...	..
Rat-lines	1½	226	...	...	...	1½	210	...	...	...	1¼	190	...	..
Stays	16	42	H.	19	2	15	40	H.	18	2	14	34	H.	1
Collars (if used)	8	9	H.	19	2	8	8	H.	18	2	7	8	H.	1
Seizings: Stay	1¾	40	...	...	...	1¾	40	...	...	...	1½	30	...	..
Seizings: Collar	1½	5	...	...	...	1½	4	...	...	...	1½	4	...	..
Laniards	5	14	...	...	...	5	14	...	...	...	4½	14	...	..
MAIN-YARD.														
Truss-pendants	7½	16	S.	8	2	7	14	S.	8	2	6½	12	S.	
Falls	3	60	...	...	...	2½	60	...	...	...	2½	55	...	..
Straps	3½	7	T.	..	2	3½	6½	T.	...	2	3½	6	T.	..
Jackstay	3½	15	T.	...	2	3½	14	T.	...	2	3	13	T.	..
Laniards	1½	2	...	...	...	1½	2	...	...	...	1¼	2	...	.
Foot-ropes	5	16	T.	...	2	4½	15	T.	...	2	4	14	T.	..
Laniards	2	6	. .	...	...	2	5	...	...	...	2	5	...	..
Stirrups	4	14	T.	...	6	3	12	T.	...	6	3	10	T.	.
Clue-garnets	3½	70	St.bd.	11	2	3½	65	St.bd.	11	2	3	58	St.bd.	1
Straps for Yard & Straps	3½	10	S.	11	2	3½	9½	S.	11	2	3	9	S.	1
Lashing	1¼	10	...	...	...	1¼	10	...	...	...	1	10	...	.
Seizings	¾	10	...	...	...	¾	10	...	...	...	¾	10	...	.
Bunt-lines and Falls	3	95	D. / S.	10 / 10	4 / 8	3	84	D. / S.	10 / 10	4 / 8	3	80	D. / S.	1 / 1
Strapping	3½	12	..	...	...	3	12	...	...	...	3	11	...	.
Seizings	½	30	...	...	...	½	30	...	...	...	½	30	...	.
Leech-lines	2½	49	S.	8	4	2½	47	S.	8	4	2½	44	S.	
Strapping	2½	2	...	...	...	2½	2	...	...	...	2	2	...	.
Seizings ... *Marline*	—	—	—	—	—	—	—	—	—	—	—	—	—	—
Slab-line and Strapping	2	40	S.	7	1	2	36	S.	7	1	2	32	S.	
Bow-line, Pendant, & Bridles	5	13	T.	...	4	4½	12	T.	...	4	4	11	T.	.
Tackle-fall and Strapping	2½	22	D.	8	2	2½	20	D.	8	2	2	20	D.	
Seizings ... *Marline*	—	—	—	—	—	—	—	—	—	—	—	—	—	—
Earings (4 in No.)	2½	20	...	...	...	2	20	...	...	...	1¾	20	...	.
Sheets (tapered)	5	85	C.	10	2	5	75	C.	10	2	5	68	C.	1
Tacks (tapered)	5	80	C.	10	4	5	70	C.	10	4	5	64	C.	1

* Merchant-ships generally use double-blocks, lashing the upper one to the pendants.

600 Tons.				450 Tons.					300 Tons.					BRIG. 200 Tons.				
Length in Fathoms.	Species.	Sz.inIn.	Number.	Size in Inches.	Length in Fathoms.	Species.	Sz.inIn.	Number.	Size in Inches.	Length in Fathoms.	Species.	Sz.inIn.	Number.	Size in Inches.	Length in Fathoms.	Species.	Sz.inIn.	Number.
1	...	...	...	—	*Marline*	—	—		—	—	—	—		—	—	—	—	
7	T.	...	2	7½	6½	T.	...	2	7	6	T.	...	2	6	6	T.	...	2
140	D.	11	4	3	130	D.	11	4	3	110	D.	10	4	3	100	D.	10	4
3	{ * / T.	...	2 / 2	3	3	{ * / T.	...	2 / 2	3	2½	{ * / T.	...	2 / 2	3	2½	{ * / T.	...	2 / 2
7	...	...	...	¾	6	...	...	...	¾	6	...	...	...	¾	6	...	...	...
120	D.E.	11	12	7½	105	D.E.	11	10	7	100	D.E.	10	10	6	80	D.E.	8	8
40	...	...	...	1¼	35	...	...	...	1¼	30	...	...	...	1¼	20	...	...	...
60	...	...	...	1¼	50	...	...	...	1	50	...	...	...	1¼	45	...	...	...
6	...	...	...	1	50	...	...	...	1	50	...	...	...	¾	40	...	...	...
60	...	...	...	4	50	...	...	...	3½	50	...	...	...	3	40	...	...	...
160	...	...	...	1¼	140	...	...	...	1	105	...	...	...	1	90	...	...	...
32	H.	15	2	12	28	H.	12	2	10	26	H.	10	2	8	28	H.	9	2
7	H.	15	2	5½	6	H.	12	2	5½	6	H.	10	2	5½	6	H.	9	2
30	...	...	...	1¼	30	...	...	...	1¼	25	...	...	...	1¼	25	...	...	...
4	...	...	..	1	4	...	...	...	¾	4	...	...	...	¾	4	...	...	...
14	...	...	...	3½	14	...	...	...	3	14	...	...	...	3	14	...	...	...
12	S.	8	2	5½	10	S.	7	2	5	9	S.	7	2	4	7	S.	7	2
50	...	...	...	2	45	...	...	...	2	40	...	...	...	2	36	...	...	...
6	T.	...	2	3	5½	T.	...	2	2½	5	T.	...	2	2	4½	T.	...	2
11	T.	...	2	2½	10	T.	...	2	2½	9	T.	...	2	2½	9	T.	...	2
2	...	...	...	1	1½	...	...	...	1	1½	...	...	...	1	1½	...	...	...
13	T.	...	2	3	12	T.	...	2	3	11	T.	...	2	3	11	T.	...	2
5	...	...	...	1¼	5	...	...	...	1	5	...	...	...	1	4	...	...	...
10	T.	...	6	2½	9	T.	...	6	2½	8	T.	...	6	2½	6	T.	...	4
53	St.bd.	10	2	2½	50	St.bd.	9	2	2	45	St.bd.	8	2	2	44	St.bd.	8	2
8	S.	10	2	2½	7	S.	9	2	2	7	S.	8	2	2	7	S.	8	2
9	...	...	...	¾	8	...	..		¾	7	...	...	...	¾	6	...	...	...
10	...	...	...	½	10	...	...	...	½	10	...	...	...	½	10	...	...	...
72	{ D. / S.	9 / 9	4 / 8	2½	68	{ D. / S.	9 / 9	4 / 8	2½	54	{ D. / S.	9 / 8	2 / 4	2	52	{ D. / S.	7 / 7	2 / 4
10	...	...	...	3	10	...	...	...	2½	10	...	...	...	2½	7	...	...	...
28	...	...	...	—	*Marline*				—					—				
38	S.	8	4	2½	35	S.	8	4	2	32	S.	7	4	2	30	S.	7	4
2	...	...	...	2	2	...	...	...	2	2	...	...	...	2	2	...	...	...
26	S.	7	1	2	22	S.	7	1	2	20	S.	7	1	2	18	S.	7	1
10	T.	...	4	3	10	T.	...	4	2½	10	T.	...	4	2½	10	T.	...	4
18	D.	7	2	2	16	D.	7	2	1½	14	D.	6	2	1½	14	D.	6	2
18	...	...	...	1¼	18	...	...	...	1¼	17	...	...	...	1¼	16	...	...	...
63	C.	9	2	4	60	C.	8	2		54	C.	8	2	3½	50	C.	8	2
60	C.	9	4	4	56	C.	9	4	4	50	C.	8	4	3½	50	C.	8	4

MAIN-YARD (*continued*) AND MAIN-TOP-MAST.	SHIPS.												
	1250 Tons.					1000 Tons.					800 Tons.		
	Size in Inches.	Length in Fathoms.	Blocks, &c. Species.	Blocks, &c. Sz. in In.	Blocks, &c. Number	Size in Inches.	Length in Fathoms.	Blocks, &c. Species.	Blocks, &c. Sz. in In.	Blocks, &c. Number	Size in Inches.	Length in Fathoms.	Blocks, &c. Species.
Strapping	5	11	...	...	...	5	11	...	...	...	5	11	...
Seizings	1¼	24	...	...	...	1¼	24	...	...	...	1¼	24	...
Braces	4	110	S.	16	4	4	100	S.	16	4	3½	90	S.
Strapping	5	6	T.	...	6	5	6	T.	...	6	4½	6	T.
	3	12				3	10				3	10	
Seizings	1¼	20	...	...	...	1¼	18	...	...	...	1¼	17	...
Strapping, quarter-blocks	4	11	D.	16	2	4	10	D.	16	2	4	10	D.
Lashing	2½	6	...	...	...	2½	6	...	...	...	2	5	...
Seizings	1½	6	...	...	...	1½	6	...	...	...	1¼	6	...
Lifts	4	104	S.	13	2	4	94	S.	13	2	3½	84	S.
Strapping	4½	5	...	...	...	4½	4	...	...	...	4	3	...
Short Span	5	5	C.	13	2	4½	4	C.	13	2	4	4	C.
Seizings	¾	12	...	...	...	¾	12	...	...	...	¾	12	...
Jigger-falls and Strapping	2½	40	D.*	8	2	2½	35	D.*	8	2	2	30	D.*
			S.*	8	2			S.*	8	2			S.*
Seizings	½	5	...	...	...	½	5	...	...	...	½	4	...
Main-stay-sail-stay	6	21	C.	12	1	6	19	C.	12	1	5½	18	C.
Halliards	3½	55	S.	11	2	3½	50	S.	11	2	3	46	S.
Sheets	3	35	D.*	10	2	3	33	D.*	10	2	3	30	D.*
			S.*	10	2			S.*	10	2			S.*
Tack-lashing	2	4	...	...	...	2	4	...	...	...	2	4	...
Downhauller	2½	35	S.	8	1	2½	30	S.	8	1	2½	26	S.
Strapping { Mast-head	3	4	...	...	...	3	4	...	...	...	3	4	...
Strapping { Sheet	2	1	...	...	...	2	1	...	...	...	2	1	...
Seizings ... *Marline*	—	—	—	—	—	—	—	—	—	—	—	—	—
MAIN-TOP-MAST.													
Burton Pendants	5	6	T.	...	2	4½	6	T.	...	2	4	5	T.
Burton-falls and Strapping	2½	64	D.*	9	2	2½	58	D.*	9	2	2	48	D.*
			S.*	9	2			S.*	9	2			S.*
Seizings ... *Marline*	—	—	—	—	—	—	—	—	—	—	—	—	—
Shrouds	6½	66	D. E.	10	8	6	55	D. E.	9	8	5½	50	D. E.
Seizings { Eye	1	16	...	...	...	1	12	...	...	...	1	12	...
Seizings { Throat	1	28	...	...	...	1	25	...	...	...	1	24	...
Seizings { End	¾	24	...	...	...	¾	20	...	...	...	¾	20	...
Laniards	3½	32	...	...	...	3	32	...	...	...	2½	32	...
Rat-lines	1	100	...	...	...	1	94	...	...	...	1	84	...
Backstays	7	120	D. E.	10	6	7	114	D. E.	10	6	6½	105	D. E.
Seizings { Eye	1¼	13	...	...	...	1¼	12	...	...	...	1	12	...
Seizings { Throat	1¼	24	...	...	...	1¼	24	...	...	...	1	24	...
Seizings { End	¾	20	...	...	...	½	24	...	...	...	½	24	...
Laniards	3½	20	...	...	...	3¼	20	...	...	...	3	20	...
Futtock-shrouds	7	28	Pl.DE.	9	8	6½	26	Pl.DE.	9	8	6	25	Pl.DE.
Lashings	1½	24	...	...	...	1½	20	...	...	...	1¼	20	...
Rat-lines	1	30	...	...	...	1	30	...	...	...	1	30	...
Stays	7½	48	T.	...	2	7	46	T.	...	2	6½	44	T.
Seizings { Throat	1½	6	...	...	...	1¼	6	...	...	...	1	6	...
Seizings { End	¾	6	...	...	...	¾	6	...	...	...	½	6	...
Laniards	3	10	...	...	...	3	10	...	...	...	3	10	...

	600 Tons.				450 Tons.					300 Tons.					BRIG. 200 Tons.				
		Blocks, &c.					*Blocks, &c.*					*Blocks, &c.*					*Blocks, &c.*		
[Size in] Inches.	Length in Fathoms.	Species.	Sz. in In.	Number	Size in Inches.	Length in Fathoms.	Species.	Sz. in In.	Number	Size in Inches.	Length in Fathoms.	Species.	Sz. in In.	Number	Size in Inches.	Length in Fathoms.	Species.	Sz. in In.	Number
	11	...	...	...	4	10	...	...	...	4	10	...	...	...	3½	9	...	...	...
	22	...	...	...	1	22	...	...	...	1	22	...	...	...	¾	20	...	...	...
	80	S.	14	4	3	70	S.	12	4	2½	60	S.	10	4	2¼	64	S.	8	4
	5	T.	...	6	4	4	T.	...	6	4	4	T.	...	6	3	3	T.	...	6
	9				2½	9				2	9				2	8			
	16	...	...	...	1	14	...	...	...	¾	12	...	...	...	½	12	...	...	...
	9	D.	14	2	3½	9	D.	14	2	3	8	D.	13	2	2½	6	D.	12	2
	5	...	...	...	2	4	...	...	...	2	4	...	...	...	1½	4	...	...	...
	5	...	...	...	1	4	...	...	...	¾	4	...	...	...	¾	4	...	...	...
	37	...	...	...	4½	32	...	...	...	4	30	...	...	...	3	27	...	...	...
	...	...	...	...	...	...	...	...	...	...	...	...	...	...	...	...	...	...	...
	3½	C.	10	2	4	3½	C.	9	2	4	3	C.	8	2	4	3	C.	8	2
¾	6	...	...	...	½	6	...	...	...	½	5	...	...	...	½	5	...	...	...
	28	D.*	7	2	2	28	D.*	7	2	2	26	D.*	7	2	2	26	D.*	7	2
		S.*	7	2			S.*	7	2			S.*	7	2			S.*	7	2
½	4	...	...	...	½	4	...	...	...	½	4	...	...	...	½	4	...	...	...
	17	C.	10	1	5	16	C.	10	1	4½	15	C.	9	1	4½	16	C.	9	1
	44	S.	9	2	2½	42	S.	8	2	2½	40	S.	8	2	2¼	40	S.	8	2
	28	D.*	10	2	3	26	D.*	10	2	2½	24	D.*	9	2	2	24	D.*	9	2
		S.*	10	2			S.*	10	2			S.*	9	2			S.*	9	2
½	4	...	...	...	1½	4	...	...	...	1¼	4	...	...	...	1¼	4	...	...	...
½	24	S.	8	1	2	22	S.	7	1	2	20	S.	7	1	2	20	S.	7	1
	4	...	...	...	2½	4	...	...	...	2½	4	...	...	...	2½	4	...	...	...
	1	...	...	...	2	1	...	...	...	2	1	...	...	...	2	1	...	...	...
—	—	—	—	—	—	—	—	—	—	—	—	—	—	—	—	—	—	—	—
	4½	T.	...	2	...	...	...	...	...	...	...	...	...	...	...	...	...	...	...
	45	D.*	7	2	...	...	...	...	...	...	...	...	...	...	...	...	...	...	...
		S.*	7	2	...	...	...	...	...	...	...	...	...	...	...	...	...	...	...
—	—	—	—	—	...	...	...	...	...	...	...	...	...	...	...	...	...	...	...
	45	D. E.	7	6	4½	42	. E.	6	6	4¼	40	L. E.	6	6	4	36	D. E.	6	6
¾	10	...	...	...	¾	8	...	...	...	½	8	...	...	...	½	8	...	...	...
¾	22	...	...	...	¾	20	...	...	...	½	20	...	...	...	½	18	...	...	...
½	18	...	...	...	½	16	...	...	...	½	16	...	...	...	½	14	...	...	...
2½	24	...	...	...	2	24	...	...	...	2	24	...	...	...	2	24	...	...	...
	80	...	...	...	¾	75	...	...	...	¾	70	...	...	...	¾	65	...	...	...
	94	D. E.	8	6	5½	62	D. E.	8	4	5½	58	D. E.	8	4	5	56	. E.	8	4
	12	...	...	...	1	8	...	...	...	1	8	...	...	...	1	8	...	...	...
1	24	...	...	...	1	12	...	...	...	1	12	...	...	...	1	12	...	...	...
½	24	...	...	...	¾	12	...	...	...	¾	12	...	...	...	¾	12	...	...	...
3	20	...	...	...	3	16	...	...	...	3	16	...	...	...	3	16	...	...	...
6	24	Pl.DE.	7	6	5	21	Pl.DE.	6	6	4½	20	Pl.DE.	6	6	4¼	20	Pl.DE.	6	6
1¼	18	...	...	...	1¼	18	...	...	...	1¼	18	...	...	...	1¼	18	...	...	...
1	30	...	...	...	¾	26	...	...	...	¾	24	...	...	...	¾	24	...	...	...
6	42	T.	...	2	5½	38	T.	...	2	5½	34	T.	...	2	5	30	T.	...	2
¾	6	...	...	...	¾	6	...	...	...	¾	6	...	...	...	¾	6	...	...	...
½	4	...	...	...	½	4	...	...	...	½	4	...	...	...	½	4	...	...	
2½	9	...	...	...	2½	8	...	...	...	2	8	...	...	...	2	8	...	...	

MAIN-TOP-SAIL-YARD.	SHIPS.													
	1250 Tons.					1000 Tons.					800 Tons.			
	Size in Inches.	Length in Fathoms.	Blocks, &c. Species.	Blocks, &c. Sz. in In.	Blocks, &c. Number	Size in Inches.	Length in Fathoms.	Blocks, &c. Species.	Blocks, &c. Sz. in In.	Blocks, &c. Number	Size in Inches.	Length in Fathoms.	Blocks, &c. Species.	Blocks, &c. Sz. in In.
Tye (if not chain)	5½	40	S. I.bd.	18	1	5	33	S. I.bd.	17	1	4	28	S. I.bd.	14
Strapping, Bullock-blocks	5½	18	S.	18	2	5	6	S.	17	2	4½	4	S.	14
Lashing	2½	12	...	...	...	2	12	...	...	...	2	10	...	...
Seizings	1	8	...	...	...	1	6	...	...	...	1	6	...	...
Halliards	3½	110	D. S.*	15 15	2 2	3¼	100	D. S.*	13 13	2 2	3	90	D. S.*	13 13
Strapping	4½	6	...	...	...	4	4	...	...	...	3½	4	...	...
Seizings	¾	16	...	...	...	¾	16	...	...	...	½	14	...	...
Jackstays	3	13	T.	...	2	3	12	T.	...	2	2½	11	T.	...
Laniards	¾	2	...	...	...	¾	2	...	...	...	½	2	...	...
Foot-ropes	4	14	...	...	...	3½	13	...	...	...	3½	12	...	...
Laniards	1½	4	...	...	...	1¼	4	...	...	...	1¼	4	...	...
Stirrups	2½	6	T.	...	4	2	6	T.	...	4	2	6	T.	...
Flemish-horses	3	6	...	...	...	2½	5	...	...	...	2½	4	...	...
Seizings	¾	2	...	...	...	½	2	...	...	...	½	2	...	...
Braces	3½	80	S.	11	4	3½	75	S.	11	4	3	70	S.	10
Strapping Yard	2½	5	T.	...	6	2½	5	T.	...	6	2½	4½	T.	...
Strapping Mast	4	3	...	...	...	4	3	...	...	...	3½	3	...	...
Seizings	1	6	...	...	...	1	5	...	...	...	¾	5	...	...
Lifts	3½	66	Sis.	14	2	3½	58	Sis.	14	2	3¼	54	Sis.	12
Laniards	1½	4	T.	...	2	1½	4	T.	...	2	1¼	4	T.	...
Jiggers	2	25	S.*	7	2	2	20	S.*	7	2	2	20	S.*	7
Strapping	2½	2	...	...	...	2½	2	...	...	...	2½	2	...	...
Seizings ... *Marline*	—	—	—	—	—	—	—	—	—	—	—	—	—	—
Parral-rope	4	6	...	...	...	4	5	...	...	...	4	5	...	...
Lashing	1¼	16	...	...	...	1¼	15	...	...	...	1	14	...	...
Clue-lines and Strapping	3½	88	St.bd.	11	2	3½	79	St. bd.	11	2	3	75	St.bd.	10
Seizings ... *Marline*	—	—	—	—	—	—	—	—	—	—	—	—	—	—
Bunt-lines and Strapping	3	74	S.	9	2	3	58	S.	9	2	3	52	S.	9
Seizings ... *Marline*	—	—	—	—	—	—	—	—	—	—	—	—	—	—
Span	3	2	T.	...	2	3	2	T.	...	2	3	2	T.	...
Bow-lines and Strapping	3	62	S.	9	2	3	54	S.	9	2	3	48	S.	9
Bridles	3	8	T.	...	2	3	6	T.	...	2	3	6	T.	...
Seizings ... *Marline*	—	—	—	—	—	—	—	—	—	—	—	—	—	—
Reef-tackle and Strapping	3½	66	S. T.	11	2 2	3	62	S. T.	11	2 2	3	58	S. T.	11
Earings	1½	38	...	...	...	1½	36	...	...	...	1½	34	...	...
Sheets (if not chain)	5½	57	C.	12	2	5	54	C.	11	2	5	50	C.	11
Strapping, quarter-blocks	3½	6	D.	12	2	3½	6	D.	11	2	3½	6	D.	11
Lashing	1½	6	...	...	...	1¼	5	...	...	...	1	5	...	...
Seizings	¾	6	...	...	...	¾	6	...	...	...	¾	6	...	...
Studding-sail Halliards	3½	95	S.	11	4	3½	85	S.	11	4	3½	80	S.	11
Sheets	3½	35	...	...	...	3¼	30	...	...	...	3	25	...	...
Tacks	3½	100	S.	11	4	3½	95	S.	11	4	3½	90	S.	11
Downhauller	2	55	S.	6	2	2	45	S.	6	2	2	43	S.	6
Boom-jiggers	2	75	D. S.	7 7	2 2	2	70	D. S.	7 7	2 2	2	65	D. S.	7 7
Heel-lashing	3	7	...	...	...	3	6	...	...	...	3	6	...	...

Inches.	600 Tons. Length in Fathoms.	Blocks, &c. Species.	Sz. in In.	Number	450 Tons. Size in Inches.	Length in Fathoms.	Blocks, &c. Species.	Sz. in In.	Number	300 Tons. Size in Inches.	Length in Fathoms.	Blocks, &c. Species.	Sz. in In.	Number	BRIG. 200 Tons. Size in Inches.	Length in Fathoms.	Blocks, &c. Species.	Sz. in In.	Number
	26	S. I.bd.	14	1	4	24	S. I.bd.	14	1	3½	22	S. I.bd.	12	1	3½	20	S. I.bd.	12	1
½	4	S.	14	2	4	4	S.	14	2	3½	4	S.	12	2	3½	4	S.	12	2
	9	...	...	...	1½	9	...	...	...	1½	8	...	...	...	1½	6	...	...	...
	6	...	...	...	1	5	...	...	...	¾	5	...	...	...	¾	5	...	...	...
	85	D. S.*	13 13	2 2	2½	80	D. S.*	11 11	2 2	2½	75	D. S.*	11 11	2 2	2	60	D. S.*	11 11	2 2
½	3½	...	...	...	3½	3	...	...	...	3	3	...	...	...	...	...	...	...	...
½	12	...	...	...	½	10	...	...	...	½	10	...	...	...	...	...	...	...	...
½	10	T.	...	2	2½	9	T.	...	2	2	8	T.	...	2	2	8	T.	...	2
½	2	...	...	...	½	2	...	...	...	½	2	...	...	...	½	2	...	...	...
	11	...	...	...	3	10½	...	...	...	2½	10	...	...	...	2½	9½	...	...	...
	4	...	...	...	1	3½	. .	...	...	1	3	...	...	...	1	3	...	...	...
	6	T.	...	4	2	3	T.	...	2	2	3	T.	...	2	2	3	T.	...	2
	4	...	...	...	2	4	...	...	...	2	3	...	...	...	2	3	...	...	...
½	1½	...	...	...	½	1½	...	...	...	½	1½	...	...	...	½	1½	...	...	...
	60	S.	10	4	2½	57	S.	9	4	2½	52	S.	9	4	2	64	S.	9	4
	4	T.	...	6	2	4	T.	...	6	2	4	T.	...	6	2	4	T.	...	6
3½	3	...	...	...	3	3	...	...	...	3	3	...	...	...	3	3	...	...	...
¾	4	...	...	...	½	4	...	...	...	½	4	...	...	...	½	3	...	...	...
3¼	48	Sis.	12	2	3	40	Sis.	12	2	3	35	Sis.	12	2	2½	30	Sis.	10	2
¼	4	T.	...	2	1	4	T.	...	2	1	4	T.	...	2	¾	4	T.	...	2
¾	18	S.*	6	2	1¾	16	S.*	6	2	1½	15	S.*	6	2	1½	15	S.*	6	2
2	1½	...	...	...	2	1½	...	. .	...	2	1½	...	...	...	2	1½	...	...	...
—	—	—	—	—	—	—	—	—	—	—	—	—	—	—	—	—	—	—	—
3½	4	...	...	...	3½	3½	...	...	...	3	3	...	...	...	3	3	...	...	...
1	12	...	...	...	1	10	...	...	...	1	8	...	...	...	1	8	...	...	...
3	72	St.bd.	10	2	2½	68	St.bd.	9	2	2¼	64	St.bd.	9	2	2	58	St.bd.	7	2
—	—	—	—	—	—	—	—	—	—	—	—	—	—	—	—	—	—	—	—
3	48	S.	9	2	2½	42	S.	8	2	2¼	40	S.	8	2	2	40	S.	8	2
—	—	—	—	—	—	—	—	—	—	—	—	—	—	—	—	—	—	—	—
2½	2	T.	...	2	2½	2	T.	...	...	2	2	T.	...	2	2	2	T.	...	2
3	42	S.	9	2	2½	38	S.	8	2	2¼	36	S.	8	2	2	38	S.	7	2
3	6	T.	...	2	2½	6	T.	...	2	2½	6	T.	...	2	2	6	T.	...	2
—	—	—	—	—	—	—	—	—	—	—	—	—	—	—	—	—	—	—	—
3	56	S. T.	11	2 2	2½	52	S. T.	8	2 2	2½	48	S. T.	8	2 2	2	46	S. T.	7	2 2
1¼	32	...	...	...	1¼	32	...	...	...	1	32	...	...	...	1	32	...	...	...
4½	48	C.	10	2	4½	44	C.	10	2	4	42	C.	8	2	3½	40	C.	7	2
3	5	D.	10	2	3	5	D.	10	2	3	5	D.	8	2	2½	5	D.	7	2
¾	4	...	...	...	¾	4	...	...	...	¾	4	...	...	...	½	4	...	...	...
¾	6	...	...	...	½	6	...	...	...	½	6	...	...	...	½	6	...	...	...
3	70	S.	11	4	2¾	65	S.	10	4	2½	60	S.	10	4	2	55	S.	9	4
3	22	...	...	...	2¾	18	...	...	...	2½	16	...	...	...	2	14	...	...	...
3	75	S.	11	4	2¾	65	S.	10	4	2½	55	S.	10	4	2	50	S.	9	4
1½	40	S.	5	2	1½	38	S.	5	2	1½	36	S.	5	2	1½	34	S.	5	2
2	60	D. S.	7 7	2 2	2	55	D. S.	7 7	2 2	...	...	...	...	...	...	...	...	...	...
2½	5	...	...	...	2½	5	...	...	...	2	4	...	...	...	2	4	...	...	...

MAIN-TOP-SAIL-YARD (*continued*), MAIN-TOP-GALLANT-MAST, AND MAIN-ROYAL-YARD.	SHIPS. 1250 Tons.					1000 Tons.					800 Tons.			
	Size in Inches.	Length in Fathoms.	*Blocks, &c.* Species.	Sz. in In	Number	Size in Inches.	Length in Fathoms.	*Blocks, &c.* Species.	Sz. in In.	Number	Size in Inches.	Length in Fathoms.	*Blocks,* Species.	Sz. in In.
Strapping for all the blocks	3½	18	...	...	...	3½	16	...	...	...	3½	15	...	..
	2½	8	...	...	...	2½	6	...	...	...	2	6	...	.
Seizings	½	10	..	...	...	½	9	...	...	..	½	8	...	.
MAIN-TOP-GALLANT-MAST.														
Shrouds	4½	54	T.	...	8	4	48	T.	...	8	3½	44	T.	..
Laniards	2	12	...	...	...	2	12	...	...	...	1½	12	...	..
Backstays	4½	92	D. E.	6	4	4½	88	D. E.	6	4	4	82	D. E.	
Seizings	¾	6	...	...	...	¾	6	...	...	...	½	6	...	..
Laniards	2	12	...	...	...	2	12	...	...	...	2	12	...	..
Stay	4½	36	..	...	...	4	32	...	...	...	3½	30	...	..
Laniard	2	12	...	...	...	2	12	...	...	...	2	12	...	..
Seizings ... *Marline*	—	—	—	—	—	—	—	—	—	—	—	—	—	—
Royal-stay	2½	40	...	...	...	2½	35	...	...	...	2½	32	...	..
Backstay	2½	108	T.	...	4	2½	100	T.	...	4	2½	95	T.	..
Laniards	1	6	...	...	...	1	6	...	...	...	1	6	...	..
MAIN-TOP-GALLANT-YARD.														
Halliards and Strapping	3½	56	D. S.*	11 11	1 1	3½	50	D. S.*	11 11	1 1	3	45	D. S.*	9 9
Jackstay	2	9	T.	...	2	2	8	T.	...	2	1½	8	T.	...
Laniards	¾	2	...	...	...	¾	2	...	...	...	¾	2	...	...
Foot-ropes	2½	10	...	...	...	2½	9	...	...	...	2½	9	...	...
Laniards ... *Marline*	—	—	—	—	—	—	—	—	—	—	—	—	—	—
Braces and Strapping	2½	90	S.	6	6	2½	80	S.	6	6	2¼	75	S.	6
Seizings ... *Marline*	—	—	—	—	—	—	—	—	—	—	—	—	—	—
Lifts	3	58	T.	...	2	3	55	T.	...	2	2½	50	T.	...
Laniards	1½	3	T.	...	2	1¼	3	T.	...	2	1	3	T.	...
Parral-rope	2	2	...	...	...	2	2	...	...	...	2	2	...	...
Seizings	1	1	...	...	...	¾	1	...	...	...	1½	1	...	...
Clue-lines	2¼	86	S.	6	2	2¼	80	S.	6	2	2	76	S.	6
Strapping for quarter-blocks	2	2½	D.	6	2	2	2½	D.	6	2	2	2½	D.	6
Lashings	1	3	...	...		1	3	...	...	...	1	2½	...	...
Seizings ... *Marline*	—	—	—	—	—	—	—	—	—	—	—	—	—	—
Bow-lines and Strapping	2	78	S.	6	2	2	74	S.	6	2	2	68	S.	6
Bridles	2	3	T.	...	2	2	3	T.	...	2	2	3	T.	...
Seizings ... *Marline*	—	—	—	—	—	—	—	—	—	—	—	—	—	—
Sheets	3½	60	...	...	...	3½	56	...	...	...	3¼	50	...	...
Earings	1¼	3	...	...	...	1	3	...	...	...	¾	2½	..	...
Studg.-sail Halliards & Strapg.	2½	80	S.	7	4	2½	76	S.	7	4	2	72	S.	7
Sheets	2	44	...	...	...	2	40	...	...	...	2	36	...	...
Tacks and Strapping	2	57	S.	6	2	2	52	S.	6	2	2	48	S.	6
Downhauller and Strapping	1½	47	S.	5	2	1½	42	S.	5	2	1½	40	S.	5
Seizings ... *Marline*	—	—	—	—	—	—	—	—	—	—	—	—	—	—
MAIN-ROYAL-YARD.														
Halliards	2¾	70	...	...	...	2¾	66	...	...	...	2½	60	...	...
Jackstay	¾	7	T.	...	2	¾	6	T.	...	2	¾	5½	T.	...

																BRIG.			
	600 Tons.				450 Tons.					300 Tons.					200 Tons.				
Inches.	Length in Fathoms.	Blocks, &c.			Size in Inches.	Length in Fathoms.	Blocks, &c.			Size in Inches.	Length in Fathoms.	Blocks, &c.			Size in Inches.	Length in Fathoms.	Blocks, &c.		
		Species.	Sz. in In.	Number			Species.	Sz. in In.	Number			Species.	Sz. in In.	Number			Species.	Sz. in In.	Number
	15	...	...	...	3	12	...	...	...	3	11	...	...	...	2½	10	...	...	...
	6	...	...	...	2	5	...	...	...	2	5	...	...	...	1½	5	...	...	...
	7	...	...	...	½	7	...	...	...	½	6	...	...	...	—	*Marline*		—	—
	42	T.	...	8	3¼	38	T.	..	8	3	36	T.	...	8	2½	34	T.	...	8
	12	...	...	...	1¼	10	...	...	...	1	10	...	...	...	1	9	...	...	...
	76	D. E.	6	4	3¼	70	T.	...	4	3	65	T.	...	4	2½	65	T.	...	4
	6	...	...	...	—	*Marline*		—	—	—	—	—	—	—	—	—	—	—	—
	12	...	...	...	1½	10	...	...	...	1¼	10	...	...	...	1¼	8	...	...	...
	27	...	...	...	3¼	27	...	...	...	3	25	...	...	...	2½	25	...	...	...
	12	...	...	...	1½	10	...	...	...	1¼	10	...	...	...	1¼	8	...	...	...
	—	—	—	—	—	—	—	—	—	—	—	—	—	—	—	—	—	—	—
	30	...	...	...	2¼	29	...	...	...	2	27	...	...	...	1½	27	...	...	...
	90	T.	...	4	2¼	85	T.	...	4	2	80	T.	...	4	1½	80	T.	...	4
	6	...	...	...	¾	6	.	...	...	½	6	...	...	...	½	6	...	...	...
	40	{ D.	9	1	2½	38	{ D.	7	1	2½	36	{ D.	7	1	2½	34	{ D.	7	1
		{ S.*	9	1			{ S.*	7	1			{ S.*	7	1			{ S.*	7	1
	7	T.	...	2	1¼	6½	T.	...	2	1¼	6	T.	...	2	1	5	T.	...	2
	2	...	...	...	½	2	...	...	...	½	2	...	...	...	½	2	...	...	...
	8	...	...	...	2	8	...	...	...	2	7	...	...	...	2	7	...	...	...
	—	—	—	—	—	—	—	—	—	—	—	—	—	—	—	—	—	—	—
	70	S.	6	6	2	54	S.	6	4	1¾	48	S.	6	4	1½	48	S.	6	4
	—	—	—	—	—	—	—	—	—	—	—	—	—	—	—	—	—	—	—
	45	T.	...	2	2	40	T.	...	2	2	36	T.	...	2	2	34	T.	...	2
	3	T.	...	2	¾	3	T.	...	2	¾	2	T.	...	2	¾	2	T.	...	2
	2	...	...	...	1½	1½	...	...	...	1	1½	...	...	...	1	1½	...	...	...
	1	...	...	...	½	1	...	...	...	—	*Marline*		—	—	—	—	—	—	—
	70	S.	6	2	1¾	54	...	...	...	1½	50	...	...	...	1½	48	...	...	...
	2½	D.	6	2	2	1½	D.	6	2	2	1½	D.	6	2	2	1½	D.	6	2
	2	...	...	...	1	2	...	...	...	¾	2	...	...	...	¾	2	...	...	...
	—	—	—	—	—	—	—	—	—	—	—	—	—	—	—	—	—	—	—
	65	S.	5	2	1½	60	S.	5	2	1½	55	S.	5	2	1½	55	S.	5	2
	2½	T.	...	2	1½	2½	T.	...	2	1½	2	T.	...	2	1½	2	T.	...	2
	—	—	—	—	—	—	—	—	—	—	—	—	—	—	—	—	—	—	—
	46	...	...	...	2½	42	...	...	...	2½	40	...	...	...	2	40	...	...	...
	2	...	...	...	¾	2	...	...	...	¾	2	...	...	...	¾	2	...	...	...
	70	S.	7	4	1½	66	S.	7	4	1½	60	S.	7	4	1¼	56	S.	7	4
	32	...	...	...	1½	28	...	...	...	1½	24	...	..	...	1¼	24	...	...	...
	44	S.	6	2	2	38	S.	6	2	2	36	S.	6	2	2	36	S.	6	2
	...	...	...	...	...	...	...	...	...	...	...	...	...	...	...	...	...	...	...
	—	—	—	—	—	—	—	—	—	—	—	—	—	—	—	—	—	—	—
	56	...	...	...	2½	50	...	...	...	2	46	...	...	...	1½	46	...	...	...
	5	T	...	2	¾	4½	T.	...	2	½	4	T.	...	2	½	4	T.	...	2

MAIN-ROYAL-YARD (continued), MIZEN-MAST, AND CROSS-JACK-YARD.	SHIPS. 1250 Tons. Size in Inches.	Length in Fathoms.	Blocks, &c. Species.	Sz. in In.	Number	1000 Tons. Size in Inches.	Length in Fathoms.	Blocks, &c. Species.	Sz. in In.	Number	800 Tons. Size in Inches.	Length in Fathoms.	Blocks, &c. Species.	Sz. in In.
Laniards .... *Marline*	—	—	—	—	—	—	—	—	—	—	—	—	—	—
Foot-ropes	1	8	...	...	...	1	7	...	...	...	1	[illegible]	...	...
Braces and Strapping	2	75	S.	5	2	2	70	S.	5	2	1½	66	S.	[illegible]
Lifts	2	29	T.	...	2	2	27	T.	...	2	2	24	T.	..
Parral-lashing	1	1	...	...	...	1	1	...	...	...	1	1	...	...
Clue-lines and Strapping	1	82	S.	4	2	1	78	S.	4	2	1	74	S.	4
Bowlines	1	80	S.	4	2	2	75	S.	4	2	1	70	S.	4
Sheets	2	80	...	...	...	2	76	...	...	...	2	70	...	...
Earings	½	1	...	...	...	½	1	...	...	...	½	1	...	...
Seizings .... *Marline*	—	—	—	—	—	—	—	—	—	—	—	—	—	—
MIZEN-MAST.														
Burton-pendants	5	6	T.	...	2	4½	6	T.	...	2	4	5	T.	...
Falls and Strapping	3	60	D.*	10	2	3	52	D.*	10	2	2½	45	D.*	8
			S.*	10	2			S.*	10	2			S.*	8
Seizings .... *Marline*	—	—	—	—	—	—	—	—	—	—	—	—	—	—
Shrouds	7	100	D. E.	10	12	6½	90	D. E.	9	12	6	76	D. E.	8
Seizings: Eye	1	18	...	...	...	1	18	...	...	...	1	12	...	...
Seizings: Throat	1	36	...	...	...	1	36	...	...	...	1	24	...	...
Seizings: End	¾	36	...	...	...	¾	36	...	...	...	¾	24	...	...
Laniards	¾	50	...	...	...	3	50	...	...	...	3	42	...	...
Ratlines	1¼	120	...	...	...	1¼	114	...	...	...	1	100	...	...
Stay	8	15	T.	...	1	7½	14	T.	...	1	7	14	T.	...
Seizings	1½	3	...	...	...	1¼	3	...	...	...	1¼	3	...	...
	¾	3	...	...	...	¾	3	...	...	...	¾	3	...	...
Laniards	3	5	...	...	...	3	5	...	...	...	2½	5	...	...
CROSS-JACK-YARD.														
Truss-pendant	5	6	S.	6	1	4½	6	S.	6	1	4½	5	S.	6
Fall	2	28	S.	...	...	2	25	...	...	...	2	23	...	...
Strap	2½	3	T.	...	1	2½	3	T.	...	1	2½	3	T.	...
Foot-ropes	3½	14	...	...	...	3	12	...	...	...	3	11	...	...
Laniard	3	1	...	...	...	3	1	...	...	...	2½	1	...	...
Stirrups	3	1½	T.	...	2	2½	1½	T.	...	2	2	1½	T.	...
Braces and Strapping	2½	75	S.	8	4	2½	70	S.	8	4	2½	65	S.	8
Strapping, quarter blocks ...	3½	3	D.	9	1	3½	3	D.	9	1	3	3	D.	8
Lashing	1¼	1	...	...	...	1	1	...	...	...	1	1	...	...
Seizings .... *Marline*	—	—	—	—	—	—	—	—	—	—	—	—	—	—
Lifts	3	52	...	...	...	2½	50	...	...	...	2½	45	...	...
Laniards	1¼	2	T.	...	2	1	2	T.	...	2	1	2	T.	...
Short-span	3	3	C.	9	2	3	3	C.	8	2	2½	3	C.	8
Seizings	¾	3	...	...	...	¾	3	...	...	...	¾	3	...	...
Mizen-stay-sail-stay	5	15	T.	...	1	5	14	T.	...	1	5	14	T.	...
Seizings	1¼	3	...	...	...	1¼	3	...	...	...	1	3	...	...
	½	3	...	...	...	½	3	...	...	...	½	3	...	...
Laniard	3	5	...	...	...	3	5	...	...	...	2½	5	...	...
Halliards	2½	45	S.	8	2	2½	40	S.	8	2	2½	38	S.	8
Sheets	3	25	S.	9	2	3	24	S.	9	2	2½	22	S.	8
Tack-lashing	1	2	...	...	...	1	2	...	...	...	1	1½	...	...

															BRIG.				
	600 Tons.				450 Tons.					300 Tons.					200 Tons.				
		Blocks, &c.					Blocks, &c.					Blocks, &c.					Blocks, &c.		
Inches.	Length in Fathoms.	Species.	Sz. in In.	Number	Size in Inches.	Length in Fathoms.	Species.	Sz. in In.	Number	Size in Inches.	Length in Fathoms.	Species.	Sz. in In.	Number	Size in Inches.	Length in Fathoms.	Species.	Sz. in In.	Number
	—	—	—	—	—	—	—	—	—	—	—	—	—	—	—	—	—	—	—
	6	…	…	…	1	5	…	…	…	1	5	…	…	…	1	5	…	…	…
	62	S.	5	2	1¼	58	S.	4	2	1	56	S.	4	2	1	54	S.	4	2
	22	T.	…	2	1½	22	T.	…	2	1½	21	T.	…	2	1½	21	T.	…	2
	1	…	…	…	¾	1	…	…	…	½	1	…	…	…	½	1	…	…	…
	70	S.	4	2	1	66	S.	4	2	1	60	S.	4	2	1	60	S.	4	2
	65	S.	4	2	¾	60	S.	4	2	¾	55	S.	4	2	¾	55	S.	4	2
	65	…	…	…	1½	58	…	…	…	1¼	48	…	…	…	1	48	…	…	…
	1	…	…	…	—	*Marline*		—	—	—	—	—	—	—	—	—	—	—	—
	—	—	—	—	—	—	—	—	—	—	—	—	—	—	—	—	—	—	—
	4½	T.	…	2	4	4	T.	…	2	3½	4	T.	…	2	…	…	…	…	…
	40	D.*	7	2	2	40	D.*	7	2	2	40	D.*	7	2	…	…	…	…	…
		S.*	7	2			S.*	7	2			S.*	7	2	…	…	…	…	…
	—	—	—	—	—	—	—	—	—	—	—	—	—	—	…	…	…	…	…
	64	D. E.	8	8	5½	60	D. E.	8	8	5	56	D. E.	8	8	…	…	…	…	…
	12	…	…	…	1	12	…	…	…	1	12	…	…	…	…	…	…	…	…
	24	…	…	…	1	24	…	…	…	1	24	…	…	…	…	…	…	…	…
	24	…	…	…	½	24	…	…	…	½	24	…	…	…	…	…	…	…	…
	36	…	…	…	2½	36	…	…	…	2½	36	…	…	…	…	…	…	…	…
	90	…	…	…	1	80	…	…	…	1	70	…	…	…	…	…	…	…	…
	13	T.	…	1	6	12	T.	…	1	6	12	T.	…	1	…	…	…	…	…
	3	…	…	…	1	3	…	…	…	¾	3	…	…	…	…	…	…	…	…
	3	…	…	…	½	3	…	…	…	½	2	…	…	…	…	…	…	…	…
	5	…	…	…	2	5	…	…	…	2	5	…	…	…	…	…	…	…	…
	5	S.	6	1	4	5	S.	6	1	3	5	S.	6	1	…	…	…	…	…
	21	…	…	…	2	20	…	…	…	2	18	…	…	…	…	…	…	…	…
	3	T.	…	1	2	3	T.	…	1	2	2½	T.	…	1	…	…	…	…	…
	10	…	…	…	2	9	…	…	…	2	8	…	…	…	…	…	…	…	…
	1	…	…	…	2	1	…	…	…	2	1	…	…	…	…	…	…	…	…
	…	…	…	…	…	…	…	…	…	…	…	…	…	…	…	…	…	…	…
	60	S.	6	4	2	55	S.	6	4	2	50	S.	6	4	…	…	…	…	…
	3	D.	8	1	3	2½	D.	8	1	2½	2	D.	8	1	…	…	…	…	…
	1	…	…	…	¾	1	…	…	…	¾	1	…	…	…	…	…	…	…	…
	—	—	—	—	—	—	—	—	—	—	—	—	—	—	…	…	…	…	…
	43	…	…	…	2½	40	…	…	…	2	36	…	…	…	…	…	…	…	…
	2	T.	…	2	¾	2	T.	…	2	¾	2	T.	…	2	…	…	…	…	…
	3	C.	8	2	2	2	C.	8	2	2	2	C.	6	2	…	…	…	…	…
	3	…	…	…	½	3	…	…	…	½	2	…	…	…	…	…	…	…	…
	13	T.	…	1	4½	12	T.	…	1	4½	12	T.	…	1	…	…	…	…	…
	3	…	…	…	¾	3	…	…	…	¾	3	…	…	…	…	…	…	…	…
	3	…	…	…	½	3	…	…	…	½	3	…	…	…	…	…	…	…	…
	5	…	…	…	2	5	…	…	…	2	4	…	…	…	…	…	…	…	…
	35	S.	6	2	2	33	S.	6	2	2	30	S.	6	2	…	…	…	…	…
	20	S.	8	2	2	18	S.	6	2	2	18	S.	6	2	…	…	…	…	…
	1½	…	…	…	¾	1	…	…	…	¾	1	…	…	…	…	…	…	…	…

CROSS-JACK-YARD (*continued*), MIZEN-TOP-MAST, AND MIZEN-TOP-SAIL-YARD.	SHIPS.													
	1250 Tons.					1000 Tons.					800 Tons.			
	Size in Inches.	Length in Fathoms.	*Blocks, &c.* Species.	Sz. in In.	Number	Size in Inches.	Length in Fathoms.	*Blocks, &c.* Species.	Sz. in In.	Number	Size in Inches.	Length in Fathoms.	*Blocks, &c.* Species.	Sz. in In.
Downhauller and Strapping .	2	22	S.	6	1	2	21	S.	6	1	2	20	S.	6
Seizings ....*Marline*	—	—	—	—	—	—	—	—	—	—	—	—	—	—
MIZEN- OP-MAST.														
Shrouds...........................	5	47	D. E.	8	8	5	45	D. E.	8	8	4½	42	D. E.	7
Seizings { Eye	1½	16	...	...	...	½	16	...	...	...	½	16	...	...
Seizings { Throat..............	¾	24	...	...	...	¾	24	...	...	...	¾	22	...	...
Seizings { End ......*Marline*	—	—	—	—	—	—	—	—	—	—	—	—	—	—
Laniards	2½	32	...	...	...	2½	32	...	...	...	2	28	...	...
Rat-lines	1	60	...	...	.	1	55	...	...	...	1	50	...	...
Backstays	5	60	D. E.	8	4	4½	55	D. E.	8	4	4½	52	D. E.	7
Seizings { Eye ....*Marline*	—	—	—	—	—	—	—	—	—	—	—	—	—	—
Seizings { Throat	¾	12	...	...	...	¾	12	...	...	...	¾	12	...	...
Seizings { End ......*Marline*	—	—	—	—	—	—	—	—	—	—	—	—	—	—
Laniards	2½	14	...	...	...	2½	14	...	...	...	2	14	...	..
Futtock-shrouds	4½	16	Pl.DE.	8	8	4½	15	Pl.DE.	8	8	4	14	Pl.DE.	7
Lashings	¾	12	...	...	...	¾	12	...	...	...	¾	12	...	...
Rat-lines	1	15	...	...	...	1	14	...	...	...	1	13	...	...
Stay	5	12	...	...	...	5	11	...	...	...	4½	10	...	...
Seizing	1	1½	T.	...	1	¾	1	T.	...	1	¾	1	T.	...
Laniard	1½	2	...	...	...	1½	2	...	...	...	1¼	2	...	...
MIZEN-TOP-SAIL-YARD.														
Tie (if not chain)	4½	17	S.I. bd.	12	1	4½	15	S.I. bd.	12	1	4	14	S.I. bd.	11
Halliards and Strapping .	2½	45	{ D. / S.*	8 / 8	1 / 1	2½	38	{ D. / S.*	8 / 8	1 / 1	2½	35	{ D. / S.*	8 / 8
Seizings ....*Marline*	—	—	—	—	—	—	—	—	—	—	—	—	—	—
Jackstays	2½	9	T.	...	2	2½	8	T.	...	2	2	8	T.	...
Laniards	¾	2	...	...	...	¾	2	...	...	...	¾	2	...	...
Foot-ropes	2	10	...	...	...	2	9½	...	...	...	2	9	...	...
Laniards ....*Marline*	—	—	—	—	—	—	—	—	—	—	—	—	...	...
Stirrups	2½	2	T.	...	2	2½	2	T.	...	2	2	2	T.	...
Flemish Horses	2	4	...	...	...	2	4	...	...	...	2	3½	...	...
Seizings ....*Marline*	—	—	—	—	—	—	—	—	—	—	—	—	—	—
Braces	2½	80	S.	8	4	2½	75	S.	8	4	2½	70	S.	8
Strapping	2	3	T.	...	4	2	3	T.	...	4	2	3	T.	...
Seizings ....*Marline*	—	—	—	—	—	—	—	—	—	—	—	—	—	—
Lifts	3¼	50	Sis.	9	2	3	45	Sis.	8	2	3	40	Sis.	8
Laniards	1	3	T.	...	2	1	3	T.	.	2	1	3	T.	...
Parral-rope	3	3	...	...	...	3	3	...	...	...	2½	3	...	...
Lashing	1	5	...	...	...	1	5	...	...	...	1	4	...	...
Clue-lines and Strapping ...	2	66	St.bd.	7	2	2	60	St.bd.	7	2	2	55	St.bd.	7
Seizings ....*Marline*	—	—	—	—	—	—	—	—	—	—	—	—	—	—
Bunt-lines and Strapping ...	2	52	S.	7	2	2	50	S.	7	2	2	48	S.	7
Span	2	1½	T.	...	2	2	1½	T.	...	2	2	1½	T.	...
Bow-lines and Strapping	2	44	S.	7	2	2	42	S.	7	2	2	38	S.	7
Bridles	2	2	T.	...	2	2	2	T.	...	2	2	2	T.	...
Seizings ....*Marline*	—	—	—	—	—	—	—	—	—	—	—	—	—	—
Reef-Tackles	2¼	42	...	...	...	2¼	40	...	...	...	2¼	36	...	...
Earings	1½	28	...	...	...	1½	28	...	...	...	1½	28	...	...

														BRIG.				
600 Tons.				450 Tons.					300 Tons.					200 Tons.				
Length in Fathoms.	Blocks, &c. Species.	Sz. in In.	Number	Size in Inches.	Length in Fathoms.	Blocks, &c. Species.	Sz. in In.	Number	Size in Inches.	Length in Fathoms.	Blocks, &c. Species.	Sz. in In.	Number	Size in Inches.	Length in Fathoms.	Blocks, &c. Species.	Sz. in In.	Number
19	S.	6	1	1½	18	S.	5	2	1½	18	S.	5	2	...	...	...	...	...
—	—	—	—	—	—	—	—	—	—	—	—	—	—	...	...	...	...	...
34	D. E.	7	6	3½	32	D. E.	6	6	3¼	28	D. E.	6	6	...	...	...	...	...
12	...	...	—	—		Marline	—	—	—	—	—	—	—	...	...	...	...	...
16	..	...	...	½	16	...	...	...	½	16	...	...	...	...	...	...	...	...
—	—	—	—	—	—	—	—	—	—	—	—	—	—	...	...	...	...	...
19	...	...	...	2	19	...	...	...	1½	19	...	...	...	...	...	...	...	...
45	...	...	...	¾	40	...	...	...	¾	35	...	...	...	...	...	...	...	...
48	D. E.	7	4	4	44	D. E.	6	4	3½	38	D. E.	6	4	...	...	...	...	...
—	—	—	—	—	—	—	—	—	—	—	—	—	—	...	...	...	...	...
12	...	...	...	½	12	...	...	...	½	12	...	...	...	...	...	...	...	...
—	—	—	—	—	—	—	—	—	—	—	—	—	—	...	...	...	...	...
14	...	...	...	1¾	14	...	...	...	1½	14	...	...	...	...	...	...	...	...
12	Pl.DE.	7	6	3½	10	Pl.DE.	6	6	3	8	Pl.DE.	6	6	...	...	...	...	...
12	...	...	..	½	10	...	...	...	½	10	...	...	...	...	...	...	...	...
12	...	...	...	¾	11	...	...	...	¾	10	...	...	...	...	...	...	...	...
9½	...	...	...	4	9	...	...	...	3½	8½	...	...	...	...	...	...	...	...
1	T.	...	1	½	1	T.	...	1	½	1	T.	...	1	...	...	...	...	...
2	...	...	...	1	2	...	...	...	1	2	...	...	...	...	...	...	...	...
12	S.I. bd.	11	1	3½	11	S.I. bd.	10	1	3	10	S.I. bd.	10	1	...	...	...	...	...
33	{ D.	8	1	2	31	{ D.	7	1	2	28	{ D.	7	1	...	...	...	...	...
	{ S.*	8	1			{ S.*	7	1			{ S.*	7	1	...	...	...	...	...
—	—	—	—	—	—	—	—	—	—	—	—	—	—	...	...	...	...	...
7	T.	...	2	1¾	6	T.	...	2	1½	6	T.	...	2	...	...	...	...	...
2	...	...	...	½	2	...	...	...	½	2	...	...	...	...	...	...	...	...
8	...	...	...	2	7	...	...	...	2	7	...	...	...	...	...	...	...	...
—	—	—	—	—	—	—	—	—	—	—	—	—	—	...	...	...	...	...
2	T.	...	2	1½	2	T.	...	2	1½	2	T.	...	2	...	...	...	...	...
3	...	...	...	1½	3	...	...	...	1½	3	...	...	...	...	...	...	...	...
—	—	—	—	—	—	—	—	—	—	—	—	—	—	...	...	...	...	...
64	S.	6	4	2	60	S.	6	4	1½	55	S.	6	4	...	...	...	...	...
2½	T.	...	4	1½	2	T.	...	4	1½	2	T.	...	4	...	...	...	...	...
—	—	—	—	—	—	—	—	—	—	—	—	—	—	...	...	...	...	...
36	Sis.	8	2	2½	32	Sis.	8	2	2½	28	Sis.	6	2	...	...	...	...	...
3	T.	...	2	¾	3	T.	...	2	¾	3	T.	...	2	...	...	...	...	...
2½	...	...	...	2	2	...	...	...	2	2	...	...	...	...	...	...	...	...
4	...	...	...	¾	3	...	...	...	¾	3	...	...	...	...	...	...	...	...
50	St.bd.	5	2	1½	46	St.bd.	5	2	1½	42	St.bd.	5	2	...	...	...	...	...
—	—	—	—	—	—	—	—	—	—	—	—	—	—	...	...	...	...	...
36	S.	7	1	1½	30	S.	5	1	1½	28	S.	5	1	...	...	...	...	...
1½	T.	...	2	1½	1	T.	...	2	1½	1	T.	...	2	...	...	...	...	...
36	S.	5	2	1½	32	S.	5	2	1½	28	S.	5	2	...	...	...	...	...
2	T.	...	2	1½	2	T.	...	2	1½	1½	T.	...	2	...	...	...	...	...
—	—	—	—	—	—	—	—	—	—	—	—	—	—	...	...	...	...	...
34	...	...	...	2	33	...	...	...	2	30	...	...	...	...	...	...	...	...
28	...	...	...	1	26	...	...	...	1	26	...	...	...	...	...	...	...	...

SHIPS.

MIZEN-TOP-SAIL-YARD (continued), MIZEN-TOP-GALLANT-MAST, MIZEN-TOP-GALLANT-YARD, MIZEN-ROYAL-YARD, AND SPANKER-BOOM.	1250 Tons.					1000 Tons.					800 Tons.			
	Size in Inches.	Length in Fathoms.	Species.	Sz.inIn.	Number	Size in Inches.	Length in Fathoms.	Species.	Sz.inIn.	Number	Size in Inches.	Length in Fathoms.	Species.	Sz.inIn
Sheets (if not chain)	3½	45	C.	7	2	3½	40	C.	7	2	3½	36	C.	
Strapping, quarter-blocks ...	3½	3	D.	8	2	3½	3	D.	8	2	3	3	D.	
Lashings......................	1	2	...	...	...	1	2	...	...	...	1	2	...	
Seizings............*Marline*	—	—	—			—	—	—			—	—		
MIZEN-TOP-GAL-MAST.														
Shrouds......................	3	44	T.	...	8	3	40	T.	...	8	3	36	T.	
Laniards......................	1½	8	...	...	...	1½	8	...	...	...	1¼	7	...	
Backstays	3	30	T.	...	2	3	28	T.	...	2	3	26	T.	
Seizings............*Marline*	—	—	—			—	—	—			—	—		
Laniards	1½	6	...	...	...	1½	6	...	...	...	1¼	6	...	
Stay	3	17	...	...	...	3	16	...	...	...	3	14		
Laniard	1½	1½	T.	...	1	1¼	1½	T.	...	1	1	1½	T.	
Royal-stay	2	20	...	...	...	2	18	...	...	...	1¾	16	...	
Backstays	2	34	T.	...	2	2	32	T.	...	2	2	30	T.	
Laniards	1	1½	...	...	...	1	1½	...	...	...	¾	1	...	
MIZEN-TOP-GAL-YARD.														
Halliards and Strapping......	2¼	34	S.*	6	2	2¼	32	S.*	6	2	2¼	30	S.*	
Jackstays	¾	7	T.	...	2	¾	6	T.	...	2	¾	5½	T.	
Laniards ....*Marline*	—	—	—			—	—	—			—	—		
Foot-ropes	1½	8	...	...	...	1½	7	...	...	...	1¼	7	...	
Laniards ....*Marline*	—	—	—			—	—	—			—	—		
Lifts	2	30	T.	...	2	2	28	T.	...	2	2	26	T.	
Laniards......................	1	2	T.	...	2	1	2	T.	...	2	1	2	T.	
Parral-lashing	1½	1	...	...	...	1½	1	...	...	...	1	1		
Clue-lines	1½	58	...	...	...	1½	55	...	...	...	1½	50	...	
Strapping, quarter-blocks ...	2	2	D.	4	2	2	2	D.	4	2	1½	2	D.	
Lashing	½	1	...	...	...	½	1	...	...	...	1½	1	...	
Seizings............*Marline*	—	—	—			—	—	—			—	—		
Bow-lines and Strapping......	1½	58	S.	5	2	1½	52	S.	5	2	1½	48	S.	
Bridles.......................	1½	2	T.	...	2	1½	2	T.	...	2	1½	1½	T.	
Seizings............*Marline*	—	—	—			—	—	—			—	—		
Sheets	2	46	...	...	...	2	44	...	...	...	2	42	...	
Earings	½	1½	...	...	...	½	1½	...	...	...	½	1		
MIZEN-ROYAL-YARD.														
Halliards.	2	34	...	...	...	2	33	...	...	...	1½	32	...	
Jackstays	½	5	T.	...	2	½	4	T.	...	2	½	4	T.	
Foot-ropes	1	6	...	...	...	1	5	...	...	...	1	5	...	
Braces and Strapping	1	52	S.	4	2	1	50	S.	4	2	1	46	S.	4
Lifts	1½	20	T.	...	2	1½	19	T.	...	2	1½	18	T.	
Parral-lashing	½	1	...	...	...	½	1	...	...	...	½	1		
Clue-lines and Strapping	1	60	S.	4	2	1	57	S.	4	2	1	52	S.	4
Bow-lines	1	50	T.	...	2	¾	48	T.	...	2	¾	44	T.	
Sheets	1	60	...	...	...	1	57				1	52	...	
Earings ....*Marline*	—	—				—	—				—	—		
Seizings ....*Marline*	—	—				—	—				—	—		
SPANKER-BOOM														
Topping-lifts	5	34	S.	15	2	4½	32	S.	13	2	4½	30	S.	13

															BRIG.				
	600 Tons.				450 Tons.					300 Tons.					200 Tons.				
		Blocks, &c.					*Blocks, &c.*					*Blocks, &c.*					*Blocks, &c.*		
Inches.	Length in Fathoms.	Species.	Sz. in In.	Number	Size in Inches.	Length in Fathoms.	Species.	Sz. in In.	Number	Size in Inches.	Length in Fathoms.	Species.	Sz. in In.	Number	Size in Inches.	Length in Fathoms.	Species.	Sz. in In.	Number
	34	C.	6	2	3	30	C.	6	2	2½	26	C.	5	2	...	...	...	...	...
	2½	D.	8	2	2½	2	D.	7	2	2½	2	D.	7	2	...	...	...	...	...
¾	2	...	...	...	¾	2	...	...	...	½	2	...	...	...	...	...	...	...	...
—	—	—	—	—	—	—	—	—	—	—	—	—	—	—	...	...	...	...	...
½	32	T.	...	8	2½	30	T.	...	8	2¼	28	T.	...	8	...	...	...	...	...
¼	7	...	...	...	1	6	...	...	...	1	6	...	...	...	...	...	...	...	...
½	24	T.	...	2	2	22	T.	...	2	2	21	T.	...	2	...	...	...	...	...
—	—	—	—	—	—	—	—	—	—	—	—	—	—	—	...	...	...	...	...
	6	...	...	...	1	5	...	...	...	1	5	...	...	...	...	...	...	...	...
½	13	...	...	...	2½	12	...	...	...	2	11	...	...	...	...	...	...	...	...
	1	T.	...	1	¾	1	T.	...	1	½	1	T.	...	1	...	...	...	...	...
½	15	...	...	...	1½	14	...	...	...	1½	12	...	...	...	...	...	...	...	...
½	28	T.	...	2	1¼	26	T.	...	2	1¼	25	T.	...	2	...	...	...	...	...
¾	1	...	...	...	½	1	...	...	...	½	1	...	...	...	...	...	...	...	...
	28	S.*	5	2	2	26	S.*	5	2	1½	24	S.*	5	2	...	...	...	...	...
¾	5	T.	...	2	½	4½	T.	...	2	½	4	T.	...	2	...	...	...	...	...
—	—	—	—	—	—	—	—	—	—	—	—	—	—	—	...	...	...	...	...
	6	...	...	...	1	6	...	...	...	1	5	...	...	...	...	...	...	...	...
—	—	—	—	—	—	—	—	—	—	—	—	—	—	—	...	...	...	...	...
	24	T.	...	2	1½	22	T.	...	2	1½	20	T.	...	2	...	...	...	...	...
¾	1	T.	...	2	¾	1	T.	...	2	¾	1	T.	...	2	...	...	...	...	...
	1	...	...	...	1	1	...	...	...	1	1	...	...	...	...	...	...	...	...
½	45	...	...	...	1½	42	...	...	...	1	40	...	...	...	...	...	...	...	...
½	1½	D.	4	2	1½	1½	D.	4	2	1½	1½	D.	4	2	...	...	...	...	...
½	1	...	...	...	—		*Marline*	—	—	—	—	—	—	—	...	...	...	...	...
—	—	—	—	—	—	—	—	—	—	—	—	—	—	—	...	...	...	...	...
½	46	S.	5	2	1	43	S.	4	2	1	40	S.	4	2	...	...	...	...	...
½	1½	T.	...	2	1	1½	T.	...	2	1	1½	T.	...	2	...	...	...	...	...
—	—	—	—	—	—	—	—	—	—	—	—	—	—	—	...	...	...	...	...
½	40	...	...	...	1½	38	...	...	...	1½	36	...	...	...	...	...	...	...	...
½	1	...	...	...	—		*Marline*	—	—	—	—	—	—	—	...	...	...	...	...
¼	30	...	...	...	1	28	...	...	...	1	26	...	...	...	...	...	...	...	...
½	4	T.	...	2	½	3½	T.	...	2	½	3½	T.	...	2	...	...	...	...	...
	5	...	...	...	1	4½	...	...	...	1	4½	...	...	...	...	...	...	...	...
¾	42	S.	4	2	¾	38	S.	4	2	¾	36	S.	4	2	...	...	...	...	...
¼	17	T.	...	2	1¼	16	T.	...	2	1¼	16	T.	...	2	...	...	...	...	...
½	1	...	...	...	½	1	...	...	...	½	1	...	...	...	...	...	...	...	...
	47	S.	4	2	1	44	S.	4	2	1	42	S.	4	2	...	...	...	...	...
¾	40	T.	...	2	¾	36	T.	...	2	¾	34	T.	...	2	...	...	...	...	...
	47	...	...	...	1	44	...	...	...	1	42	...	...	...	...	...	...	...	...
—	—	—	—	—	—	—	—	—	—	—	—	—	—	—	...	...	...	...	...
—	—	—	—	—	—	—	—	—	—	—	—	—	—	—	...	...	...	...	...
	27	S.	11	2	3½	25	S.	10	2	3	21	S.	9	2	4	40	S.	12	2

SPANKER-BOOM AND BOOM-MAIN-SAIL (*continued*), GAFF, AND NECESSARY ROPES.	SHIPS.														
	1250 Tons.					1000 Tons.					800 Tons.				
	Size in Inches.	Length in Fathoms.	*Blocks, &c.* Species.	Sz. in In.	Number	Size in Inches.	Length in Fathoms.	*Blocks, &c.* Species.	Sz. in In.	Number	Size in Inches.	Length in Fathoms.	*Blocks,* Species.	Sz. in In	
Span	5	4	...	...	...	4½	4	...	...	...	4½	4	...	..	
Falls and Strapping	3	50	D. S.*	9 9	2 2	3	45	D. S.*	9 9	2 2	3	43	D. S.*		
Seizings *Marline*	—	—	—	—	—	—	—	—	—	—	—	—	—	—	
Guy-pendants	3½	15	...	...	...	3½	14	...	...	...	3½	12	...	..	
Falls and Strapping	2½	52	D. S.*	8 8	2 2	2½	50	D. S.*	8 8	2 2	2	48	D. S.*		
Pendant-strap	...	...	...	...	...	...	...	...	...	...	...	...	...	..	
Reef-pendant	...	...	...	...	...	...	...	...	...	..	...	...	...	..	
Reef-tackles	...	...	...	...	...	...	...	...	...	...	...	...	...	..	
Seizings *Marline*	—	—	—	—	—	—	—	—	—	—	—	—	—	—	
Outhauller	3½	26	C.	7	1	3½	25	C.	7	1	3	24	C.		
Boom-sheet	3½	38	D.	11	2	3½	36	D.	11	2	3½	34	D.	1	
Strapping	3½	4½	T.	...	1	3½	4	T.	...	1	3½	3½	T.	..	
Seizings	¾	4	...	...	...	¾	4	...	...	...	¾	4	...	..	
GAFF.															
Throat Halliards	4	55	D. T.	12 ...	1 1	4	50	D. T.	12 ...	1 1	3½	45	D. T.	1 ..	
Peak Halliards & Strapping	4	66	DIbd S.	12 12	1 2	4	60	DIbd S.	12 12	1 2	3½	55	DIbd S.	1 1	
Seizings	½	4	...	...	...	½	4	...	...	...	½	3½	...	..	
Vang Pendants	3½	11	...	...	...	3½	10	...	...	...	3	10	...	..	
Falls and Strapping	2	30	D. S.*	7 7	2 2	2	28	D. S.*	7 7	2 2	2	25	D. S.*		
Seizings *Marline*	—	—	—	—	—	—	—	—	—	—	—	—	—	—	
Peak Downhauller	...	...	...	...	...	...	...	...	...	...	...	...	...	..	
Earings	1½	10	...	...	...	1½	8	...	...	...	1¼	8	...	..	
Lacing to Gaff	1¼	32	...	...	...	1¼	30	...	...	...	1¼	28	...	..	
Lacing to Mast	2½	8	...	...	...	2½	7	...	...	...	2	7	...	..	
Brails { Peak	2	38	S.	7	2	2	36	S.	7	2	2	34	S.		
Brails { Middle	2	38	D.	7	2	2	36	D.	7	2	2	34	D.		
Brails { Throat	2½	42	Tr.	8	2	2½	40	Tr.	8	2	2½	37	Tr.		
Brails { Hook	2	40	S.	7	2	2	38	S.	7	2	1½	35	S.		
Strapping	2	7½	...	...	...	2	7½	...	...	...	2	7	...	..	
Seizings *Marline*	—	—	—	—	—	—	—	—	—	—	—	—	—	—	
Tack-tackle and Strapping	2	24	D.* S.*	6 6	1 1	2	22	D.* S.*	6 6	1 1	2	20	D.* S.*		
Seizings *Marline*	—	—	—	—	—	—	—	—	—	—	—	—	—	—	
NECESSARY ROPES.															
Hawsers	6	112	...	...	1	6	112	...	...	1	6	112	...	..	
	7	112	...	...	2	7	112	...	...	2	7	112	...	..	
	10	112	...	...	1	10	112	...	...	1	9	112	...	..	
Messenger	11	45	...	...	...	10½	42	...	...	...	10	40	...	..	
Lashing	5	5	...	...	...	4½	5	...	...	...	4½	5	...	..	
Cat-falls	4½	90	TrI.bd	17	2	4	80	TrI.bd	16	2	4	75	TrI.bd	1	

															BRIG.				
	600 Tons.				450 Tons.					300 Tons.					200 Tons.				
		Blocks, &c.					Blocks, &c.					Blocks, &c.					Blocks, &c.		
Inches.	Length in Fathoms.	Species.	Sz. in In.	Number	Size in Inches.	Length in Fathoms.	Species.	Sz. in In.	Number	Size in Inches.	Length in Fathoms.	Species.	Sz. in In.	Number	Size in Inches.	Length in Fathoms.	Species.	Sz. in In.	Number
	4	...	...	...	$3\frac{1}{2}$	4	...	...	...	3	4	...	...	...	4	4	...	...	...
$\frac{1}{2}$	40	D.	8	2	2	38	D.	7	2	2	38	D.	7	2	2	40	D.	7	2
		S.*	8	2			S.*	7	2			S.*	7	2			S.*	7	2
-	—	—	—	—	—	—	—	—	—	—	—	—	—	—	—	—	—	—	—
	12	...	...	...	3	10	...	...	—	3	10	...	...	...	4	5	*	...	1
																	T.	...	1
	44	D.	7	2	2	40	D.	7	2	$1\frac{1}{2}$	36	D.	5	2	2	45	D.*	7	2
		S.*	7	2			S.*	7	2			S.*	5	2			S.*	7	2
.	...	...	...	...	...	...	...	...	...	...	...	...	...	...	4	2	T.	...	1
.	...	...	...	...	...	...	...	...	...	...	...	...	...	...	$3\frac{1}{2}$	15	...	...	...
.	...	...	...	...	...	...	...	...	...	...	...	...	...	...	2	18	D.*	7	1
																	S.*	7	1
-	—	—	—	—	—	—	—	—	—	—	—	—	—	—	—	—	—	—	—
	22	C.	6	1	$2\frac{1}{2}$	20	C.	5	1	2	20	C.	5	1	$2\frac{1}{2}$	24	C.	7	1
	30	D.	10	1	3	27	D.	10	1	$2\frac{1}{2}$	25	D.	8	1	3	50	D.	10	4
		S.	10	1			S.	10	1			S.	8	1					
	3	T.	...	1	3	3	T.	...	1	$2\frac{1}{2}$	$2\frac{1}{2}$	T.	...	1	3	6	T.	...	2
$\frac{1}{2}$	4	...	...	..	$\frac{1}{2}$	3	...	...	...	$\frac{1}{2}$	$2\frac{1}{2}$	...	...	...	$\frac{3}{4}$	12	...	...	...
	43	D.	9	1	$2\frac{1}{2}$	36	D.	9	1	$2\frac{1}{2}$	30	S.	9	1	$2\frac{1}{2}$	32	D.I. bd	9	1
		T.	...	1			T.	...	1			T.	...	1					
	50	DIbd	10	1	3	45	DIbd	10	1	$2\frac{1}{2}$	40	DIbd	10	1	$2\frac{1}{2}$	46	S. I. bd	9	4
		S.	10	2			S.	10	2			S.	10	2					
$\frac{1}{2}$	3	...	...	...	$\frac{1}{2}$	3	...	...	...	$\frac{1}{2}$	3	...	...	...	...	...	...	...	...
$\frac{1}{2}$	9	...	...	...	$2\frac{1}{2}$	8	...	...	...	$2\frac{1}{2}$	8	...	...	...	...	...	...	...	...
	20	D.	7	2	2	18	D.	7	2	2	16	D.	7	2	...	...	...	...	...
		S.*	7	2			S.*	7	2			S.*	7	2					
-	—	—	—	—	—	—	—	—	—	—	—	—	—	—	—	—	—	—	—
.	...	...	...	...	...	...	...	...	...	...	...	...	...	...	$1\frac{1}{2}$	40	S.	6	2
$\frac{1}{4}$	8	...	...	...	1	7	...	...	...	1	7	...	...	...	$1\frac{1}{2}$	8	...	...	...
	26	...	...	...	1	25	...	...	...	1	24	...	...	...	$1\frac{1}{2}$	25	...	...	..
	6	...	...	...	2	6	...	...	...	2	6	...	...	...	$2\frac{1}{2}$	7	...	...	...
	30	S.	7	2	$1\frac{1}{2}$	26	S.	6	2	$1\frac{1}{2}$	24	S.	6	2	...	...	...	...	...
	30	D.	7	2	$1\frac{1}{2}$	26	D.	6	2	$1\frac{1}{2}$	24	D.	6	2	...	...	...	...	...
	33	Tr.	7	2	2	30	Tr.	7	2	2	28	Tr.	7	2	$2\frac{1}{2}$	40	C.	6	2
$\frac{1}{2}$	30	S.	6	2	$1\frac{1}{2}$	28	S.	6	2	$1\frac{1}{2}$	25	S.	6	2	...	...	...	...	...
	7	...	...	...	$1\frac{1}{2}$	7	...	...	...	$1\frac{1}{2}$	7	...	...	...	$2\frac{1}{2}$	2	...	...	...
-	—	—	—	—	—	—	—	—	—	—	—	—	—	—	—	—	—	—	—
	18	D.*	6	1	$1\frac{1}{2}$	16	D.*	5	1	$1\frac{1}{2}$	12	D.*	5	1	2	8	D.*	6	1
		S.*	6	1			S.*	5	1			S.*	5	1			S.*	6	1
-	—	—	—	—	—	—	—	—	—	—	—	—	—	—	—	—	—	—	—
$\frac{1}{2}$	112	...	...	1	5	112	...	...	1	5	112	...	...	1	4	112	...	...	1
$\frac{1}{2}$	112	...	...	2	6	112	...	...	2	6	112	...	...	2	5	112	...	...	2
$\frac{1}{2}$	112	...	...	1	8	112	...	...	1	$7\frac{1}{2}$	112	...	...	1	6	112	...	...	1
	36	...	...	...	$7\frac{1}{2}$	34	...	...	...	7	33	...	...	...	$6\frac{1}{2}$	32	...	...	...
	5	...	...	...	4	5	...	...	...	$3\frac{1}{2}$	5	...	...	...	3	5	...	...	...
$\frac{1}{2}$	70	Tr I.bd	14	2	3	65	Tr I.bd	12	2	$2\frac{1}{2}$	60	Tr I.bd	12	2	2	46	Tr I.bd	12	2

NECESSARY ROPES *(continued)*.	SHIPS. 1250 Tons. Size in Inches.	Length in Fathoms.	Blocks, &c. Species.	Sz. in In.	Number	1000 Tons. Size in Inches.	Length in Fathoms.	Blocks, &c. Species.	Sz. in In.	Number	800 Tons. Size in Inches.	Length in Fathoms.	Blocks, &c. Species.
Cables.													
Stream Cable.													
Fish-pendant	6	7½	T. Hook	... ...	2 1	6	7	T. Hook	... ...	2 1	5½	7	T. Hook
Fall	3½	33	D.* S.*	12 12	1 1	3½	30	D.* S.*	12 12	1 1	3	28	D.* S.*
Strapping	3½	3	...	...	...	3½	3	...	...	...	3	3	...
Seizings	1	4	...	...	...	1	4	...	...	...	1	4	...
Cat-head Stoppers	6	10	...	...	...	5½	10	...	...	...	5	10	...
Shank Painters	6	10	...	...	...	5½	10	...	...	...	5	10	...
Deck Stoppers	9	14	T.	...	6	9	13	T.	...	6	8	13	T.
Lashings	4	10	...	...	...	4	9	...	...	...	3½	9	...
Laniards	4	18	...	...	...	3½	18	...	...	...	3	18	...
Bitt Stoppers	5	7	...	...	...	5	7	...	...	...	4½	7	...
Buoy-ropes	7	40	...	...	...	6	40	...	...	...	6	40	...
Junk for Nippers...... ½ Cwt.	—	—	—	—	—	—	—	—	—	—	—	—	—
Fore Jeers and Strapping	6	85	Tr. D.	18 18	1 1	5½	75	Tr. D.	16 16	1 1	5	70	D.
Lashing	2½	5	...	...	...	2	4	...	...	...	2	4	...
Seizings	1½	8	...	...	...	1½	8	...	...	...	1¼	8	...
Main Jeers and Strapping	6	95	Tr. D.	18 18	1 1	5½	85	Tr. D.	16 16	1 1	5	76	D.
Lashing	2½	5	...	...	...	2	4	...	...	...	2	4	...
Seizings	1½	8	...	...	...	1½	8	...	...	...	1¼	8	...
Fore-top-tackle-pendant	7½	18	T.	...	1	7	17	T.	...	1	6½	15	T.
Fall	3½	70	TrIbd D.Ibd	11 11	1 1	3	65	TrIbd D.Ibd	10 10	1 1	3	60	TrIbd D.Ibd
Main-top-tackle-pendant	7½	20	...	...	...	7	19	...	...	...	6½	17	...
Fall	3½	75	TrIbd D.Ibd	11 11	1 1	3	70	TrIbd D.Ibd	10 10	1 1	3	60	TrIbd D.Ibd
Fore-yard-tackle-pendant	6½	5	*	...	1	5	5	*	...	1	4½	4½	*
Fall and Strapping	3	50	D. S.*	10 10	1 1	3	45	D. S.*	10 10	1 1	2½	40	D. S.*
Seizings	¾	5	...	...	...	¾	5	...	...	...	¾	4	...
Main-yard-tackle-pendant	6½	5	*	...	1	5	5	*	...	1	4½	5	*
Fall and Strapping	3	56	D. S.*	10 10	1 1	3	50	D. S.*	10 10	1 1	2½	46	D. S.*
Seizings	¾	5	...	...	...	¾	5	...	...	...	¾	4	...
Fore-stay-tackle-pendant	6½	6	*	...	1	5	6	*	...	1	4½	5	*
Fall and Strapping	3	50	D. S.*	10 10	1 1	3	45	D. S.*	10 10	1 1	2½	40	D. S.*
Seizings	¾	5	...	...	...	¾	5	...	...	...	¾	4	...
Span	6	6	...	...	...	5½	6	...	...	...	5	5	...
Main-stay-tackle-pendant	6½	6½	*	...	1	5	6½	*	...	1	4½	5½	*
Fall and Strapping	3	50	D. S.*	10 10	1 1	3	45	D. S.*	10 10	1 1	2½	40	D. S.*
Seizings	¾	5	...	...	...	¾	5	...	...	...	¾	4	...
Quarter-davit Falls & Straps	3½	120	D.*	12	4	3	120	D.*	10	4	3	110	D.*
Stern-davit Falls & Straps	3	40	S.*	10	2	3	38	S.*	10	2	2½	35	S.*
Seizings .... *Marline*	—	—	—	—	—	—	—	—	—	—	—	—	—
Signal Halliards	...	200	...	...	...	...	200	...	...	...	...	180	...

600 Tons.				450 Tons.					300 Tons.					BRIG. 200 Tons.				
Length in Fathoms.	Blocks, &c. Species.	Sz. in In.	Number	Size in Inches.	Length in Fathoms.	Blocks, &c. Species.	Sz. in In.	Number	Size in Inches.	Length in Fathoms.	Blocks, &c. Species.	Sz. in In.	Number	Size in Inches.	Length in Fathoms.	Blocks, &c. Species.	Sz. in In.	Number
6	T. Hook	... ...	2 1	5	6	T. Hook	... ...	2 1	4½	5	T. Hook	... ...	2 1	4½	5	T. Hook	... ...	2 1
25	D.* S.*	10 10	1 1	2½	23	D.* S.*	9 9	1 1	2½	22	D.* S.*	9 9	1 1	2½	22	D.* S.*	9 9	1 1
2½	...	...	...	3	2½	...	...	...	2½	3	...	...	...	2½	2½	...	...	...
4	...	...	...	¾	4	...	...	...	¾	...	. .	...	...	½	4	...	...	...
9	...	...	...	4½	9	...	...	...	4	9	...	...	...	4	8	...	...	...
9	...	...	...	4½	9	...	...	...	4	9	...	...	...	4	8	...	...	...
13	T.	...	6	7	13	T.	...	6	6	12	T.	...	6	5	10	T.	...	6
9	...	...	...	2½	9	...	...	...	2½	8	...	...	...	2½	8	...	...	...
16	...	...	...	2½	15	...	...	...	2½	15	...	...	...	2½	14	...	...	...
—	*None*	—	—	—	—	—	—	—	—	—	—	—	—	—	—	—	—	—
40	...	...	...	5	35	...	...	...	4	30	...	...	...	4	30	...	...	...
—	—	—	—	—	—	—	—	—	—	—	—	—	—	—	—	—	—	—
...	...	...	...	...	...	...	...	...	...	...	...	...	...	...	...	...	...	...
...	...	...	...	...	...	...	...	...	...	...	...	...	...	...	...	...	...	...
...	...	...	...	...	...	...	...	...	...	...	...	...	...	...	...	...	...	...
...	...	...	...	...	...	...	...	...	...	...	...	...	...	...	...	...	...	...
...	...	...	...	...	...	...	...	...	...	...	...	...	...	...	...	...	...	...
...	...	...	...	...	...	...	...	...	...	...	...	...	...	...	...	...	...	...
14	T.	...	1	5½	13	T.	...	1	5½	13	T.	...	1	5	12	T.	...	1
56	D. I.bd	9	2	2½	54	D. I.bd	9	2	2½	50	D. I.bd	9	2	2	48	D. I.bd	8	2
16	...	...	...	5½	15	...	...	...	5½	14	...	...	...	5	13	...	...	...
60	D.I. bd	9	2	2½	58	D. I.bd	9	2	2½	56	D. I.bd	9	2	2	52	D. I.bd	8	2
4½	*	...	1	4	4	*	...	1	3½	4	*	...	1	3½	4	*	...	1
38	D. S.*	9 9	1 1	2½	36	D. S.*	9 9	1 1	2	34	D. S.*	8 8	1 1	2	36	D. S.*	8 8	1 1
4	...	...	...	½	4	...	...	...	½	4	...	...	...	½	4	...	...	...
4½	*	...	1	4	4	*	...	1	3½	4	*	...	1	3½	4	*	...	1
45	D. S.*	9 9	1 1	2½	40	D. S.*	9 9	1 1	2	38	D. S.*	8 8	1 1	2	40	D. S.*	8 8	1 1
4	...	...	...	½	4	...	...	...	½	4	...	...	...	½	4	...	...	...
5	*	...	1	4	5	*	...	1	3½	5	*	...	1	3½	5	*	...	1
38	D. S.*	9 9	1 1	2½	36	D. S.*	9 9	1 1	2	34	D. S.*	8 8	1 1	2	36	D. S.*	8 8	1 1
4	...	...	...	½	4	...	...	...	1½	4	...	...	...	½	4	...	...	...
5	...	...	...	4	5	...	...	...	3½	5	...	...	...	3½	5	...	...	...
5½	*	...	1	4	5½	*	...	1	3½	5½	*	...	1	3½	5½	*	...	1
38	D. S.*	9 9	1 1	2½	36	D. S.*	9 9	1 1	2	34	D. S.*	8 8	1 1	2	36	D. S.*	8 8	1 1
4	...	...	...	½	4	...	...	...	½	4	...	...	...	½	4	...	...	...
100	D.*	9	4	2½	95	D.*	9	4	2	80	S.*	7	4	2	80	S.*	7	4
33	S.*	9	2	2	30	S.*	7	2	2	30	S.*	7	2	2	28	S.*	7	2
—	—	—	—	—	—	—	—	—	—	—	—	—	—	—	—	—	—	—
170	...	...	...	...	160	...	...	...	...	150	...	...	...	...	150	...	...	...

SIZE AND DIMENSIONS OF THE RIGGING FOR

FORE-AND-AFT SCHOONERS.

	120 to 130 Tons							160 Tons							200 Tons						
	Size in Inches.	Length in Fms.	Blocks, &c.	Inches	Number	Hooks	Thimbles	Size in Inches.	Length in Fms.	Blocks, &c.	Inches	Number	Hooks	Thimbles	Size in Inches.	Length in Fms.	Blocks, &c.	Inches	Number	Hooks	Thimbles
BOWSPRIT.																					
Gammoning	...	...	Iron Clamp	...	...	...	...	...	...	Iron Clamp	...	...	...	...	...	...	Iron Clamp	...	...	...	...
Shrouds	$\frac{5}{16}$	6	Chain	...	...	...	...	$\frac{5}{16}$	7	Chain	...	...	...	...	$\frac{5}{8}$	8	Chain	...	...	...	...
Bobstays	$\frac{9}{16}$	4	Chain	...	...	...	...	$\frac{9}{16}$	5	Chain	...	...	...	...	$\frac{9}{16}$	$5\frac{1}{2}$	Chain	...	...	...	...
JIB-BOOM.																					
Jib-stay	$4\frac{1}{4}$	17	.....	7	2			$4\frac{3}{4}$	$19\frac{1}{2}$	.....	7	2			5	23	.....	7	2		
Purchase	2	16	D.I.B.	7	2	2		2	16	D.I.B.	7	2	2		$2\frac{1}{4}$	16	D.I.B.	7	2	2	
Guys	$4\frac{1}{4}$	13	Single C.	6	2			$4\frac{3}{4}$	15	Single C.	7	2			5	19	Single C.	7	2		
Runners	3	$4\frac{1}{2}$						$3\frac{1}{2}$	$4\frac{1}{2}$						$3\frac{3}{4}$	$4\frac{1}{2}$					
Falls	2	12	{ S.I.B. / Fiddle	6 / 10	2 / 2		2	$2\frac{1}{4}$	14	{ S.I.B. / Fiddle	7 / 11	2 / 2		2	$2\frac{1}{4}$	14	{ S.I.B. / Fiddle	7 / 12	2 / 2		2
Martingale	$\frac{3}{8}$	3	Chain					$\frac{7}{8}$	$3\frac{3}{4}$	Chain					$\frac{1}{16}$	$4\frac{1}{2}$	Chain				
Back ropes	$3\frac{1}{4}$	$3\frac{1}{2}$	{ Double / S.I.B.	6 / 6	2 / 2			$4\frac{1}{4}$	$3\frac{1}{2}$	{ Double / S.I.B.	7 / 7	2 / 2			$4\frac{1}{2}$	5	{ Double / S.I.B.	7 / 7	2 / 2		
Falls	2	21	.....					$2\frac{1}{4}$	19	.....					$2\frac{1}{4}$	20	.....				
Foot-ropes	$2\frac{1}{4}$	7						$2\frac{1}{2}$	8						$2\frac{1}{2}$	$10\frac{1}{2}$					
Heel-rope	$2\frac{1}{4}$	10	S.I.B.	7	1		1	3	$10\frac{1}{2}$	S.I.B.	8	1		1	3	14	S.I.B.	9	1		1
Jib Halliards	2	31	Single	7	2		1	$2\frac{1}{4}$	37	Single	7	2		1	$2\frac{1}{2}$	43	Single	8	2		1
Tack	3	4	Traveller					$3\frac{1}{2}$	4	Traveller					$3\frac{3}{4}$	$6\frac{1}{2}$	Traveller				
Downhaul	$1\frac{3}{4}$	20	Single	6	1		1	2	20	Single	6	1		1	$2\frac{1}{4}$	24	Single	6	1		1
Outhaul	$2\frac{1}{4}$	10	Single	7	1		1	$2\frac{1}{2}$	10	Single	7	1		1	$2\frac{1}{2}$	$11\frac{1}{2}$	Single	9	1		1
Sheet Pendants	$3\frac{1}{4}$	4	Single	7	2			4	4	Single	7	2		1	$4\frac{1}{2}$	$4\frac{1}{2}$	Single	8	1		1
Sheets	$2\frac{1}{4}$	16	.....		2		2	$2\frac{1}{2}$	16	.....		2		2	$2\frac{1}{2}$	18	.....		2		2

SIZE AND DIMENSIONS OF THE RIGGING FOR FORE-AND-AFT SCHOONERS.

120 to 130 Tons.

	Size in Inches.	Length in Fms.	*Blocks, &c.*	Inches.	Number.	Hooks.	Thimbles
Jib-Boom *(continued).*							
Jib Top-sail Halliards*	...	...	......	...	...	...	...
Tack	1½	24	......	...	...	...	...
Sheets	2	18	......	...	...	...	...
FORE-MAST.							
Shrouds and Pendants	5¼	59	Dead-Eyes	7	6	...	...
			Single C.	7	2	...	...
Ratlines	9-thr	46	......	...	...	...	...
Runners of Tackles	4¼	6	......	...	...	2	2
Falls	2¼	14	Double	7	2	...	...
			S. I. B.	7	2	...	...
Fore-stay	7	12	......	...	...	...	...
Laniard	2	8	......	...	...	...	...
Storm-stay	3¼	10	......	...	...	...	...
Laniard	1¾	6	......	...	...	...	...
Lacing	1¾	14	......	...	...	...	...
Halliard	2¼	26	S. I. B.	7	2	...	...
Tack	2¾	2	......	...	...	1	1
Fall	1¾	8	D. I. B.	6	1	1	1
			S. I. B.	6	1	...	...
Downhaul	1¾	13	Single	6	1	...	...
Sheets	2¼	34	Double	7	2	...	...
			D. I. B.	7	2	...	...
FORE-YARD.							
Square-sail Halliards	2	35	D. I. B.	6	2	...	...
Jack-stay	2½	7	Bull's-Eye	...	...	1	1
Laniard	1	4	......	...	...	...	...
Braces	1¾	104	S. I. B.	5	2	4	...

160 Tons.

	Size in Inches.	Length in Fms.	*Blocks, &c.*	Inches.	Number.	Hooks.	Thimbles
Jib-Boom *(continued).*							
Jib Top-sail Halliards*	...	...	......	...	...	...	...
Tack	1½	25	......	...	...	...	...
Sheets	2	20	......	...	...	...	...
FORE-MAST.							
Shrouds and Pendants	6	63	Dead-Eyes	7½	6	...	...
			Single C.	8	2	...	...
Ratlines	9-thr	50	......	...	...	...	...
Runners of Tackles	4½	8½	......	...	...	2	2
Falls	2½	15	Double	7	2	...	...
			S. I. B.	7	2	...	...
Fore-stay	8½	13	......	...	...	...	...
Laniard	2	8	......	...	...	...	...
Storm-stay	4¼	10	......	...	...	...	...
Laniard	2	7	......	...	...	...	...
Lacing	2	15	......	...	...	...	...
Halliard	2½	29	S. I. B.	8	2	...	...
Tack	3¼	2	......	...	...	1	1
Fall	2	8½	D. I. B.	7	1	1	1
			S. I. B.	7	1	...	...
Downhaul	2	14½	Single	7	1	...	...
Sheets	2½	38	Double	8	2	...	...
			D. I. B.	8	2	...	...
FORE-YARD.							
Square-sail Halliards	2	38	D. I. B.	7	2	...	...
Jack-stay	3	7½	Bull's-Eye	...	...	1	1
Laniard	1	4	......	...	...	...	...
Braces	2	116	S. I. B.	5	2	4	...

200 Tons.

	Size in Inches.	Leugth in Fms.	*Blocks, &c.*	Inches.	Number.	Hooks.	Thimbles
Jib-Boom *(continued).*							
Jib Top-sail Halliards*	...	...	......	...	...	...	...
Tack	1¾	30	......	...	...	...	...
Sheets	2¼	25	......	...	...	...	...
FORE-MAST.							
Shrouds and Pendants	6¼	70	Dead-Eyes	8	6	...	...
			Single C.	8	2	...	...
Ratlines	9-thr	55	......	...	...	...	...
Runners of Tackles	4¾	10	......	...	...	2	2
Falls	2½	16	Double	8	2	...	...
			S. I. B.	8	2	...	...
Fore-stay	9	15½	......	...	...	...	...
Laniard	2½	8	......	...	...	...	...
Storm-stay	4¾	12	......	...	...	...	...
Laniard	2	7	......	...	...	...	...
Lacing	2¼	20	......	...	...	...	...
Halliard	2¾	34	S. I. B.	9	2	...	...
Tack	3¾	2	......	...	...	1	1
Fall	2¼	9	D. I. B.	7	1	1	1
			S. I. B.	7	1	...	...
Downhaul	2¼	18	Single	7	1	...	...
Sheets	2¾	40	Double	9	2	...	...
			D. I. B.	9	2	...	...
FORE-YARD.							
Square-sail Halliards	2½	40	D. I. B.	8	2	...	...
Jack-stay	3½	8½	Bull's-Eye	...	...	1	1
Laniard	1	4	......	...	...	...	...
Braces	2¼	126	S. I. B.	6	2	4	...

* Square-sail Halliards always used.

FORE-YARD (*continued*).																					
Lifts	2	36	......	...	...	...	...	2	40	......	...	...	...	...	2½	42	......	...	...	...	...
Yard-ropes	2¾	42	Double	7	2	...	...	3	47	Double	8	2	...	...	3½	50	Double	9	2	...	...
TOP-SAIL-YARD.																					
Square Top-sail Sheets	2	24	Double	6	1	...	...	2¼	35	Double	7	1	...	...	2½	40	Double	7	1	...	...
Halliards	2½	24	......	...	...	...	...	2¾	29	......	...	...	...	...	3	30	......	...	...	...	...
FORE-TOP-MAST.																					
Shrouds	2¾	18	......	...	...	...	4	3	20	......	...	...	...	4	3¼	24	......	...	...	...	4
Stay	2¾	21	......	...	...	...	...	3	24	......	...	...	...	...	3¼	29	......	...	...	...	...
Tackle	1½	5	Double	5	1	...	...	1¾	6	Double	6	1	...	...	1¾	6	Double	6	1	...	...
			S. I. B.	5	1	...	...			S. I. B.	6	1	...	...			S. I. B.	6	1	...	...
Backstays	2¾	23	......	...	...	...	2	3	27	......	...	...	...	2	3¼	30	......	...	...	...	2
Tackle	1½	12	D. I. B.	5	4	...	2	1¾	12	D. I. B.	6	4	...	...	1¾	12	D. I. B.	6	4	...	...
Mast-rope	2½	16	......	...	...	...	...	2½	17	......	...	...	...	...	2¾	19	......	...	...	...	...
GAFF FORE-SAIL.																					
Throat Halliards	3	40	D. I. B.	8	2	...	...	3½	45	D. I. B.	9	2	...	...	3¾	50	D. I. B.	10	2	...	...
Tricing Line	1¾	22	Single	6	2	2	...	2	24	Single	7	2	2	...	2	26	Single	7	2	2	...
Peak Halliards	3	34½	S. I. B.	8	3	...	...	3½	50	S. I. B.	9	5	...	...	3¾	52	S. I. B.	10	5	...	...
Purchase	...	...	......	...	...	...	...	1¾	24	S. I. B.	6	1	...	...	2	25	S. I. B.	7	1	...	...
										Double	6	1	...	...			Double	7	1	...	...
Downhaul	1¾	21	Single	6	1	...	...	1¾	24	Single	6	1	...	...	1¾	26	Single	6	1	...	...
Fore-sheets	2½	44	D. I. B.	7	2	...	...	2¾	60	D. I. B.	8	2	...	...	3	70	D. I. B.	9	2	...	...
			Double	7	2	...	...			Double	8	2	...	...			Double	9	2	...	...
FORE-GAFF-TOP-SAIL.																					
Halliards	2½	23	Traveller	...	...	...	...	2¾	27½	Traveller	...	...	...	...	3	29	Traveller	...	...	...	...
Sheet	2	15½	Single	6	1	...	...	2¼	18	Single	7	1	...	...	2½	21	Single	7	1	...	...
Tack	2	5½	......	...	...	1	1	2¼	6½	......	...	...	1	1	2½	8	......	...	...	1	1
Tackle	1½	6	Double	5	1	...	...	1¾	6	Double	6	1	...	...	1¾	6	Double	6	1	...	...
			S. I. B.	5	1	...	...			S. I. B.	6	1	...	...			S. I. B.	6	1	...	...
Downhaul	1½	15	Single	5	1	...	...	1½	17	Single	5	1	...	...	1½	20	Single	5	1	...	...
MAIN-MAST.																					
Main Shrouds	5¼	32	Dead-Eyes	7	4	...	...	6	35	Dead-Eyes	7½	4	...	...	6½	40	Dead-Eyes	8	4	...	...

SIZE AND DIMENSIONS OF THE RIGGING FOR FORE-AND-AFT SCHOONERS.

Main-Mast (*continued.*)	120 to 130 Tons.							160 Tons.							200 Tons.						
	Size in Inches.	Length in Fms.	*Blocks, &c.*	Inches.	Number.	Hooks.	Thimbles.	Size in Inches.	Length in Fms.	*Blocks, &c.*	Inches.	Number.	Hooks.	Thimbles.	Size in Inches.	Length in Fms.	*Blocks, &c.*	Inches.	Number.	Hooks.	Thimbles.
Pendants	4¼	11	Single C.	7	2	...	...	4¾	12	Single C.	8	2	...	...	5	15	Single C.	8	2	...	...
Runners	3¼	7½	......	...	...	2	...	3½	9	......	...	...	2	...	4	9	......	...	...	2	...
Falls	2	13	{ Double	6	2	...	...	2¼	14	{ Double	7	2	...	...	2½	14	{ Double	8	2	...	...
			{ S. I. B.	6	2	...	...			{ S. I. B.	7	2	...	...			{ S. I. B.	8	2	...	...
Jumper-stays	5¼	18½	S. I. B. C.	7	2	...	...	6	22	S. I. B. C.	9	2	...	...	6¼	26	S. I. B. C.	11	2	...	...
Runners	3¾	4½	......	...	...	2	...	4¼	4½	......	...	...	2	...	4½	5	......	...	...	2	...
Tackles	2	19	{ D. I. B.	7	2	...	...	2¼	21	D. I. B.	8	4	...	...	2¾	22	D. I. B.	9	4	...	...
			{ S. I. B.	7	2	...	...														
BOOM-MAIN-SAIL.																					
Main Halliards	3	41	D. I. B.	8	2	...	...	3½	46	D. I. B.	9	2	...	...	3¾	53	D. I. B.	10	2	...	...
Peak Halliards	3	46	S. I. B.	8	5	...	...	3½	51	S. I. B.	9	5	...	...	3¾	60	S. I. B.	10	5	...	...
Purchase	1¾	24	{ Double	6	1	...	...	2	24	{ Double	6	1	...	...	2	26	{ Double	7	1	...	...
			{ S. I. B.	6	1	...	...			{ S. I. B.	6	1	...	...			{ S. I. B.	7	1	...	...
Downhaul	1¾	21	Single	6	1	...	...	1¾	25	Single	6	1	...	...	1¾	28	Single	6	1	...	...
Tack Tackle	1¾	5	{ D. I. B.	6	1	...	...	1¾	6	{ D. I. B.	6	1	...	...	2	7	{ D. I. B.	6	1	...	...
			{ S. I. B.	6	1	...	...			{ S. I. B.	6	1	...	...			{ S. I. B.	6	1	...	...
Tack Tricing-line	1¾	24	Single	6	2	2	...	2	28	Single	7	2	2	...	2	31	Single	7	2	2	...
Reef-Earings	3	24	......	...	...	...	...	4	25	......	...	...	...	...	4¼	26	......	...	...	...	...
Lacing	¾	30	......	...	...	...	...	1	34	......	...	...	...	...	1	40	......	...	...	...	...
MAIN-BOOM.																					
Topping-lifts	3	43	S. I. B. C.	7	4	...	...	3½	51	S. I. B. C.	8	4	...	...	5	35	S. I. B. C.	9	2	2	2
Tackle-falls	1¾	22	{ Double	6	1	...	...	2	26	{ Double	6	2	...	...	2½	25	{ Double	8	2	...	...
			{ S. I. B.	6	1	...	...			{ S. I. B.	6	2	...	...			{ S. I. B.	8	2	...	...
Boom-sheets	3	30	{ Double	9	2	...	...	3¼	30	{ Double	10	2	...	...	3½	32	{ Double	12	2	...	...
			{ Single C.	6	1	...	...			{ Single C.	7	1	...	...			{ Single C.	8	1	...	...
Reef-tackle	2	18	{ Fiddle	10	1	...	...	2¼	20	{ Fiddle	12	1	...	...	2¼	23	{ Fiddle	12	1	...	...
			{ S. I. B.	6	1	...	...			{ S. I. B.	7	1	...	...			{ S. I. B.	7	1	...	...

MAIN-BOOM (*continued.*)																		
Boom Guy Pendant	3½	4	......	...	...	1	1	3½	5	......	...	...	1	1	4	6	......	...	...	1	1
Guy-tackle	2	22	Double	7	1	...	...	2¼	24	Double	7	1	...	...	2¼	24	Double	7	1	...	...
			Single	7	1	...	...			Single	7	1	...	...			Single	7	1	...	...
MAIN-TOP-MAST.																		
Shrouds	2¾	48	......	...	...	...	4	3	54	......	...	...	...	4	3¼	64	......	...	...	...	4
Backstays	2¾	23	......	...	...	...	2	3	27	......	...	...	...	2	3¼	32	......	...	...	...	2
Tackles	1¾	11	D. I. B.	5	2	...	...	1¾	12	D. I. B.	5	2	...	...	1¾	12	D. I. B.	6	4	...	...
			S. I. B.	5	2	...	...			S. I. B.	5	2	...	...							
Jumper-stays	2¾	25	......	...	...	...	...	3	28	......	...	...	...	...	3¼	33	......	...	...	...	...
Tackles	1½	17	Single	5	4	...	...	1¾	18	Single	6	4	...	...	1¾	18	Single	6	4	...	...
Mast-rope	2½	16	......	...	...	...	...	2¾	17	......	...	...	...	...	3	20	......	...	...	...	...
MAIN-GAFF-TOP-SAIL.																		
Halliards	2½	24	Traveller	...	...	...	...	2¾	28	Traveller	...	...	...	...	3	31	Traveller	...	...	...	...
Sheets	2	17	Single	6	1	...	...	2½	19	Single	7	1	...	...	2½	22	Single	7	1	...	...
Tack	2	6	......	...	...	1	1	2½	6	......	...	...	1	1	2½	8	......	...	...	1	1
Tackle	1½	6	Double	5	1	...	...	1¾	6	Double	6	1	...	...	1¾	6	Double	6	1	...	...
			S. I. B.	5	1	...	...			S. I. B.	6	1	...	...			S. I. B.	6	1	...	...
Downhaul	1½	16	Single	5	1	...	...	1½	19	Single	5	1	...	...	1½	35	Single	5	1	...	...
NECESSARY ROPES.																		
Try-sail Sheets	2½	42	Double	8	4	2	2	2¾	45	Double	9	4	2	2	3	49	Double	10	4	2	2
Square-sail Guys and Sheets	2¼	30	Single	6	2	...	...	2½	33	Single	7	4	...	...	2½	35	Single	7	4	...	...
Deck Tackle	2¼	14	Double	7	1	1	1	2½	15	Double	8	1	1	1	2½	16	Double	8	1	1	1
			Single	7	1	1	1			Single	8	1	1	1			Single	8	1	1	1
Fish Burton Pendant	3½	2	......	...	...	1	1	3¾	2½	......	...	...	1	1	4	2½	......	...	...	1	1
Fall	2¼	24	Single	7	2	2	2	2¼	29	Single	7	2	2	2	2½	34	Single	8	2	2	2
Hook Pendant	3½	3	......	...	...	fish	1	3¾	3½	......	...	...	fish	1	4	4	......	...	...	fish	1
Cat Falls	2¼	26	D. I. B.	7	2	...	...	2¼	28	D. I. B.	9	2	...	...	2¾	30	D. I. B.	10	2	...	...
Boat's Tackles	2¼	40	S. I. B.	7	4	...	...	2¼	40	S. I. B.	7	4	...	...	2½	44	S. I. B.	8	4	...	...
Signal Halliards	...	112	......	...	...	...	...	...	120	......	...	...	...	...	...	150	......	...	...	...	...
Bending Gaff-top-sails	¼	20	......	...	...	...	...	¼	24	......	...	...	...	...	¼	30	......	...	...	...	...

CUTTER-YACHTS.

30 Tons.

	Size in Inches.	Length in Fms.	*Blocks, &c.*	Inches.	Number.	Hooks.	Thimbles
BOWSPRIT.							
Shrouds	3	9	I. B. D. I. B. S.	6 6	2 2	2	2
Falls	1½	12	......	...	...	...	...
Bobstay Pendants	4	2¼	I. B. D. I. B. S.	6 6	1 1	1	1
Fall	2	12	......	...	...	...	...
Heel Rope	2	8	S. I. B.	6	1	1	1
Jib Tack	2¾	4½	......	...	...	...	...
Whip	1½	8½	Single	6	1	...	...
Halliards	3	18	S. I. B. C. Single C.	6 6	1 2	...	...
Purchase	1½	20	S. I. B. Single	5 5	1 1	...	...
Downhaul	1	12	......	...	...	...	...
Inhaul	1¼	5½	......	...	...	...	...
Sheets	3½	9	......	...	...	...	...
Bobstay Tricing-line	1	2	......	...	...	...	...
THE MAST.							
Mast-head Pendants	4½	8	Single C.	6	2	...	...
Runners	3	7	Single	5	2	2	2
Falls	1¾	12	S. I. B.	5	2	2	2
Shrouds	4½	44	Dead-Eyes	5	6	...	...
Laniards	1¾	18	......	...	...	...	...
Stay	5½	8½	......	...	...	...	1
Worming	...	34	......	...	...	...	...
Laniard	2	4	......	...	...	...	...
Fore Halliard	1¼	21	S. I. B.	5	2	...	...
Downhaul	1¼	8½	......	...	...	...	...

60 Tons.

	Size in Inches.	Length in Fms.	*Blocks, &c.*	Inches.	Number.	Hooks.	Thimbles
BOWSPRIT.							
Shrouds	4	11	D. I. B.	7	4	2	2
Falls	2¼	18	......	...	...	...	...
Bobstay Pendants	5¼	3	Shackle	...	...	...	...
Fall	3	15	D. I. B. S. I. B.	8 8	1 1	1 ...	1 ...
Heel Rope	3	9½	S. I. B.	8	1	1	1
Jib Tack	4	6	......	...	...	...	...
Whip	2½	11½	Single	7	1	...	...
Halliards	4	24	S. I. B. C. Single C.	9 9	1 2	...	...
Purchase	1¾	25	D. I. B.	7	2	...	...
Downhaul	1½	14½	Single	5	1	...	...
Inhaul	1½	6½	......	...	...	...	...
Sheets	2½	18	Single C.	7	2	...	...
Bobstay Tricing-line	1¼	3½	Single	5	1	...	...
THE MAST.							
Mast-head Pendants	4	22½	S. I. B. C.	8	22	...	...
Runners	4	9	Fiddle	11	2	2	2
Falls	2	18	Single	7	2	2	2
Shrouds	5¼	55	Dead-Eyes	6½	8	...	...
Laniards	3	24	......	...	...	...	...
Stay	7½	10	Heart	8	1	...	...
Worming	...	38	......	...	...	...	...
Laniard	2¼	5	......	...	...	...	...
Fore Halliard	2¼	21	S. I. B.	6	2	...	...
Downhaul	1¾	10	......	...	...	...	...

90 Tons.

	Size in Inches.	Length in Fms.	*Blocks, &c.*	Inches.	Number.	Hooks.	Thimbles
BOWSPRIT.							
Shrouds	4½	13	D. I. B.	8	4	2	2
Falls	2½	20	......	...	...	...	...
Bobstay Pendants	5¾	3½	Shackle	...	...	...	...
Fall	3½	19	D. I. B. S. I. B.	9 9	1 1	1 ...	1 ...
Heel Rope	3½	11	S. I. B.	9	1	1	1
Jib Tack	4½	7	......	...	...	...	...
Whip	2¾	15	Single	8	1	...	...
Halliards	4½	26	S. I. B. C. Single C.	10 10	1 2	...	...
Purchase	2	30	D. I. B.	8	2	...	...
Downhaul	1½	17	Single	5	1	...	...
Inhaul	1¾	8	......	...	...	...	...
Sheets	2¾	19	Single C.	8	2	...	...
Bobstay Tricing-line	1½	3½	Single	5	1	...	...
THE MAST.							
Mast-head Pendants	4½	24	S. I. B. C.	10	2	...	...
Runners	4½	10	Fiddle	12	2	2	2
Falls	2½	20	Single	8	2	2	2
Shrouds	5¾	60	Dead-Eyes	8	8	...	...
Laniards	3¼	24	......	...	...	...	...
Stay	10	11½	Heart	9	1	...	...
Worming	...	42	......	...	...	...	...
Laniard	2½	5	......	...	...	...	...
Fore Halliard	2¾	24	S. I. B.	8	2	...	...
Downhaul	1¾	11¼	......	...	...	...	...

Tack	2	1½	......	...	...	...	...	2½	1⅔	......	...	...	...	...	3	2½	......	...	...	...	...
Fall	*none*	—	—	—	—	—	—	1½	8	S. I. B.	5	2	...	...	1¾	9	D. I. B.	5	2	...	...
Sheets	1¾	15	S. I. B.	5	2	2	4	2	35½	D. I. B.	6	2	2	4	2¼	40	D. I. B.	7	2	2	4
			Single	5	2	...	...														
Jack-stay	1½	5	......	...	...	...	...	3	6¼	......	...	...	1	2	3½	7	......	...	...	1	2
Laniard	1¼	1½	......	...	...	...	...	1½	1½	......	...	...	...	...	1¾	2	......	...	...	...	...
CROSS-JACK-YARD.																					
Square-sail Braces	1	58	......	...	...	...	...	1½	86	S. I. B.	5	2	...	...	1¾	90	S. I. B.	6	2	...	...
Halliards	1¼	16½	S. I. B.	4	2	...	...	2	31	S. I. B.	5	2	...	...	2¼	35	S. I. B.	6	2	...	...
Sheets and Guys	1½	15	......	...	...	...	...	2	18	......	...	...	...	...	2½	22	......	...	...	...	...
Yard Ropes	1½	34	Single	5	2	2	2	2¼	38	Single	6	2	2	2	3	44	Single	8	2	2	2
BOOM-MAIN-SAIL.																					
Throat Halliards	2½	24	D. I. B.	5	1	...	...	3¼	32	D. I. B.	9	2	...	...	3½	37	D. I. B.	10	2	...	...
			S. I. B.	5	1	...	...														
Peak Halliards	2½	27	S. I. B.	6	5	...	...	3¼	42	S. I. B.	9	5	...	...	3½	49	S. I. B.	10	5	...	...
Purchase	*none*	—	—	—	—	—	—	1¾	30	D. I. B.	7	1	...	...	1¾	35	D. I. B.	7	1	...	...
										S. I. B.	7	1	...	...			S. I. B.	7	1	...	...
Tack-tackle	1	4	Single	4	2	2	2	1½	5	Double	6	1	1	1	1¾	6	Double	6	1	...	...
										S. I. B.	6	1	...	...			Single	6	1	...	...
Tack Tricing-line	1	16½	Single	5	2	...	...	1¾	19½	Single	6	2	...	...	1¾	23	Single	6	2	...	...
Peak Downhaul	1	17	Single	4	1	...	...	1½	21	Single	5	1	...	...	1¾	23	Single	5	1	...	...
Reef Pendants	2	16	......	...	...	...	...	3¼	20	......	...	...	...	...	4	24	......	...	...	...	...
Lacing and Earings	1	20	......	...	...	...	...	1½	24	......	...	...	...	...	1¾	27	......	...	...	...	...
Tackle	1	10	S. I. B.	5	1	...	...	1¾	20	Fiddle	7	1	...	...	2	24	Fiddle	10	1	...	...
			Single	5	1	...	...			Single	6	1	...	...			Single	6	1	...	...
Boom-guy Pendant	2¾	3	......	...	...	1	2	4	4	......	...	...	1	2	4½	6	......	...	...	1	2
Tackle	1½	8	Single	5	2	2	2	1¾	10	Double	7	1	...	...	2	12	Double	7	1	...	...
										Single	7	1	...	...			Single	7	1	...	...
Topping-lifts	3	16	Single	5	2	2	2	3½	23	S. I. B.	7	4	...	...	3¾	25	S. I. B.	7	4	...	...
Fall	1½	9	S. I. B.	5	2	...	...	2	16	S. I. B.	7	4	...	...	2½	18	D. I. B.	8	4	...	...
																	S. I. B.	8	4	...	...
Main-sheet	2	25	Double	7	1	...	...	3	32	Double	10	1	...	...	3¼	34	Double	11	1	...	...
			S. I. B. C.	7	1	...	...			D. I. B.	10	1	...	...			D. I. B.	11	1	...	...
										S. I. B. C.	7	1	...	...			S. I. B. C.	7	1	...	...
Try-sail-sheets	1½	18	D. I. B.	7	2	...	...	2¼	20	D. I. B.	8	4	4	...	2½	22	D. I. B.	8	4	4	...
			S. I. B.	7	2	...	...														
Downhaul	1	13	Single	4	1	...	...	1½	15	Single	5	1	...	...	1¾	17	Single	5	1	...	...

SIZE AND DIMENSIONS OF THE RIGGING FOR CUTTER-YACHTS.

TOP-MAST.	30 Tons. Size in Inches	Length in Fms.	Blocks, &c.	Inches	Number	Hooks	Thimbles	60 Tons. Size in Inches	Length in Fms.	Blocks, &c.	Inches	Number	Hooks	Thimbles	90 Tons. Size in Inches	Length in Fms.	Blocks, &c.	Inches	Number	Hooks	Thimbles
Shrouds	2¼	20		4	4		2	3	55	D.I.B.		5	8		4	3¾	56	D.I.B.		6	8	4
Tackle	1	4	S.I.B.	4	4			1½	15	S.I.B.C.	5	5	1		1¼	16	S.I.B.C.	5	5	1	
Stay	2¼	17	S.I.B.C.	5	1	1		3	22	} Double { S.I.B.	5	5	1		3¾	24	} Double { S.I.B.	5	5	1	
Tackle	none	—						1½	6						1¼	6					
Mast-rope	2	8	—					3	10	} D.I.B. { S.I.B.	5	5	1		3¾	10	} D.I.B. { S.I.B.	6	6	1	
Tackle	none	—						1½	22						1¾	35		6	6	1	
Gaff-top-sail Halliards	2	20	—		4			none	—	Single	6	6	1		3¼	15	Single	6	6	1	
Tye	none	—						3	13						2¼	28				1	1
Whip	none	—	Single	4	1	1		1½	26	Single	5	5	1		1¾	18	Single	5	5	1	
Clue-line	1½	13½						1½	28½	Single C.	5	5	2		1¾	19	Single C.	5	5	2	
Sheet	1¼	13½						2½	16						2¾	10½					
Tack	1½	5½						2½	9						2¼	8					
Tackle	none	—						1½	8	} D.I.B. { S.I.B.	6	6	1		1¾	28	} D.I.B. { S.I.B.	6	6	1	
Half-top-sail Halliards	1	20						2¼	25	Single	5	5	1	1	2¼	18	Single	6	6	1	1
Downhaul	1	13½						1½	16						1¼	31					
Tack	1¾	24			2			2	28½			2			2¼	28				2	
Jib-top-sail Halliards	1¾	19	—	5	1			1½	25						1¼	11					
Downhaul	none	—						1¼	10	Single	5	5	1		1¼	30	Single	5	5	1	
Tack	1	6½	Single		1			1¼	25	Single	5	5	2		1¾	18	Single	5	5	2	
Sheets	1	12						1¼	16						1¾	60					
Signal Halliards	1½	25		5		fishl	1	1¼	40				fishl	1	4	4ft.				fishl	1
Fish-hook Pendant	2	2			5	2	1	3¼	21	Single	6	6	2	1	3¼	21	Single	6	6	2	1
Burton Pendant	1¾	16	Single					2½	18				1	1	2¾	23				1	1
Best Bower Stopper	2	2						2¼							2½	2¾					
Small Bower Stopper	…	…						1¾							2½	2½					
Tiller Ropes	1⅝	3						1¾							3½	5					
Ridge Ropes	1¾	3						2							3	4					
Laniards	¾	1						¾							2½	1¾					

A CATALOG OF SELECTED DOVER
BOOKS IN ALL FIELDS OF INTEREST

CONCERNING THE SPIRITUAL IN ART, Wassily Kandinsky. Pioneering work by father of abstract art. Thoughts on color theory, nature of art. Analysis of earlier masters. 12 illustrations. 80pp. of text. 5⅜ x 8½. 23411-8 Pa. $4.95

ANIMALS: 1,419 Copyright-Free Illustrations of Mammals, Birds, Fish, Insects, etc., Jim Harter (ed.). Clear wood engravings present, in extremely lifelike poses, over 1,000 species of animals. One of the most extensive pictorial sourcebooks of its kind. Captions. Index. 284pp. 9 x 12. 23766-4 Pa. $14.95

CELTIC ART: The Methods of Construction, George Bain. Simple geometric techniques for making Celtic interlacements, spirals, Kells-type initials, animals, humans, etc. Over 500 illustrations. 160pp. 9 x 12. (Available in U.S. only.) 22923-8 Pa. $9.95

AN ATLAS OF ANATOMY FOR ARTISTS, Fritz Schider. Most thorough reference work on art anatomy in the world. Hundreds of illustrations, including selections from works by Vesalius, Leonardo, Goya, Ingres, Michelangelo, others. 593 illustrations. 192pp. 7⅛ x 10¼. 20241-0 Pa. $9.95

CELTIC HAND STROKE-BY-STROKE (Irish Half-Uncial from "The Book of Kells"): An Arthur Baker Calligraphy Manual, Arthur Baker. Complete guide to creating each letter of the alphabet in distinctive Celtic manner. Covers hand position, strokes, pens, inks, paper, more. Illustrated. 48pp. 8¼ x 11. 24336-2 Pa. $3.95

EASY ORIGAMI, John Montroll. Charming collection of 32 projects (hat, cup, pelican, piano, swan, many more) specially designed for the novice origami hobbyist. Clearly illustrated easy-to-follow instructions insure that even beginning papercrafters will achieve successful results. 48pp. 8¼ x 11. 27298-2 Pa. $3.50

THE COMPLETE BOOK OF BIRDHOUSE CONSTRUCTION FOR WOOD-WORKERS, Scott D. Campbell. Detailed instructions, illustrations, tables. Also data on bird habitat and instinct patterns. Bibliography. 3 tables. 63 illustrations in 15 figures. 48pp. 5¼ x 8½. 24407-5 Pa. $2.50

BLOOMINGDALE'S ILLUSTRATED 1886 CATALOG: Fashions, Dry Goods and Housewares, Bloomingdale Brothers. Famed merchants' extremely rare catalog depicting about 1,700 products: clothing, housewares, firearms, dry goods, jewelry, more. Invaluable for dating, identifying vintage items. Also, copyright-free graphics for artists, designers. Co-published with Henry Ford Museum & Greenfield Village. 160pp. 8¼ x 11. 25780-0 Pa. $10.95

HISTORIC COSTUME IN PICTURES, Braun & Schneider. Over 1,450 costumed figures in clearly detailed engravings—from dawn of civilization to end of 19th century. Captions. Many folk costumes. 256pp. 8⅜ x 11¼. 23150-X Pa. $12.95

STICKLEY CRAFTSMAN FURNITURE CATALOGS, Gustav Stickley and L. & J. G. Stickley. Beautiful, functional furniture in two authentic catalogs from 1910. 594 illustrations, including 277 photos, show settles, rockers, armchairs, reclining chairs, bookcases, desks, tables. 183pp. 6½ x 9¼.   23838-5 Pa. $11.95

AMERICAN LOCOMOTIVES IN HISTORIC PHOTOGRAPHS: 1858 to 1949, Ron Ziel (ed.). A rare collection of 126 meticulously detailed official photographs, called "builder portraits," of American locomotives that majestically chronicle the rise of steam locomotive power in America. Introduction. Detailed captions. xi+ 129pp. 9 x 12.   27393-8 Pa. $13.95

AMERICA'S LIGHTHOUSES: An Illustrated History, Francis Ross Holland, Jr. Delightfully written, profusely illustrated fact-filled survey of over 200 American light-houses since 1716. History, anecdotes, technological advances, more. 240pp. 8 x 10¾.
25576-X Pa. $12.95

TOWARDS A NEW ARCHITECTURE, Le Corbusier. Pioneering manifesto by founder of "International School." Technical and aesthetic theories, views of industry, eco-nomics, relation of form to function, "mass-production split" and much more. Profusely illustrated. 320pp. 6⅛ x 9¼. (Available in U.S. only.)   25023-7 Pa. $10.95

HOW THE OTHER HALF LIVES, Jacob Riis. Famous journalistic record, expos-ing poverty and degradation of New York slums around 1900, by major social reformer. 100 striking and influential photographs. 233pp. 10 x 7⅞.
22012-5 Pa. $11.95

FRUIT KEY AND TWIG KEY TO TREES AND SHRUBS, William M. Harlow. One of the handiest and most widely used identification aids. Fruit key covers 120 deciduous and evergreen species; twig key 160 deciduous species. Easily used. Over 300 photographs. 126pp. 5⅜ x 8½.   20511-8 Pa. $3.95

COMMON BIRD SONGS, Dr. Donald J. Borror. Songs of 60 most common U.S. birds: robins, sparrows, cardinals, bluejays, finches, more—arranged in order of increasing complexity. Up to 9 variations of songs of each species.
Cassette and manual 99911-4 $8.95

ORCHIDS AS HOUSE PLANTS, Rebecca Tyson Northen. Grow cattleyas and many other kinds of orchids—in a window, in a case, or under artificial light. 63 illus-trations. 148pp. 5⅜ x 8½.   23261-1 Pa. $7.95

MONSTER MAZES, Dave Phillips. Masterful mazes at four levels of difficulty. Avoid deadly perils and evil creatures to find magical treasures. Solutions for all 32 exciting illustrated puzzles. 48pp. 8¼ x 11.   26005-4 Pa. $2.95

MOZART'S DON GIOVANNI (DOVER OPERA LIBRETTO SERIES), Wolfgang Amadeus Mozart. Introduced and translated by Ellen H. Bleiler. Standard Italian libretto, with complete English translation. Convenient and thoroughly portable—an ideal companion for reading along with a recording or the performance itself. Introduction. List of characters. Plot summary. 121pp. 5¼ x 8½.
24944-1 Pa. $3.95

TECHNICAL MANUAL AND DICTIONARY OF CLASSICAL BALLET, Gail Grant. Defines, explains, comments on steps, movements, poses and concepts. 15-page pictorial section. Basic book for student, viewer. 127pp. 5⅜ x 8½.
21843-0 Pa. $4.95

THE CLARINET AND CLARINET PLAYING, David Pino. Lively, comprehensive work features suggestions about technique, musicianship, and musical interpretation, as well as guidelines for teaching, making your own reeds, and preparing for public performance. Includes an intriguing look at clarinet history. "A godsend," *The Clarinet*, Journal of the International Clarinet Society. Appendixes. 7 illus. 320pp. 5⅜ x 8½. 40270-3 Pa. $9.95

HOLLYWOOD GLAMOR PORTRAITS, John Kobal (ed.). 145 photos from 1926-49. Harlow, Gable, Bogart, Bacall; 94 stars in all. Full background on photographers, technical aspects. 160pp. 8⅜ x 11¼. 23352-9 Pa. $12.95

THE ANNOTATED CASEY AT THE BAT: A Collection of Ballads about the Mighty Casey/Third, Revised Edition, Martin Gardner (ed.). Amusing sequels and parodies of one of America's best-loved poems: Casey's Revenge, Why Casey Whiffed, Casey's Sister at the Bat, others. 256pp. 5⅜ x 8½. 28598-7 Pa. $8.95

THE RAVEN AND OTHER FAVORITE POEMS, Edgar Allan Poe. Over 40 of the author's most memorable poems: "The Bells," "Ulalume," "Israfel," "To Helen," "The Conqueror Worm," "Eldorado," "Annabel Lee," many more. Alphabetic lists of titles and first lines. 64pp. $5\frac{3}{16}$ x 8¼. 26685-0 Pa. $1.00

PERSONAL MEMOIRS OF U. S. GRANT, Ulysses Simpson Grant. Intelligent, deeply moving firsthand account of Civil War campaigns, considered by many the finest military memoirs ever written. Includes letters, historic photographs, maps and more. 528pp. 6⅛ x 9¼. 28587-1 Pa. $12.95

ANCIENT EGYPTIAN MATERIALS AND INDUSTRIES, A. Lucas and J. Harris. Fascinating, comprehensive, thoroughly documented text describes this ancient civilization's vast resources and the processes that incorporated them in daily life, including the use of animal products, building materials, cosmetics, perfumes and incense, fibers, glazed ware, glass and its manufacture, materials used in the mummification process, and much more. 544pp. 6⅛ x 9¼. (Available in U.S. only.) 40446-3 Pa. $16.95

RUSSIAN STORIES/PYCCKNE PACCKA3bl: A Dual-Language Book, edited by Gleb Struve. Twelve tales by such masters as Chekhov, Tolstoy, Dostoevsky, Pushkin, others. Excellent word-for-word English translations on facing pages, plus teaching and study aids, Russian/English vocabulary, biographical/critical introductions, more. 416pp. 5⅜ x 8½. 26244-8 Pa. $9.95

PHILADELPHIA THEN AND NOW: 60 Sites Photographed in the Past and Present, Kenneth Finkel and Susan Oyama. Rare photographs of City Hall, Logan Square, Independence Hall, Betsy Ross House, other landmarks juxtaposed with contemporary views. Captures changing face of historic city. Introduction. Captions. 128pp. 8¼ x 11. 25790-8 Pa. $9.95

AIA ARCHITECTURAL GUIDE TO NASSAU AND SUFFOLK COUNTIES, LONG ISLAND, The American Institute of Architects, Long Island Chapter, and the Society for the Preservation of Long Island Antiquities. Comprehensive, well-researched and generously illustrated volume brings to life over three centuries of Long Island's great architectural heritage. More than 240 photographs with authoritative, extensively detailed captions. 176pp. 8¼ x 11. 26946-9 Pa. $14.95

NORTH AMERICAN INDIAN LIFE: Customs and Traditions of 23 Tribes, Elsie Clews Parsons (ed.). 27 fictionalized essays by noted anthropologists examine religion, customs, government, additional facets of life among the Winnebago, Crow, Zuni, Eskimo, other tribes. 480pp. 6⅛ x 9¼. 27377-6 Pa. $10.95

FRANK LLOYD WRIGHT'S DANA HOUSE, Donald Hoffmann. Pictorial essay of residential masterpiece with over 160 interior and exterior photos, plans, elevations, sketches and studies. 128pp. 9¼ x 10¾. 29120-0 Pa. $14.95

THE MALE AND FEMALE FIGURE IN MOTION: 60 Classic Photographic Sequences, Eadweard Muybridge. 60 true-action photographs of men and women walking, running, climbing, bending, turning, etc., reproduced from rare 19th-century masterpiece. vi + 121pp. 9 x 12. 24745-7 Pa. $12.95

1001 QUESTIONS ANSWERED ABOUT THE SEASHORE, N. J. Berrill and Jacquelyn Berrill. Queries answered about dolphins, sea snails, sponges, starfish, fishes, shore birds, many others. Covers appearance, breeding, growth, feeding, much more. 305pp. 5¼ x 8¼. 23366-9 Pa. $9.95

ATTRACTING BIRDS TO YOUR YARD, William J. Weber. Easy-to-follow guide offers advice on how to attract the greatest diversity of birds: birdhouses, feeders, water and waterers, much more. 96pp. 5³⁄₁₆ x 8¼. 28927-3 Pa. $2.50

MEDICINAL AND OTHER USES OF NORTH AMERICAN PLANTS: A Historical Survey with Special Reference to the Eastern Indian Tribes, Charlotte Erichsen-Brown. Chronological historical citations document 500 years of usage of plants, trees, shrubs native to eastern Canada, northeastern U.S. Also complete identifying information. 343 illustrations. 544pp. 6½ x 9¼. 25951-X Pa. $12.95

STORYBOOK MAZES, Dave Phillips. 23 stories and mazes on two-page spreads: Wizard of Oz, Treasure Island, Robin Hood, etc. Solutions. 64pp. 8¼ x 11. 23628-5 Pa. $2.95

AMERICAN NEGRO SONGS: 230 Folk Songs and Spirituals, Religious and Secular, John W. Work. This authoritative study traces the African influences of songs sung and played by black Americans at work, in church, and as entertainment. The author discusses the lyric significance of such songs as "Swing Low, Sweet Chariot," "John Henry," and others and offers the words and music for 230 songs. Bibliography. Index of Song Titles. 272pp. 6½ x 9¼. 40271-1 Pa. $9.95

MOVIE-STAR PORTRAITS OF THE FORTIES, John Kobal (ed.). 163 glamor, studio photos of 106 stars of the 1940s: Rita Hayworth, Ava Gardner, Marlon Brando, Clark Gable, many more. 176pp. 8⅜ x 11¼. 23546-7 Pa. $14.95

BENCHLEY LOST AND FOUND, Robert Benchley. Finest humor from early 30s, about pet peeves, child psychologists, post office and others. Mostly unavailable elsewhere. 73 illustrations by Peter Arno and others. 183pp. 5⅜ x 8½. 22410-4 Pa. $6.95

YEKL and THE IMPORTED BRIDEGROOM AND OTHER STORIES OF YIDDISH NEW YORK, Abraham Cahan. Film Hester Street based on *Yekl* (1896). Novel, other stories among first about Jewish immigrants on N.Y.'s East Side. 240pp. 5⅜ x 8½. 22427-9 Pa. $7.95

SELECTED POEMS, Walt Whitman. Generous sampling from *Leaves of Grass*. Twenty-four poems include "I Hear America Singing," "Song of the Open Road," "I Sing the Body Electric," "When Lilacs Last in the Dooryard Bloom'd," "O Captain! My Captain!"–all reprinted from an authoritative edition. Lists of titles and first lines. 128pp. 5³⁄₁₆ x 8¼. 26878-0 Pa. $1.00

THE BEST TALES OF HOFFMANN, E. T. A. Hoffmann. 10 of Hoffmann's most important stories: "Nutcracker and the King of Mice," "The Golden Flowerpot," etc. 458pp. 5⅜ x 8½.   21793-0 Pa. $9.95

FROM FETISH TO GOD IN ANCIENT EGYPT, E. A. Wallis Budge. Rich detailed survey of Egyptian conception of "God" and gods, magic, cult of animals, Osiris, more. Also, superb English translations of hymns and legends. 240 illustrations. 545pp. 5⅜ x 8½.   25803-3 Pa. $13.95

FRENCH STORIES/CONTES FRANÇAIS: A Dual-Language Book, Wallace Fowlie. Ten stories by French masters, Voltaire to Camus: "Micromegas" by Voltaire; "The Atheist's Mass" by Balzac; "Minuet" by de Maupassant; "The Guest" by Camus, six more. Excellent English translations on facing pages. Also French-English vocabulary list, exercises, more. 352pp. 5⅜ x 8½.   26443-2 Pa. $9.95

CHICAGO AT THE TURN OF THE CENTURY IN PHOTOGRAPHS: 122 Historic Views from the Collections of the Chicago Historical Society, Larry A. Viskochil. Rare large-format prints offer detailed views of City Hall, State Street, the Loop, Hull House, Union Station, many other landmarks, circa 1904-1913. Introduction. Captions. Maps. 144pp. 9⅜ x 12¼.   24656-6 Pa. $12.95

OLD BROOKLYN IN EARLY PHOTOGRAPHS, 1865-1929, William Lee Younger. Luna Park, Gravesend race track, construction of Grand Army Plaza, moving of Hotel Brighton, etc. 157 previously unpublished photographs. 165pp. 8⅞ x 11¾.   23587-4 Pa. $13.95

THE MYTHS OF THE NORTH AMERICAN INDIANS, Lewis Spence. Rich anthology of the myths and legends of the Algonquins, Iroquois, Pawnees and Sioux, prefaced by an extensive historical and ethnological commentary. 36 illustrations. 480pp. 5⅜ x 8½.   25967-6 Pa. $10.95

AN ENCYCLOPEDIA OF BATTLES: Accounts of Over 1,560 Battles from 1479 B.C. to the Present, David Eggenberger. Essential details of every major battle in recorded history from the first battle of Megiddo in 1479 B.C. to Grenada in 1984. List of Battle Maps. New Appendix covering the years 1967-1984. Index. 99 illustrations. 544pp. 6½ x 9¼.   24913-1 Pa. $16.95

SAILING ALONE AROUND THE WORLD, Captain Joshua Slocum. First man to sail around the world, alone, in small boat. One of great feats of seamanship told in delightful manner. 67 illustrations. 294pp. 5⅜ x 8½.   20326-3 Pa. $6.95

ANARCHISM AND OTHER ESSAYS, Emma Goldman. Powerful, penetrating, prophetic essays on direct action, role of minorities, prison reform, puritan hypocrisy, violence, etc. 271pp. 5⅜ x 8½.   22484-8 Pa. $8.95

MYTHS OF THE HINDUS AND BUDDHISTS, Ananda K. Coomaraswamy and Sister Nivedita. Great stories of the epics; deeds of Krishna, Shiva, taken from puranas, Vedas, folk tales; etc. 32 illustrations. 400pp. 5⅜ x 8½.   21759-0 Pa. $12.95

THE TRAUMA OF BIRTH, Otto Rank. Rank's controversial thesis that anxiety neurosis is caused by profound psychological trauma which occurs at birth. 256pp. 5⅜ x 8½.   27974-X Pa. $7.95

A THEOLOGICO-POLITICAL TREATISE, Benedict Spinoza. Also contains unfinished Political Treatise. Great classic on religious liberty, theory of government on common consent. R. Elwes translation. Total of 421pp. 5⅜ x 8½. 20249-6 Pa. $10.95

MY BONDAGE AND MY FREEDOM, Frederick Douglass. Born a slave, Douglass became outspoken force in antislavery movement. The best of Douglass' autobiographies. Graphic description of slave life. 464pp. 5⅜ x 8½. 22457-0 Pa. $8.95

FOLLOWING THE EQUATOR: A Journey Around the World, Mark Twain. Fascinating humorous account of 1897 voyage to Hawaii, Australia, India, New Zealand, etc. Ironic, bemused reports on peoples, customs, climate, flora and fauna, politics, much more. 197 illustrations. 720pp. 5⅜ x 8½. 26113-1 Pa. $15.95

THE PEOPLE CALLED SHAKERS, Edward D. Andrews. Definitive study of Shakers: origins, beliefs, practices, dances, social organization, furniture and crafts, etc. 33 illustrations. 351pp. 5⅜ x 8½. 21081-2 Pa. $12.95

THE MYTHS OF GREECE AND ROME, H. A. Guerber. A classic of mythology, generously illustrated, long prized for its simple, graphic, accurate retelling of the principal myths of Greece and Rome, and for its commentary on their origins and significance. With 64 illustrations by Michelangelo, Raphael, Titian, Rubens, Canova, Bernini and others. 480pp. 5⅜ x 8½. 27584-1 Pa. $10.95

PSYCHOLOGY OF MUSIC, Carl E. Seashore. Classic work discusses music as a medium from psychological viewpoint. Clear treatment of physical acoustics, auditory apparatus, sound perception, development of musical skills, nature of musical feeling, host of other topics. 88 figures. 408pp. 5⅜ x 8½. 21851-1 Pa. $11.95

THE PHILOSOPHY OF HISTORY, Georg W. Hegel. Great classic of Western thought develops concept that history is not chance but rational process, the evolution of freedom. 457pp. 5⅜ x 8½. 20112-0 Pa. $9.95

THE BOOK OF TEA, Kakuzo Okakura. Minor classic of the Orient: entertaining, charming explanation, interpretation of traditional Japanese culture in terms of tea ceremony. 94pp. 5⅜ x 8½. 20070-1 Pa. $3.95

LIFE IN ANCIENT EGYPT, Adolf Erman. Fullest, most thorough, detailed older account with much not in more recent books, domestic life, religion, magic, medicine, commerce, much more. Many illustrations reproduce tomb paintings, carvings, hieroglyphs, etc. 597pp. 5⅜ x 8½. 22632-8 Pa. $12.95

SUNDIALS, Their Theory and Construction, Albert Waugh. Far and away the best, most thorough coverage of ideas, mathematics concerned, types, construction, adjusting anywhere. Simple, nontechnical treatment allows even children to build several of these dials. Over 100 illustrations. 230pp. 5⅜ x 8½. 22947-5 Pa. $8.95

THEORETICAL HYDRODYNAMICS, L. M. Milne-Thomson. Classic exposition of the mathematical theory of fluid motion, applicable to both hydrodynamics and aerodynamics. Over 600 exercises. 768pp. 6⅛ x 9¼. 68970-0 Pa. $20.95

SONGS OF EXPERIENCE: Facsimile Reproduction with 26 Plates in Full Color, William Blake. 26 full-color plates from a rare 1826 edition. Includes "The Tyger," "London," "Holy Thursday," and other poems. Printed text of poems. 48pp. 5¼ x 7. 24636-1 Pa. $4.95

OLD-TIME VIGNETTES IN FULL COLOR, Carol Belanger Grafton (ed.). Over 390 charming, often sentimental illustrations, selected from archives of Victorian graphics—pretty women posing, children playing, food, flowers, kittens and puppies, smiling cherubs, birds and butterflies, much more. All copyright-free. 48pp. 9¼ x 12¼. 27269-9 Pa. $7.95

PERSPECTIVE FOR ARTISTS, Rex Vicat Cole. Depth, perspective of sky and sea, shadows, much more, not usually covered. 391 diagrams, 81 reproductions of drawings and paintings. 279pp. 5⅜ x 8½. 22487-2 Pa. $9.95

DRAWING THE LIVING FIGURE, Joseph Sheppard. Innovative approach to artistic anatomy focuses on specifics of surface anatomy, rather than muscles and bones. Over 170 drawings of live models in front, back and side views, and in widely varying poses. Accompanying diagrams. 177 illustrations. Introduction. Index. 144pp. 8⅜ x11¼. 26723-7 Pa. $9.95

GOTHIC AND OLD ENGLISH ALPHABETS: 100 Complete Fonts, Dan X. Solo. Add power, elegance to posters, signs, other graphics with 100 stunning copyright-free alphabets: Blackstone, Dolbey, Germania, 97 more–including many lower-case, numerals, punctuation marks. 104pp. 8⅛ x 11. 24695-7 Pa. $9.95

HOW TO DO BEADWORK, Mary White. Fundamental book on craft from simple projects to five-bead chains and woven works. 106 illustrations. 142pp. 5⅜ x 8. 20697-1 Pa. $5.95

THE BOOK OF WOOD CARVING, Charles Marshall Sayers. Finest book for beginners discusses fundamentals and offers 34 designs. "Absolutely first rate . . . well thought out and well executed."–E. J. Tangerman. 118pp. 7¾ x 10⅝. 23654-4 Pa. $7.95

ILLUSTRATED CATALOG OF CIVIL WAR MILITARY GOODS: Union Army Weapons, Insignia, Uniform Accessories, and Other Equipment, Schuyler, Hartley, and Graham. Rare, profusely illustrated 1846 catalog includes Union Army uniform and dress regulations, arms and ammunition, coats, insignia, flags, swords, rifles, etc. 226 illustrations. 160pp. 9 x 12. 24939-5 Pa. $12.95

WOMEN'S FASHIONS OF THE EARLY 1900s: An Unabridged Republication of "New York Fashions, 1909," National Cloak & Suit Co. Rare catalog of mail-order fashions documents women's and children's clothing styles shortly after the turn of the century. Captions offer full descriptions, prices. Invaluable resource for fashion, costume historians. Approximately 725 illustrations. 128pp. 8⅜ x 11¼. 27276-1 Pa. $12.95

THE 1912 AND 1915 GUSTAV STICKLEY FURNITURE CATALOGS, Gustav Stickley. With over 200 detailed illustrations and descriptions, these two catalogs are essential reading and reference materials and identification guides for Stickley furniture. Captions cite materials, dimensions and prices. 112pp. 6½ x 9¼. 26676-1 Pa. $9.95

EARLY AMERICAN LOCOMOTIVES, John H. White, Jr. Finest locomotive engravings from early 19th century: historical (1804–74), main-line (after 1870), special, foreign, etc. 147 plates. 142pp. 11⅜ x 8¼. 22772-3 Pa. $12.95

THE TALL SHIPS OF TODAY IN PHOTOGRAPHS, Frank O. Braynard. Lavishly illustrated tribute to nearly 100 majestic contemporary sailing vessels: Amerigo Vespucci, Clearwater, Constitution, Eagle, Mayflower, Sea Cloud, Victory, many more. Authoritative captions provide statistics, background on each ship. 190 black-and-white photographs and illustrations. Introduction. 128pp. 8⅞ x 11¾. 27163-3 Pa. $14.95

LITTLE BOOK OF EARLY AMERICAN CRAFTS AND TRADES, Peter Stockham (ed.). 1807 children's book explains crafts and trades: baker, hatter, cooper, potter, and many others. 23 copperplate illustrations. 140pp. 4⅝ x 6.
23336-7 Pa. $4.95

VICTORIAN FASHIONS AND COSTUMES FROM HARPER'S BAZAR, 1867–1898, Stella Blum (ed.). Day costumes, evening wear, sports clothes, shoes, hats, other accessories in over 1,000 detailed engravings. 320pp. 9⅜ x 12¼.
22990-4 Pa. $16.95

GUSTAV STICKLEY, THE CRAFTSMAN, Mary Ann Smith. Superb study surveys broad scope of Stickley's achievement, especially in architecture. Design philosophy, rise and fall of the Craftsman empire, descriptions and floor plans for many Craftsman houses, more. 86 black-and-white halftones. 31 line illustrations. Introduction 208pp. 6½ x 9¼. 27210-9 Pa. $9.95

THE LONG ISLAND RAIL ROAD IN EARLY PHOTOGRAPHS, Ron Ziel. Over 220 rare photos, informative text document origin (1844) and development of rail service on Long Island. Vintage views of early trains, locomotives, stations, passengers, crews, much more. Captions. 8⅞ x 11¾. 26301-0 Pa. $14.95

VOYAGE OF THE LIBERDADE, Joshua Slocum. Great 19th-century mariner's thrilling, first-hand account of the wreck of his ship off South America, the 35-foot boat he built from the wreckage, and its remarkable voyage home. 128pp. 5⅜ x 8½.
40022-0 Pa. $5.95

TEN BOOKS ON ARCHITECTURE, Vitruvius. The most important book ever written on architecture. Early Roman aesthetics, technology, classical orders, site selection, all other aspects. Morgan translation. 331pp. 5⅜ x 8½. 20645-9 Pa. $9.95

THE HUMAN FIGURE IN MOTION, Eadweard Muybridge. More than 4,500 stopped-action photos, in action series, showing undraped men, women, children jumping, lying down, throwing, sitting, wrestling, carrying, etc. 390pp. 7⅞ x 10⅝.
20204-6 Clothbd. $29.95

TREES OF THE EASTERN AND CENTRAL UNITED STATES AND CANADA, William M. Harlow. Best one-volume guide to 140 trees. Full descriptions, woodlore, range, etc. Over 600 illustrations. Handy size. 288pp. 4½ x 6⅜.
20395-6 Pa. $6.95

SONGS OF WESTERN BIRDS, Dr. Donald J. Borror. Complete song and call repertoire of 60 western species, including flycatchers, juncoes, cactus wrens, many more–includes fully illustrated booklet. Cassette and manual 99913-0 $8.95

GROWING AND USING HERBS AND SPICES, Milo Miloradovich. Versatile handbook provides all the information needed for cultivation and use of all the herbs and spices available in North America. 4 illustrations. Index. Glossary. 236pp. 5⅜ x 8½.
25058-X Pa. $7.95

BIG BOOK OF MAZES AND LABYRINTHS, Walter Shepherd. 50 mazes and labyrinths in all–classical, solid, ripple, and more–in one great volume. Perfect inexpensive puzzler for clever youngsters. Full solutions. 112pp. 8⅛ x 11.
22951-3 Pa. $5.95

PIANO TUNING, J. Cree Fischer. Clearest, best book for beginner, amateur. Simple repairs, raising dropped notes, tuning by easy method of flattened fifths. No previous skills needed. 4 illustrations. 201pp. 5⅜ x 8½. 23267-0 Pa. $6.95

HINTS TO SINGERS, Lillian Nordica. Selecting the right teacher, developing confidence, overcoming stage fright, and many other important skills receive thoughtful discussion in this indispensible guide, written by a world-famous diva of four decades' experience. 96pp. 5³/₈ x 8½. 40094-8 Pa. $4.95

THE COMPLETE NONSENSE OF EDWARD LEAR, Edward Lear. All nonsense limericks, zany alphabets, Owl and Pussycat, songs, nonsense botany, etc., illustrated by Lear. Total of 320pp. 5⅜ x 8½. (Available in U.S. only.) 20167-8 Pa. $7.95

VICTORIAN PARLOUR POETRY: An Annotated Anthology, Michael R. Turner. 117 gems by Longfellow, Tennyson, Browning, many lesser-known poets. "The Village Blacksmith," "Curfew Must Not Ring Tonight," "Only a Baby Small," dozens more, often difficult to find elsewhere. Index of poets, titles, first lines. xxiii + 325pp. 5⅜ x 8¼. 27044-0 Pa. $12.95

DUBLINERS, James Joyce. Fifteen stories offer vivid, tightly focused observations of the lives of Dublin's poorer classes. At least one, "The Dead," is considered a masterpiece. Reprinted complete and unabridged from standard edition. 160pp. 5³/₁₆ x 8¼. 26870-5 Pa. $1.50

GREAT WEIRD TALES: 14 Stories by Lovecraft, Blackwood, Machen and Others, S. T. Joshi (ed.). 14 spellbinding tales, including "The Sin Eater," by Fiona McLeod, "The Eye Above the Mantel," by Frank Belknap Long, as well as renowned works by R. H. Barlow, Lord Dunsany, Arthur Machen, W. C. Morrow and eight other masters of the genre. 256pp. 5⅜ x 8½. (Available in U.S. only.) 40436-6 Pa. $8.95

THE BOOK OF THE SACRED MAGIC OF ABRAMELIN THE MAGE, translated by S. MacGregor Mathers. Medieval manuscript of ceremonial magic. Basic document in Aleister Crowley, Golden Dawn groups. 268pp. 5⅜ x 8½. 23211-5 Pa. $9.95

NEW RUSSIAN-ENGLISH AND ENGLISH-RUSSIAN DICTIONARY, M. A. O'Brien. This is a remarkably handy Russian dictionary, containing a surprising amount of information, including over 70,000 entries. 366pp. 4½ x 6⅛. 20208-9 Pa. $10.95

HISTORIC HOMES OF THE AMERICAN PRESIDENTS, Second, Revised Edition, Irvin Haas. A traveler's guide to American Presidential homes, most open to the public, depicting and describing homes occupied by every American President from George Washington to George Bush. With visiting hours, admission charges, travel routes. 175 photographs. Index. 160pp. 8¼ x 11. 26751-2 Pa. $13.95

NEW YORK IN THE FORTIES, Andreas Feininger. 162 brilliant photographs by the well-known photographer, formerly with *Life* magazine. Commuters, shoppers, Times Square at night, much else from city at its peak. Captions by John von Hartz. 181pp. 9¼ x 10¾. 23585-8 Pa. $13.95

INDIAN SIGN LANGUAGE, William Tomkins. Over 525 signs developed by Sioux and other tribes. Written instructions and diagrams. Also 290 pictographs. 111pp. 6⅛ x 9¼. 22029-X Pa. $3.95

ANATOMY: A Complete Guide for Artists, Joseph Sheppard. A master of figure drawing shows artists how to render human anatomy convincingly. Over 460 illustrations. 224pp. 8⅜ x 11¼. 27279-6 Pa. $11.95

MEDIEVAL CALLIGRAPHY: Its History and Technique, Marc Drogin. Spirited history, comprehensive instruction manual covers 13 styles (ca. 4th century through 15th). Excellent photographs; directions for duplicating medieval techniques with modern tools. 224pp. 8⅜ x 11¼. 26142-5 Pa. $12.95

DRIED FLOWERS: How to Prepare Them, Sarah Whitlock and Martha Rankin. Complete instructions on how to use silica gel, meal and borax, perlite aggregate, sand and borax, glycerine and water to create attractive permanent flower arrangements. 12 illustrations. 32pp. 5⅜ x 8½. 21802-3 Pa. $1.00

EASY-TO-MAKE BIRD FEEDERS FOR WOODWORKERS, Scott D. Campbell. Detailed, simple-to-use guide for designing, constructing, caring for and using feeders. Text, illustrations for 12 classic and contemporary designs. 96pp. 5⅜ x 8½. 25847-5 Pa. $3.95

SCOTTISH WONDER TALES FROM MYTH AND LEGEND, Donald A. Mackenzie. 16 lively tales tell of giants rumbling down mountainsides, of a magic wand that turns stone pillars into warriors, of gods and goddesses, evil hags, powerful forces and more. 240pp. 5⅜ x 8½. 29677-6 Pa. $6.95

THE HISTORY OF UNDERCLOTHES, C. Willett Cunnington and Phyllis Cunnington. Fascinating, well-documented survey covering six centuries of English undergarments, enhanced with over 100 illustrations: 12th-century laced-up bodice, footed long drawers (1795), 19th-century bustles, 19th-century corsets for men, Victorian "bust improvers," much more. 272pp. 5⅜ x 8¼. 27124-2 Pa. $9.95

ARTS AND CRAFTS FURNITURE: The Complete Brooks Catalog of 1912, Brooks Manufacturing Co. Photos and detailed descriptions of more than 150 now very collectible furniture designs from the Arts and Crafts movement depict davenports, settees, buffets, desks, tables, chairs, bedsteads, dressers and more, all built of solid, quarter-sawed oak. Invaluable for students and enthusiasts of antiques, Americana and the decorative arts. 80pp. 6½ x 9¼. 27471-3 Pa. $8.95

WILBUR AND ORVILLE: A Biography of the Wright Brothers, Fred Howard. Definitive, crisply written study tells the full story of the brothers' lives and work. A vividly written biography, unparalleled in scope and color, that also captures the spirit of an extraordinary era. 560pp. 6⅛ x 9¼. 40297-5 Pa. $17.95

THE ARTS OF THE SAILOR: Knotting, Splicing and Ropework, Hervey Garrett Smith. Indispensable shipboard reference covers tools, basic knots and useful hitches; handsewing and canvas work, more. Over 100 illustrations. Delightful reading for sea lovers. 256pp. 5⅜ x 8½. 26440-8 Pa. $8.95

FRANK LLOYD WRIGHT'S FALLINGWATER: The House and Its History, Second, Revised Edition, Donald Hoffmann. A total revision—both in text and illustrations—of the standard document on Fallingwater, the boldest, most personal architectural statement of Wright's mature years, updated with valuable new material from the recently opened Frank Lloyd Wright Archives. "Fascinating"—*The New York Times*. 116 illustrations. 128pp. 9¼ x 10¾. 27430-6 Pa. $12.95

PHOTOGRAPHIC SKETCHBOOK OF THE CIVIL WAR, Alexander Gardner. 100 photos taken on field during the Civil War. Famous shots of Manassas Harper's Ferry, Lincoln, Richmond, slave pens, etc. 244pp. 10⅝ x 8¼. 22731-6 Pa. $10.95

FIVE ACRES AND INDEPENDENCE, Maurice G. Kains. Great back-to-the-land classic explains basics of self-sufficient farming. The one book to get. 95 illustrations. 397pp. 5⅜ x 8½. 20974-1 Pa. $7.95

SONGS OF EASTERN BIRDS, Dr. Donald J. Borror. Songs and calls of 60 species most common to eastern U.S.: warblers, woodpeckers, flycatchers, thrushes, larks, many more in high-quality recording. Cassette and manual 99912-2 $9.95

A MODERN HERBAL, Margaret Grieve. Much the fullest, most exact, most useful compilation of herbal material. Gigantic alphabetical encyclopedia, from aconite to zedoary, gives botanical information, medical properties, folklore, economic uses, much else. Indispensable to serious reader. 161 illustrations. 888pp. 6½ x 9¼. 2-vol. set. (Available in U.S. only.) Vol. I: 22798-7 Pa. $10.95
Vol. II: 22799-5 Pa. $10.95

HIDDEN TREASURE MAZE BOOK, Dave Phillips. Solve 34 challenging mazes accompanied by heroic tales of adventure. Evil dragons, people-eating plants, bloodthirsty giants, many more dangerous adversaries lurk at every twist and turn. 34 mazes, stories, solutions. 48pp. 8¼ x 11. 24566-7 Pa. $2.95

LETTERS OF W. A. MOZART, Wolfgang A. Mozart. Remarkable letters show bawdy wit, humor, imagination, musical insights, contemporary musical world; includes some letters from Leopold Mozart. 276pp. 5⅜ x 8½. 22859-2 Pa. $9.95

BASIC PRINCIPLES OF CLASSICAL BALLET, Agrippina Vaganova. Great Russian theoretician, teacher explains methods for teaching classical ballet. 118 illustrations. 175pp. 5⅜ x 8½. 22036-2 Pa. $6.95

THE JUMPING FROG, Mark Twain. Revenge edition. The original story of The Celebrated Jumping Frog of Calaveras County, a hapless French translation, and Twain's hilarious "retranslation" from the French. 12 illustrations. 66pp. 5⅜ x 8½. 22686-7 Pa. $4.95

BEST REMEMBERED POEMS, Martin Gardner (ed.). The 126 poems in this superb collection of 19th- and 20th-century British and American verse range from Shelley's "To a Skylark" to the impassioned "Renascence" of Edna St. Vincent Millay and to Edward Lear's whimsical "The Owl and the Pussycat." 224pp. 5⅜ x 8½. 27165-X Pa. $5.95

COMPLETE SONNETS, William Shakespeare. Over 150 exquisite poems deal with love, friendship, the tyranny of time, beauty's evanescence, death and other themes in language of remarkable power, precision and beauty. Glossary of archaic terms. 80pp. 5$^{3}/_{16}$ x 8¼. 26686-9 Pa. $1.00

THE BATTLES THAT CHANGED HISTORY, Fletcher Pratt. Eminent historian profiles 16 crucial conflicts, ancient to modern, that changed the course of civilization. 352pp. 5⅜ x 8½. 41129-X Pa. $9.95

THE WIT AND HUMOR OF OSCAR WILDE, Alvin Redman (ed.). More than 1,000 ripostes, paradoxes, wisecracks: Work is the curse of the drinking classes; I can resist everything except temptation; etc. 258pp. 5⅜ x 8½. 20602-5 Pa. $6.95

SHAKESPEARE LEXICON AND QUOTATION DICTIONARY, Alexander Schmidt. Full definitions, locations, shades of meaning in every word in plays and poems. More than 50,000 exact quotations. 1,485pp. 6½ x 9¼. 2-vol. set.
Vol. 1: 22726-X Pa. $17.95
Vol. 2: 22727-8 Pa. $17.95

SELECTED POEMS, Emily Dickinson. Over 100 best-known, best-loved poems by one of America's foremost poets, reprinted from authoritative early editions. No comparable edition at this price. Index of first lines. 64pp. 5$\frac{3}{16}$ x 8¼.
26466-1 Pa. $1.00

THE INSIDIOUS DR. FU-MANCHU, Sax Rohmer. The first of the popular mystery series introduces a pair of English detectives to their archnemesis, the diabolical Dr. Fu-Manchu. Flavorful atmosphere, fast-paced action, and colorful characters enliven this classic of the genre. 208pp. 5$\frac{3}{16}$ x 8¼. 29898-1 Pa. $2.00

THE MALLEUS MALEFICARUM OF KRAMER AND SPRENGER, translated by Montague Summers. Full text of most important witchhunter's "bible," used by both Catholics and Protestants. 278pp. 6⅝ x 10. 22802-9 Pa. $12.95

SPANISH STORIES/CUENTOS ESPAÑOLES: A Dual-Language Book, Angel Flores (ed.). Unique format offers 13 great stories in Spanish by Cervantes, Borges, others. Faithful English translations on facing pages. 352pp. 5⅜ x 8½.
25399-6 Pa. $8.95

GARDEN CITY, LONG ISLAND, IN EARLY PHOTOGRAPHS, 1869–1919, Mildred H. Smith. Handsome treasury of 118 vintage pictures, accompanied by carefully researched captions, document the Garden City Hotel fire (1899), the Vanderbilt Cup Race (1908), the first airmail flight departing from the Nassau Boulevard Aerodrome (1911), and much more. 96pp. 8⅞ x 11¾. 40669-5 Pa. $12.95

OLD QUEENS, N.Y., IN EARLY PHOTOGRAPHS, Vincent F. Seyfried and William Asadorian. Over 160 rare photographs of Maspeth, Jamaica, Jackson Heights, and other areas. Vintage views of DeWitt Clinton mansion, 1939 World's Fair and more. Captions. 192pp. 8⅞ x 11. 26358-4 Pa. $14.95

CAPTURED BY THE INDIANS: 15 Firsthand Accounts, 1750-1870, Frederick Drimmer. Astounding true historical accounts of grisly torture, bloody conflicts, relentless pursuits, miraculous escapes and more, by people who lived to tell the tale. 384pp. 5⅜ x 8½. 24901-8 Pa. $9.95

THE WORLD'S GREAT SPEECHES (Fourth Enlarged Edition), Lewis Copeland, Lawrence W. Lamm, and Stephen J. McKenna. Nearly 300 speeches provide public speakers with a wealth of updated quotes and inspiration–from Pericles' funeral oration and William Jennings Bryan's "Cross of Gold Speech" to Malcolm X's powerful words on the Black Revolution and Earl of Spenser's tribute to his sister, Diana, Princess of Wales. 944pp. 5⅜ x 8⅜. 40903-1 Pa. $15.95

THE BOOK OF THE SWORD, Sir Richard F. Burton. Great Victorian scholar/adventurer's eloquent, erudite history of the "queen of weapons"–from prehistory to early Roman Empire. Evolution and development of early swords, variations (sabre, broadsword, cutlass, scimitar, etc.), much more. 336pp. 6⅛ x 9¼.
25434-8 Pa. $9.95

AUTOBIOGRAPHY: The Story of My Experiments with Truth, Mohandas K. Gandhi. Boyhood, legal studies, purification, the growth of the Satyagraha (nonviolent protest) movement. Critical, inspiring work of the man responsible for the freedom of India. 480pp. 5⅜ x 8½. (Available in U.S. only.)   24593-4 Pa. $9.95

CELTIC MYTHS AND LEGENDS, T. W. Rolleston. Masterful retelling of Irish and Welsh stories and tales. Cuchulain, King Arthur, Deirdre, the Grail, many more. First paperback edition. 58 full-page illustrations. 512pp. 5⅜ x 8½.   26507-2 Pa. $9.95

THE PRINCIPLES OF PSYCHOLOGY, William James. Famous long course complete, unabridged. Stream of thought, time perception, memory, experimental methods; great work decades ahead of its time. 94 figures. 1,391pp. 5⅜ x 8½. 2-vol. set.
Vol. I: 20381-6 Pa. $14.95
Vol. II: 20382-4 Pa. $14.95

THE WORLD AS WILL AND REPRESENTATION, Arthur Schopenhauer. Definitive English translation of Schopenhauer's life work, correcting more than 1,000 errors, omissions in earlier translations. Translated by E. F. J. Payne. Total of 1,269pp. 5⅜ x 8½. 2-vol. set.
Vol. 1: 21761-2 Pa. $12.95
Vol. 2: 21762-0 Pa. $12.95

MAGIC AND MYSTERY IN TIBET, Madame Alexandra David-Neel. Experiences among lamas, magicians, sages, sorcerers, Bonpa wizards. A true psychic discovery. 32 illustrations. 321pp. 5⅜ x 8½. (Available in U.S. only.)   22682-4 Pa. $9.95

THE EGYPTIAN BOOK OF THE DEAD, E. A. Wallis Budge. Complete reproduction of Ani's papyrus, finest ever found. Full hieroglyphic text, interlinear transliteration, word-for-word translation, smooth translation. 533pp. 6½ x 9¼.
21866-X Pa. $12.95

MATHEMATICS FOR THE NONMATHEMATICIAN, Morris Kline. Detailed, college-level treatment of mathematics in cultural and historical context, with numerous exercises. Recommended Reading Lists. Tables. Numerous figures. 641pp. 5⅜ x 8½.
24823-2 Pa. $11.95

PROBABILISTIC METHODS IN THE THEORY OF STRUCTURES, Isaac Elishakoff. Well-written introduction covers the elements of the theory of probability from two or more random variables, the reliability of such multivariable structures, the theory of random function, Monte Carlo methods of treating problems incapable of exact solution, and more. Examples. 502pp. 5³/₈ x 8¹/₂.   40691-1 Pa. $16.95

THE RIME OF THE ANCIENT MARINER, Gustave Doré, S. T. Coleridge. Doré's finest work; 34 plates capture moods, subtleties of poem. Flawless full-size reproductions printed on facing pages with authoritative text of poem. "Beautiful. Simply beautiful."–*Publisher's Weekly.* 77pp. 9¼ x 12.   22305-1 Pa. $7.95

NORTH AMERICAN INDIAN DESIGNS FOR ARTISTS AND CRAFTSPEOPLE, Eva Wilson. Over 360 authentic copyright-free designs adapted from Navajo blankets, Hopi pottery, Sioux buffalo hides, more. Geometrics, symbolic figures, plant and animal motifs, etc. 128pp. 8⅜ x 11. (Not for sale in the United Kingdom.)   25341-4 Pa. $9.95

SCULPTURE: Principles and Practice, Louis Slobodkin. Step-by-step approach to clay, plaster, metals, stone; classical and modern. 253 drawings, photos. 255pp. 8⅛ x 11.
22960-2 Pa. $11.95

THE INFLUENCE OF SEA POWER UPON HISTORY, 1660–1783, A. T. Mahan. Influential classic of naval history and tactics still used as text in war colleges. First paperback edition. 4 maps. 24 battle plans. 640pp. 5⅜ x 8½.   25509-3 Pa. $14.95

THE STORY OF THE TITANIC AS TOLD BY ITS SURVIVORS, Jack Winocour (ed.). What it was really like. Panic, despair, shocking inefficiency, and a little heroism. More thrilling than any fictional account. 26 illustrations. 320pp. 5⅜ x 8½.
20610-6 Pa. $8.95

FAIRY AND FOLK TALES OF THE IRISH PEASANTRY, William Butler Yeats (ed.). Treasury of 64 tales from the twilight world of Celtic myth and legend: "The Soul Cages," "The Kildare Pooka," "King O'Toole and his Goose," many more. Introduction and Notes by W. B. Yeats. 352pp. 5⅜ x 8½.   26941-8 Pa. $8.95

BUDDHIST MAHAYANA TEXTS, E. B. Cowell and others (eds.). Superb, accurate translations of basic documents in Mahayana Buddhism, highly important in history of religions. The Buddha-karita of Asvaghosha, Larger Sukhavativyuha, more. 448pp. 5⅜ x 8½.   25552-2 Pa. $12.95

ONE TWO THREE . . . INFINITY: Facts and Speculations of Science, George Gamow. Great physicist's fascinating, readable overview of contemporary science: number theory, relativity, fourth dimension, entropy, genes, atomic structure, much more. 128 illustrations. Index. 352pp. 5⅜ x 8½.   25664-2 Pa. $9.95

EXPERIMENTATION AND MEASUREMENT, W. J. Youden. Introductory manual explains laws of measurement in simple terms and offers tips for achieving accuracy and minimizing errors. Mathematics of measurement, use of instruments, experimenting with machines. 1994 edition. Foreword. Preface. Introduction. Epilogue. Selected Readings. Glossary. Index. Tables and figures. 128pp. 5³⁄₈ x 8¹⁄₂.
40451-X Pa. $6.95

DALÍ ON MODERN ART: The Cuckolds of Antiquated Modern Art, Salvador Dalí. Influential painter skewers modern art and its practitioners. Outrageous evaluations of Picasso, Cézanne, Turner, more. 15 renderings of paintings discussed. 44 calligraphic decorations by Dalí. 96pp. 5⅜ x 8½. (Available in U.S. only.)   29220-7 Pa. $5.95

ANTIQUE PLAYING CARDS: A Pictorial History, Henry René D'Allemagne. Over 900 elaborate, decorative images from rare playing cards (14th–20th centuries): Bacchus, death, dancing dogs, hunting scenes, royal coats of arms, players cheating, much more. 96pp. 9¼ x 12¼.   29265-7 Pa. $12.95

MAKING FURNITURE MASTERPIECES: 30 Projects with Measured Drawings, Franklin H. Gottshall. Step-by-step instructions, illustrations for constructing handsome, useful pieces, among them a Sheraton desk, Chippendale chair, Spanish desk, Queen Anne table and a William and Mary dressing mirror. 224pp. 8⅛ x 11¼.
29338-6 Pa. $13.95

THE FOSSIL BOOK: A Record of Prehistoric Life, Patricia V. Rich et al. Profusely illustrated definitive guide covers everything from single-celled organisms and dinosaurs to birds and mammals and the interplay between climate and man. Over 1,500 illustrations. 760pp. 7½ x 10⅛.   29371-8 Pa. $29.95

Prices subject to change without notice.

Available at your book dealer or write for free catalog to Dept. GI, Dover Publications, Inc., 31 East 2nd St., Mineola, N.Y. 11501. Dover publishes more than 500 books each year on science, elementary and advanced mathematics, biology, music, art, literary history, social sciences and other areas.